AN IMAG

By the same author

A Local Habitation:
Life and Times, Volume I: 1918–40
A Sort of Clowning:
Life and Times, Volume II: 1940–59
Auden: An Introductory Essay
The Uses of Literacy
W. H. Auden
Teaching Literature
Speaking to Each Other:
Volume 1: About Society
Volume 2: About Literature
Only Connect – On Culture and Communication:
The BBC Reith Lectures 1971
An Idea and Its Servants: UNESCO from Within
An English Temper
The British Council and the Arts (joint)
An Idea of Europe
(with Douglas Johnson)

As Editor

Your Sunday Paper
The Future of Broadcasting
(with Janet Morgan)
The Public Service Idea in British Broadcasting: Main Principles
Quality in Television
Liberty and Legislation

AN IMAGINED LIFE

(Life and Times, Volume III: 1959–91)

RICHARD HOGGART

OXFORD UNIVERSITY PRESS

1993

Oxford University Press, Walton Street, Oxford OX2 6DP

Oxford New York Toronto
Delhi Bombay Calcutta Madras Karachi
Kuala Lumpur Singapore Hong Kong Tokyo
Nairobi Dar es Salaam Cape Town
Melbourne Auckland Madrid
and associated companies in
Berlin Ibadan

First published 1992 by Chatto & Windus Ltd
First issued as an Oxford University Press paperback 1993

British Library Cataloguing in Publication Data
Data available

ISBN 0 19 283112-7

1 3 5 7 9 10 8 6 4 2

Printed and bound in Great Britain by
Biddles Ltd, Guildford and King's Lynn

CONTENTS

In loving memory of
Tom Longfellow Hoggart
(1917–90)

ACKNOWLEDGMENTS

For many kinds of help I am greatly indebted to: Philip Collins, Geoffrey Goodman, Michael Green, Stephen Hearst, Kenneth Lamb, Dennis Lawrence, 'Pip' Leedam, David Lodge, John Miller, Michael Orrom, Dieter Pevsner and Bernard Schilling.

I owe to Catharine Carver, as always, a huge debt for her inspired editing.

From Jenny Uglow, Carmen Callil and their colleagues at Chatto & Windus, and from Michael Shaw at Curtis Brown, I have received constant help – and an unflagging belief in this long effort.

To all members of the family – above all my wife, Mary – I am, once more, endlessly grateful.

The author and publishers would like to thank the following for the use of copyright material: Faber & Faber Ltd and Macmillan London Ltd.

PREFACE

This is the last volume of a three-volume *Life and Times* and brings the story virtually to the present. Like its predecessors, it is self-contained; you do not have to have read the others to follow this one.

The first volume was about growing up to the time of leaving university and joining the army; so it was very personal. Volume Two was personal too, especially on family and the business of writing; it was also to some extent public, and talked about army life and about the call to teaching adults.

This third volume has had to be much more public, since it covers the years from 1959 to 1991, and those three decades contained a great deal of public work. Yet they were also centred on the family. That relationship, between the public and the private, has emerged as one of the main themes of this trilogy, part of what – I see now – I have been trying to make sense of throughout. So the more professional and public chapters here are bracketed, at front and back, by more directly personal chapters. But all the chapters do try to interweave the private and the public. For several reasons I have decided, tempting though it was, not to write at length about living acquaintances.

Chapter 5, placed as we leave England for France and international life, interrupts the chronological movement so as to look at the unusual history of the universities in the Sixties.

I found my title in Logan Pearsall Smith: 'People before the public live *an imagined life* [my italics] in the thought of others, and flourish and feel faint as their self outside themselves grows bright or dwindles in that mirror.' That's a dire thought, and no doubt directed at people whose public life has been much grander than mine. I hope Logan Pearsall Smith was wrong; and, as I describe in the final chapter, I've tried so far as concerns myself to prove him wrong.

To make the story complete I have drawn on a few earlier pieces of writing, though modifying each part taken so that it fits the narrative here and is brought up to date. The most substantial element used in this way is the account of life at UNESCO head-quarters in Paris. Those five years could not be left out of the record here. But chapter 6 describes the French experience in a very different way from that used in an earlier book. Major public issues in UNESCO's activities during my time – the debates about a New International Economic Order and a New International Communications Order; the Arab–Israeli disputes; endless argu-ments about the structuring, financing and staffing of UNESCO as the origins of its many internal tensions – all these and other questions were discussed in my book on the organisation of the late Seventies. Here, the story is much more about people I knew in Paris, particularly the ever-present, brooding presence of the Director-General, René Maheu; it is about what they, and what the problems I had directly to face in my work, might have taught me about the aspirations and limitations of international organisations – and about myself. Above all, the events and judg-ments on all these things have altered greatly. I would not want to claim emotion recollected in tranquillity; but the passage of the years has certainly brought a new perspective to important elements of life in that near-anarchic Tower of Babel, UNESCO.

I have called this sequence a *Life and Times* so as to avoid the catch-all, inaccurate title 'Autobiography'. I thought of calling it 'Cultural Autobiography' but that seemed pompous. It has been about a life lived, after 1957, to some extent in the public eye, in one of the publics' eyes; but to describe that is not my main object. It has also been a life of sustained ordinariness, day by day, and that characteristic has been more important than the public.

So the many incidents I describe are not offered simply as instances of more or less important public moments, nor as homely little incidents typical of ordinary life. I may not have succeeded but my aim has been, in choosing and describing any kind of incident, to do so in a way which might bring out a somewhat more 'representative', 'telling', meaning than would have been at first assumed. This is a matter of selection, angle, tone and much else; and sometimes one succeeds more than at others. If it works, the incidents, public or private, may suggest half-hidden elements in the nature of this society, and perhaps of the changes going on in it over almost three-quarters of a century. And a few incidents found their way in just because they seemed too funny – laughable or curious – to leave out.

RICHARD HOGGART

PART ONE

⚜

PROVINCIAL AND NATIONAL: THE 1960s

❦

CHAPTER 1

THE DELTA: GOING PUBLIC

In the early Seventies I took part in a radio discussion for the BBC in Paris, with an Anglo-French group. We had lunch beforehand, at two tables near each other. I heard the most distinguished of the French members ask the programme's British chairman who I was. The reply came in a loud, professional broadcaster's voice: 'Oh, he made his name with a book years ago and has gone on saying the same things ever since.' A little clumsy of him but, though I might have entered a few caveats, not a charge I could entirely deny.

I

Looked at now, my professional life for some years after the publication of *The Uses of Literacy* seems like the view of a river from above, a river at the point of breaking into several smaller streams to form a delta.

At the time I did not have such a bird's-eye view of my own activities; self-deception by preoccupation is an effective anaesthetic. Even as late as the early Seventies, when at UNESCO in Paris, I was surprised when a friend reported that Philip Larkin had said I should have stuck to writing, and not been deflected into executive work, however important it might have seemed. Larkin was right; but also wrong, judging too much from within the checks and balances of his own personality.

The Uses of Literacy appeared when we were half-way through a year in the United States, where I taught at the University of

Rochester in upstate New York. I do not know how much attention the book would have received had we been in England at the time and I available for interviews. Probably it would, even so, have received less notice than if it had appeared in 1987. There were then few television and radio chat shows on to which authors, *faute de mieux*, could be wheeled, fewer press profiles, promotional lunches, public readings or signing sessions. The planned and predictable public-relations-laboratory creating of the best-seller of each month or season was in its infancy.

In the early Fifties my first book, on Auden, was discussed by the Third Programme's *Critics*; Auden was a big name. Half a decade later, *The Uses of Literacy* was not so chosen; I was not a well known name, this book was not directly literary and it was hard to pigeon-hole. The *Guardian* was very warm, but most reviews were favourable without being unusually enthusiastic.

It would not, in that first year and for a long time after, have occurred to journalists to call *The Uses of Literacy* a 'classic', as a fair number do today. The word has become part of a tag: 'Author of the classic *The Uses of Literacy*.' A 'classic' should be a book of exceptionally rare quality and my book does not have that stature, glad as I am that I wrote several of its pages. To some extent the sobriquet does depend on age, the age of the author and of the book; say, twenty years for the book and arriving at the age of sixty for the author. At roughly that point there begins to appear: 'The distinguished author of the classic . . .'; a small, weightless, stick-on label; not as strong as the properly much less used 'a masterpiece'.

Neither Chatto nor I expected much from the book. The many months, the labours, the worries which went into it had not been sustained by the feeling that it would make any more impact than my first book. I assumed the existence of readers who might be interested in what I had to say, not an 'audience' which would make me well known. I knew the risks of leaving the established academic tracks, but hoped that some reviewers would sufficiently approve of what I was trying to do for the enterprise to help rather than hinder such academic reputation as I was beginning to have.

The book's reputation grew slowly but steadily, apparently by word of mouth as much as or more than by public commendation.

The Pelican edition greatly accelerated the process; that appeared a year after the hardback. Allen Lane read the book very early, sitting in the sun at his place in the Balearics, and 'phoned his office or Chatto to say he wanted it for Pelican and as soon as possible. It was, he said later, exactly the kind of book he had hoped to publish when he had founded the Pelican list just before the war. It has remained in paperback to this day. Lane's decision, which encouraged the inclusion of the title on reading-lists for students at many levels, rather than the hard-cover sales, was the foundation of the book's wide impact.

I expected even less the belief of many readers that the book had caught and given shape to a moment of change in British cultural life. I see what those readers are saying and am intrigued but also surprised, especially since the book was written from back to front – first a Leavisite kind of analysis, then the description of working-class life with which it opens. When I moved from the critical analysis of parts of popular culture to the attempt to set that material in the context of the kind of life I had known as a boy, it did seem possible that the whole might form a diptych which would be more interesting to some people than its separate parts. Published ten years earlier, or later, it might have had much less effect. At the entry into the Sixties – the first decade of post-war, consumer-directed prosperity – it took on for some people an aspect of both summation and prophecy.

Some elements of the original reviews seemed odd even at the time. One was the complaint that I was obsessed with the conviction that Britain was a class-divided society, whereas all balanced people knew we were now classless. Orwell had met the same objection and noted it in *The Road to Wigan Pier* over twenty years before; other observers have met it in each succeeding decade. It is levelled today, and will be tomorrow, an incantation against accepting something we would have to recognise as shameful if we forced ourselves to face it. Yet the energy with which we reject the accusation is fed by the knowledge in our deepest hearts that it is true, that for all the patronising camaraderie of the older England when it addresses 'the chaps', and the shallow mateyness of the new when it wants to 'wow the punters' – and whatever the fuzziness of some old class-frontiers today – we are still fundamentally divided in both trivial and important ways, from recreations to family habits; apparent assimilations are usually deceptive.

This leads to an idea which will bob up again and again in this book: that late-twentieth-century British – and European – society is not destroying but re-forming and re-labelling the ridges between classes. The fact of this tenacious, deep-seated divisiveness is less troublesome than the refusal to admit it. So when the idea is yet again denied, pushed resentfully away, you have to go on saying as equably as possible: 'But, yes, England is still an unjustly divided society.' Find more emollient phrases if you will, such as that we are now less separated by indicators of birth, property and inherited wealth. You then have to go on to realise that we are as much as ever divided by status differences, consumer-group differences, life-style differences; that they are all, and there are always, new cheap clothes for the old wolf. The emotional charge behind the sense of division by class of birth has been transferred so as now to sustain the new sense of division by status. We are united more in our nastier attitudes – chauvinism, racism, suspicion of the mind at work – than in the gentler fellow-feelings; yet they too can be found in some people and places and situations, and at all social levels.

One or two of the reviewers of *The Uses of Literacy* more or less thanked me for opening their eyes to the continuing realities of class-divisions in England; but often did so in a manner which suggested that the writers still held the assumptions which underlay the differences. One reviewer began in roughly this way: 'Now we know as we travel North and look out of the train window at those small terrace houses, all seeming so much the same . . . what is really going-on behind the half-length lace curtains.' An egregious compliment, when one thinks of all the earlier works which could have introduced him to the differences between the privileges of his kind of life and the poverty in those little houses. Orwell again makes the contrast most sharply, in the image – also seen from a train, from a third-class carriage as he went south – of a beaten-down working-class housewife outside just that kind of terrace house, poking feebly with a stick at a blocked drain.

Inevitably, some reviewers described me (not usually unkindly, but in the way you might note that your cousin was unfortunately born blind in one eye) as a 'Puritan'. What different services that word is pressed into. More and more now, it is invoked to mean: 'He has dared to pass a judgment of value. He has said that some lives – in more than one part of society – are uncivilised, shameful.' One doesn't talk like that nowadays, make judgments such as that, make any judgments at all about the quality of anyone else's life – even though most of us would be at the worst shocked, at the best very sad if any members of our own families led lives so ill-endowed and ill-considered as very many people do.

A good number of readers of *The Uses of Literacy*, and more than a score wrote to me in this spirit, were not only generous but relieved. They said the book had helped them bring into the open early experiences that they had not before been able to absorb into their adult pictures of themselves. This response was especially evoked by a chapter (written with considerable difficulty because it was about particularly sensitive personal experiences) called 'Scholarship Boy', on the tensions of moving from a working-class home to the professional middle class or a classless intelligentsia (neither phrase is adequate but, together, they will have to do).

These readers had had early experiences much like my own and had usually 'gone on to higher things'. Among them were a Deputy Secretary and a Permanent Secretary in the Civil Service; there were also a couple of university vice-chancellors and a few others of that eminence. They tended to add that they had been fortunate in having admirable, loving and entirely 'supportive' parents. They mentioned the corner-shop behind which had been a warm home. I would not have guessed all that, so good were the disguises they had grown into. There was a touch of the relieved confessional about these conversations, as though the speakers were each revealing a personal strawberry mark to one who had already admitted to that inheritance, and had by that released them from an inhibition their current range of acquaintance imposed.

That most social scientists were hospitable to the book was unexpected since, and of this I had been warned, it might have been thought to encroach on their territories. There was at least one nicely crabby exception. A professor at my own *alma mater*, the University of Leeds, did not care for the book. I think he regarded it as a work of impressionism which true scientists of the social kind should stamp on. A woman once told me that in the middle Sixties she, then eighteen, had applied to study social sciences at Leeds. She lived in the South and knew nothing about either Leeds or the social sciences. Her sixth-form teacher suggested it might be useful to read in advance *The Uses of Literacy*. The professor himself interviewed her. What had she read in preparation for her possible course? She mentioned *The Uses of Literacy*. 'I mean social scientific works not bedside reading.' She was admitted in spite of this lapse.

One or two MPs, representing working-class constituencies but usually from middle-class backgrounds, told me I knew the wrong sort of working-class people. Their constituents were much doughtier, more politically active than I had suggested. The MPs may have been right in their own terms; their judgment was almost self-fulfilling. Naturally they would meet chiefly the most active kind of voter; and I had known few of those. Some more thoughtful MPs from similar constituencies said they thought my picture substantially correct; they knew that that was the ground on which they stood.

One or two readers referred to the book with resentment. This was not adverse criticism of a chapter-and-verse kind but seemed the expression of a personal resistance. Some were from working-class backgrounds, some from middle-class. The tone of their rejections suggested the book had raised in the first hidden insecurities, and in the second a resentful sense of being judged.

Even today people are likely to come up, perhaps after a lecture, and say something like: 'You must be tired of hearing this but I would like to tell you that at a difficult period in my life . . .'; and so on. Such a response is not easy to accept, especially by someone inhibited by Primitive Methodist suspicions of anything which even slightly smells of the priestly.

One evening in the Middle West of America, after I had given a lecture (about educational changes in Britain, not about anything I had written), a young woman came up and spoke in the way I have described. She was a lecturer at the local land-grant university. She had been brought up in a back-to-back house in Newcastle. I said I was going there in a few weeks' time; she asked me to call on her widowed father to confirm she was well and happy. After finishing the work in Newcastle I had an hour before the train south, took a taxi to the address and knocked on the door. Her father opened it and said simply: 'Oh, you've come then.'

2

All that was about the final broadening, through the reception of *The Uses of Literacy*, of the single professional river before it began to divide into the constituents of a delta. Before, that is, I began to receive frequent invitations to lecture, to write, to broadcast, to sit on committees. In themselves none of these need have been useless engagements; taken together they became wasteful.

Payment was infrequent and then usually slight. For the most taxing of all, the public committees, there was rightly no payment and only modest expense allowances. Nor was the work accepted, by me or by most people I met round those tables, for whatever repute it might be thought to have brought.

Some invitations were more exotic. As I was leaving home in Hull one bitter November night in 1958, for the Humber ferry and the jogging little train over the flatlands of Lincolnshire to a class and an overnight stay in Grimsby, the 'phone rang. A cultivated young woman's voice announced that its possessor was speaking on behalf of a multi-titled organisation. 'We have', she said, 'the contract for Mars.' Was I to be invited to join the space race? She went on to say they were about to launch a new confection, aimed at the 'aspirant working class'. They understood I was *the* expert on the habits, customs and aspirations of 'such people'. They were to have a 'brain-storming session' about the best shape for the campaign and would be willing to pay me a considerable sum to sit in for the day and advise. Not my line at all, I said. She was ready for me. 'We rather guessed that, but thought you might be amused to hang from the chandelier and see us at work. Still be paid.' I like hanging from chandeliers, being there and not there. But the tatty old paddle-steamer would be getting ready to cross the grey Humber for grey Grimsby, so our acquaintance ended there and then.

That fruitless conversation took its place with another in the same month, in which another young woman announced that she was speaking on behalf of the Queen. Lunch at Buck House, perhaps, to educate the table with the splendours and miseries of working-class life. But the caller went on to ask, on behalf of her editor, for a piece about working-class diets or some such.

America provided the most disconcerting incident. On my way to lecture at Amherst, two hours late into Idlewild because of bad weather, I tried to rush out of the terminal after, as I thought, clearing customs and immigration. I was stopped by a dour-faced official twirling a bunch of keys, backed by a large minder. It took a minute to interpret that he was saying: 'Come with me. US Customs' (or 'Immigration'). A long and bare corridor led to a room lighted only by the unshielded bulb one had grown used to in spy dramas. A few minutes later I was naked and being comprehensively body-searched by the minder. Eventually the other man told me I could get dressed and go. Neither had relaxed their stiff, expressionless manners throughout. I asked them why I had been chosen. They had been watching me, the senior man said, from the moment I came down the 'plane's steps. They suspected I was some kind of double agent. I told them I was an English academic, scurrying so as not to miss my connecting flight. That produced: 'All the best double agents look like you.'

Many years later came another American Technicolor occasion, for the fiftieth anniversary of D. H. Lawrence's death, a conference at the University of Santa Fe. The audience in the large lecture theatre seemed to be mainly nuns from liberal arts colleges. When the opening lecturer, speaking about *Lady Chatterley's Lover*, began: 'Let's face it. Lady C. was fucked, sucked, buggered and blown,' the nuns took notes without concern.

British memorable moments can be less inventive linguistically but no less dramatic. Six months after *The Uses of Literacy* appeared, I was invited to speak to the undergraduate students of English group, the Doughty Society, at Downing College, Cambridge. F. R. Leavis was still teaching there, to the English Literature world a looming and intransigent figure but one from whom many of us had learned more than from any other living critic, even if we had reservations about some of his views. I had first seen him, and heard him lecture but not spoken to him, at an extra-mural university tutors' conference in the early Fifties, and been fascinated by the Cambridge twang uttering without notes and with total conviction a range of complex judgments. Fascinated, too, to discover that he deployed a wicked wit; his dismissal of Lord David Cecil on that occasion was plainly slanderous. A little after that conference we had a courteous exchange of letters about my book on Auden. Perhaps this time, on Downing's own ground, I should meet him; and the at least equally redoubtable Mrs Leavis.

It was not to be; they had given their apologies to the organiser. The lecture room was packed to the window-ledges. I began by paying my respects to both the Leavises, with special reference to what I and others had learned from her about popular fiction. Afterwards, over coffee in the junior common room, a number of graduate students gathered round to talk about the study of popular culture. I became aware of an older man on the fringe of the group – I learned later he was a former student of Leavis, now taking some classes at Downing. I caught his eye in case he wanted to say something. He did. 'Would you agree', he asked, in a voice oily with malice, 'that you are the would-be intellectual's J. B. Priestley?'

As the evening at Downing came to an end, a large bearded figure introduced himself as a fellow-Yorkshireman with similar interests who proposed to become a friend. That was typical of Brian Jackson's forthrightness, and he did become a friend. He was in his early years as an imaginative and committed schoolteacher nearby. He went on to a career of practical educational innovation second only to Michael Young's, a career cut short by his death at about fifty during a sponsored run for one of his causes on behalf of children. He was a dramatic but not a stage Yorkshireman. When we first met he was living in an executive-type Span house in Cambridge but in the evening went round to the local jug-and-bottle counter because he preferred draught to bottled beer. In Paris, fifteen years later, he was persuaded to drink bottled Kronenbourg because it would have been a twenty-minute trip from our apartment to find draught. He could be a mixture of the very clumsy and the extremely delicate. After any number of pints, that night in Paris, he continued exploring the nuances of teaching children from poor backgrounds. But he broke the lavatory seat, a Second Empire chair and the curtain-rail in his bedroom.

I asked him at that first meeting after the Downing College talk why the audience had been so large. Oh, the word had gone round Cambridge that you meant to make an assault on the Leavises and in particular on Mrs Leavis's approach to popular fiction.

The memory of Brian Jackson recalls also the effect of the reception of *The Uses of Literacy* on our family life and friendships. In numbers and variety of social activities that effect was small. We did not begin to move in literary circles, to attend cocktail parties or launches or, except very rarely, to frequent the gathering-places of literary people. We were family-centred, even more anxious than before not to move out or to 'show off'. Our lives revolved around home and family, including grandparents, the few close friends we had had for years and still keep, and our immediate neighbourhood and university acquaintance. Family life remained much as it had always been. When *The Uses of Literacy* appeared the children were twelve, eight and four. At the end of the period covered by this chapter they were fifteen, eleven and seven, so we then had our first teenager. That growing-up was at the heart of things.

We came to know well half a dozen people as a result of *The Uses of Literacy*, starting that evening with Brian Jackson. Meetings with people like that (Dennis Mitchell, say), who are busy and almost certainly living and working many miles away, are never frequent. But you are at once in touch each time you meet, as though there had been no interval. You do not meet often enough to become close friends in the usual definition of that word. Yet 'acquaintance' in its normal uses does not do justice to the warmth which is carried along the years.

I wished also, it proved, to remain not only family-centred but a sort of amateur, not to belong to any identified groups, not to become a pundit (not to appear, for example, on programmes such as *Any Questions*) and not to 'put my name forward' for anything. The practice of self-promotion, whether in the search for a place on a radio talk-show, for a knighthood or an honorary degree, is regarded as normal by many climbing, or simply title-hungry, people. 'Whenever a man has cast a longing eye on offices, a rottenness begins in his conduct.' Jefferson was severe because thinking of high and influential office; those I have in mind are no more than weakly venal in their pursuit. My attitude was, as such attitudes usually are, mixed; part *amour propre*, the disinclination to push as a form of pride and to avoid a rebuff; and partly a suspicion of people who take themselves seriously as public figures, and especially as known writers.

Not, then, a member of the English Literary Happy Family. It does exist and so do, but by now only just, its links with some important parts of the circles of power and authority; thirty years ago those links were strong and manifest. You were passed on and around; your 'name was mentioned' – until unresponsiveness, which was my own normal defence, finally made them give up. Or, as also happened once or twice, until you said or wrote something which convinced them that you were not an absorbable if slightly funny outsider but that, like some harmless-looking creatures of the animal world, you could if stimulated in the wrong way exude a fluid or smell which was deeply off-putting, which put you outside that invisible pale of the at least putatively Great and Good. After the Albemarle Committee on the Youth Service had reported I gave a talk about it to a group of fairly senior civil servants and made fun of the official Youth Service's propensity to religiosity. Within a week a well-wisher 'phoned to say that a high academic proconsul, his knighthood already awarded and his peerage on the way, had literally (I use that adverb with pleasure because I had thought this particular dismissal was the invention of a satirist) delivered the judgment that 'that man Hoggart is unsound'.

I was more than once invited to let my name go forward for membership of a club. This was less surprising than the fact that it was always one of the same three or four clubs – where the arts, law, some branches of politics and some parts of the upper reaches of the Civil Service all mingled. Those who asked were pleasant, friendly and courteous people; it was like being asked to jump into a very large bed with the boys, virtually all from public schools and Oxbridge but willing to move over for you; and with, of course, no suggestion of improper conduct – just a friendly getting together.

A moment in the Athenaeum's dining room, where three members and I shared a table one day, caught well the power of puddings in the codes of this English middle- to upper-middle-class professional life. The waitress announced that today there was rice pudding – rice pudding, the standard pudding of the poor, cheap and nourishing (though, if you can afford a dash of Carnation Milk and perhaps a blob of jam, rich and creamy; if not, you settle for sugary condensed milk). But not to working-class people a treat of a pudding; not a pudding for an 'occasion', like trifle. I chose something else. The three high officials all chose rice pudding with large smiles; it brought back, they said, memories of their boarding schools.

Thinking over these events and trying to assess their effects on my sense of myself – to use a trickily self-conscious but hardly avoidable phrase – I remember Graham Greene once said that fame is 'a powerful aphrodisiac'. I didn't myself feel the sexual link but did feel for a time an increase of energy from being known about in some circles of the British intellectual family. There is also Carlyle's more sombre comment: 'For every man that can stand prosperity, there are a hundred that will stand adversity.' There speaks the Protestant Spirit in all its tight-lipped rigour.

There can also be less obvious effects from being known or known about. If people associate you with a particular kind of writing, it becomes progressively harder both to continue writing like that – are you becoming repetitive? – or to branch out into another style. Twenty-odd years after the appearance of *The Uses of Literacy* I wrote a book about UNESCO, the scientific and cultural arm of the UN, drawn from five years' work at its headquarters in Paris. It was, though this is not to say a great deal given the dullness of most books about the UN, interesting; and even had a few good jokes. Its reception could not be grumbled at. But two of the English reviewers began favourable notices by showing surprise that I had chosen an international subject. *He* writes about English working-class life, surely? There was half a suggestion I should not have stepped outside my bailiwick.

You may become even more self-conscious for a time; your wrist stiffens. You acquire your own kind of verbal and tonal tinnitus; and this is more of a problem than any urge to write what you know people expect of you. 'Public image' writing is less of a threat than self-protective writing; or than lecturing – since these pitfalls are aggravated if you accept many invitations to speak on what are thought to be 'your subjects'. Commissioned short articles, compatible articles which nevertheless you have not felt the need to write until the invitations came, have a similar effect. None of these temptations need be fatal; but they have to be recognised or you will not settle to the desk and try to recapture the sense of an entirely unknown audience which may want to eavesdrop.

The attitudes of others, of those who read or come to hear you, run through a wider range. You become used to flattering introductions from some (and pegged-nosed ones from others), knowing that whatever you say will be no better than what you would have said ten years ago, or than what several friends still working quietly in the field could have said – and both would have gone unremarked; as you would yourself have gone unremarked if you had walked into the room ten years ago, without that bit of a public aura. Even more unwished-for is the use of the phrase 'your authority' as in: 'We should like you to lend your authority to . . .' or, more likely, 'We don't think you should lend your authority to . . .'. The phrases are as unacceptable as a fancy higher-doctorate gown stolen from the wrong faculty. You have been put on a temporary pedestal for someone else's temporary purposes.

The audiences for lectures contain those who are hoping you will live up to their high opinion of your work, and those who have come to spot the clay feet. The second type have watchful, guarded, sideways airs, as though two-thirds of their minds are intent on gathering cues for the snide cracks they will deliver afterwards. At such moments a curious effect comes into play; you hear your own voice and, more, the speaker's tricks you have acquired over the years without – before – sufficiently noticing them. It's all the more bruising if you too have ever practised the guarded, sly look. All of us, whatever the merits of what we have said and no matter what nice chaps we believe ourselves to be at bottom, will be simply, instinctively, unappealing to some people in any audience.

One way of escaping all this is to speak only to audiences of the converted, closed audiences who are already on our side against the fallen world out there. Typical of these are university audiences of the convinced, Left or Right. You can quarter the country with such chosen audiences, getting away with intellectual and rhetorical murder, and never feel the chill wind of antipathy.

Some colleagues and friends, though glad you have been in this at least successful but unable to forbear straightening your new jacket, will now give a special edge to their criticisms, be ready to report that so-and-so heard you in such-and-such a town and thought you had 'gone off', were tired at best and fallen into a slack, indulgent routine at worst. There is no point in arguing. Leave it to the next attempt at writing.

About reviewing and writing other small pieces in the last three years of the Fifties, there are only a few things to say. First that, as with lecturing, I did too much. Second, I felt uneasy at being offered books for review simply because my name was for the time being in the heads of literary editors; that was a matter of fashion, a largely chance situation. For many of the books, I knew of people better equipped than I to be the reviewers, but their names were not known to the editors or their readers. The editors did not, could not afford to, know them. I wrote back several times and said that I did not feel as competent as I would have wished and offered other names, but the advice was scarcely ever taken. In the circumstances it was naïve advice. The editors wanted at that time my name, not that of someone relatively unknown.

They soon stopped approaching me because I was in most instances an over-earnest and unexciting reviewer. My mind was not free-ranging enough to allow me to write interestingly around a dull book. I had no gear-box in my writing equipment. I wanted to interest the readers but not at the cost of fairness to the book; and to do both at the same time almost entirely escaped me. I refused the advice that it was unnecessary except in rare cases to read a book all the way through, especially a long book. I worried about whether an amusing remark had won its place at the cost of some injustice to the work, and was chagrined to find that, when circumstances prompted me to attend lightly to a book, the review was often welcomed as brighter than usual, more readable. To do what I thought was full justice took more time than I could rightly spare on what could only be peripheral work. In short, I was saved by dullness as a literary journalist from even more over-extension.

Broadcasting can be more interesting than reviewing, chiefly because it allows you to try to communicate what you want to say not only by words but by tone of voice and, in television, gesture and expression. Having little ability to 'project the personality' and virtually no histrionic sense, I was not what is called a natural broadcaster. Yet once or twice in the radio and television broadcasts I did make in the late Fifties something seemed to be peeping out which made a couple of producers think there might be promise. The midwife to many television 'naturals', Grace Wyndham-Goldie, herself originally an extra-mural lecturer, was not impressed. Hearing me 'front' a pilot programme for a series on books, she gave one of her famous *ex-cathedra* judgments, in an Edith Evans style of voice which carried through the thin partition between us: 'He's not *talking* to them. He's *lecturing* them.'

Huw Wheldon in his ebullient *Monitor* days had a rather longer breath. I appeared with him in March 1958, and once or perhaps twice later. On the first occasion, ever the expansive big brother or generous uncle, he put his arm around my shoulders and boomed: 'I'm going to *make* you, my boy!' It was years later, so magisterial was his personality, that I realised he was only two and a half years older than I.

After he retired from the BBC he became in the late Seventies, to his great delight, chairman of LSE's governing board. I ran into him, both of us dressed like peacocks, at one of London University's regular honorary degree ceremonies. Over my shoulder was a splendid red silk tippet, fringed with ermine. He took hold of it and boomed in a voice which carried far into the crowded reception area: 'What's this?' 'I was given it in Paris.' 'Might have known. French. The whore's knickers.'

That early edition of *Monitor* ran late so I missed the last Sunday evening train to Hull; the next was at about five a.m. A BBC car was provided to take me to any hotel I chose near King's Cross. I had recently read that there were Turkish Baths spread under a large hotel (was it the Imperial?) in Russell Square, that you could go there at any hour, have your bath, and rest with a cup of tea and a Rich Tea biscuit, stretched under a sheet on your own upholstered bench, until it was time to leave. The cashier gave me an old-fashioned look and for the first quarter of an hour, until the sweat began pouring down my face, some of the other customers seemed curiously interested. I looked in the mirror at a streaky, parti-coloured face. In those days they made you up very heavily for television – blue-black eyebrows, white eye-sockets and jowls, pink cheeks, like a half-way mime artist.

The occasional broadcast for commercial television in those pre-Pilkington days (Pilkington sat from 1960 to 1962) gave useful insights into the ways some of the companies were then selling short their regulatory duty to provide information and education as well as entertainment; and the least regarded was education. There, most did the cheapest job they could. This came to mind during the sittings of the Pilkington Committee, when the procession of vicuna-suited, early commercial television tycoons piously declared their entire commitment to the full range of their statutory duties.

3

Work on national committees was more continuous and taxing than any other voluntary and spare-time activities, and finally more influential. Before 1957 I had had little committee experience and most of that parochial, geographically or professionally. The most useful was a small group at the Ministry of Education, assembled to decide whether to award Mature State Studentships for university to any adult students offering English Literature. Thirty scholarships a year were offered, spread over all subjects and the whole country.

It must have been in early 1958 that a letter on blue ministerial notepaper arrived inviting me to sit on a departmental committee to enquire into the future of the Youth Service in England and Wales. The chairwoman was to be Diana, Countess of Albemarle. The Countess was a handsome lady, friendly in the relaxed manner assured status can bring to those who want to be friendly, and well regarded in Whitehall for her extensive and effective public work.

The proposed chairwomen or chairmen of such committees are offered a list of possible names for members but room is left for them to choose some of their own. It mustn't be felt that the Ministry imposes only its own candidates. Conversely, it is said, you mustn't reject a sizeable number of their names in favour of your own; for if things go wrong with the committee and its report you could be blamed for having ignored the advisers and chosen unwisely. I think I was one of the Countess's proposals, prompted by her reading *The Uses of Literacy*.

I was unsure whether to accept, knowing the jokes about the Great and Good nodding somnolently over their documents. I did not want to join that sub-branch of the Establishment, even if only for the lifetime of such a committee. Yet I was concerned about the barren lives of many young people and glad to have a chance to look into whether some useful suggestions could be made. An unfashionable attitude even at that time, felt to be paternalistic. But barrenness is the right word, even though the group-lives of many young people may be more complex than adults assume.

Someone I knew had recently been invited to become a JP and, surprisingly, that helped me to agree to join the Albemarle Committee. I realised I would not have been willing to be a member of the Bench; it brought back too many memories of legitimated bossiness from above. By contrast, service on a committee with a precise and finite brief in an important area began to seem attractive.

Committees such as these are better than their conventional repute. They can become useful, though small and temporary, communities. That is less likely if the membership includes a majority with known political or commercial interests in the subject. Then they may fight with one another, and the chairman has to find compromises from the struggle. But the old style of temporary (or permanent) quango – a type which was almost destroyed in the Eighties by the confident imperatives of governments committed to conviction politics – those old-style quangos had at least a majority of members with open minds, though not all were at the start well informed in their briefs. They often did not know each other's political allegiances, if any, and did not seek to know them. They were anxious to be fair to all sides and to do a bit of good, either by helping a continuing body – such as the BBC, the Arts Council, the University Grants Committee, the British Council – to whose constitutions the service of the public interest was more important than particular political positions. Or, as with the Albemarle Committee, those invited were willing to try to reduce confusion in an area which, a government had at last recognised, needed as nearly as possible disinterested attention. The quango was an important device of consensus politics. When confrontational-ideological politics arrived, it was made to look like a dodo of public life.

That description of such committees is slightly rose-tinted; but does point to virtues often shown and rarely recognised. Even if some, perhaps most, members know little in the beginning about the arguments in the field they can, under good chairmanship and with hard work, arrive from that standing start at soundly based, sometimes bold, judgments. One observer of these processes has argued that within a few months these committees produce two or three 'gladiators' – pace-setters or scouts could be other names – who slip into the role of marshalling and presenting the arguments on the different sides, and fight them out as if between themselves but really for the edification of the others. He was not suggesting that this was a deliberate process, but that so it happened. They played out for the others, as if dramatically, the conflicting themes, and patterns of opposed positions, emerging from the mass of oral and written evidence.

It is not assumed, by the members or the sponsoring department, that the recommendations of public committees have to be accepted; they are advice to a minister. In turn, ministers remind themselves, in the self-evident but complacent formulation (often a tautology masking a disposition to brutality) that 'the business of government is to govern'. But a quango likes its report to be taken seriously. If it begins to suspect in the course of its life, or after the report has been presented, that it has been regarded only as an instrument to pipe off dissent, then it becomes angry and publicly vocal. I have twice seen ministers, meeting quango members in the ministerial conference room, become riled. They then have, at the extreme, a favourite formulation: 'Thank you for your views. But please don't try to teach me how to run my Department.' To which the chairman of the quango replies: 'And please don't expect me and my members to spend months of our time only to have our recommendations put aside in what I am forced to describe as a cavalier manner.' It is in the English style that the minister then nods curtly and business continues; but a point may have been taken.

Quite early in the life of a committee a decision has to be made about how and by whom the report will be written. The assigned civil servants will keep a record and are usually willing to prepare a first and perhaps the final draft. Some chairmen will allow no one but themselves to write the report. Others look round the committee for a few weeks and then persuade a member or two to make the draft. This was Lady Albemarle's style, and she settled on Leslie Paul and me. Leslie had not long finished a substantial report on the pay and conditions of Church of England clergy, but that had not given much scope for his abilities as a writer. His autobiographical volumes − notably *Angry Young Man*, a title later appropriated as the label for a half-generation − showed these skills better. We agreed, of course.

Drafting might have dragged on if we had met more than once to discuss the parts, but here also Lady Albemarle's patrician decisiveness and influence came into play. She asked us to meet quite soon, on a Saturday and Sunday, in the Curzon Street offices of the Ministry of Education (they now house some of the Security Services). She had obtained permission for us to work in the empty building. She fed us very well at due intervals, and by some time on the Sunday we had a complete draft for the committee to work on.

The report was a sensible document, not high-minded or romantic or nostalgic; and the minister was sensible enough to accept most of it, and to provide more money (naturally, not as much as we had hoped). It appeared in a favourable climate, when governments were first becoming aware of inner-city problems. Even so, it could have only a very slight effect on this particular range of troubles. It would have been ludicrous to expect a twelve-person, twelve-month report to bring major changes. Perhaps, though, conditions might have been worse if

Albemarle had not sat; better that than merely verbal moral Elastoplast.

The report also had some quite well written passages, much quoted, and used in 'A'-level examination papers for years afterwards. It was excoriated by some members of the House of Lords. Even the members of the committee who were communicant members of the Church of England had been led to question the formalistic piety which some Youth Clubs required as a condition of membership, such as demanding a public profession of belief before each evening's activities. We said, in a po-faced sentence we enjoyed drafting, that belief or decency could be just as well expressed in deeds as in words: 'It is on the whole better for principles to be seen shining through works than for them to be signalised by some specific spiritual assertion.' This infuriated one bishop, and the violence of his attack on our 'godlessness' gained the report far more attention than it would otherwise have been thought worth, especially by the tabloid press. Still, he was no more unattractive than the two or three other bishops, in their fifties, who used the occasion to display how much they identified with 'the young', 'the kids'.

Was it worthwhile to do so many different, but not entirely disparate, things at the cost of writing more books? The habit, started in 1957, persisted through the Sixties, was interrupted by five years (1970–5) at UNESCO in Paris, started again in the mid-Seventies and was only brought under control by 1985. The peak was in the late Seventies. Each committee brought its share of reports, enquiries, publications. I sometimes remembered Lawrence: 'Never a real or a good thing said'; but if the limitations had been as plain as that refusals would have been easier. I also felt, all the time, as I had about the narrow range from which reviewers were chosen: there are lots of people who could do these jobs as well as I could. But by then I knew why such a search was rarely made, and suggestions of other names received without interest.

Throughout, I did not think of myself as 'a committee man'; each invitation seemed to be a job worth doing. So one got up earlier, went to bed later, and learned to squeeze work into hitherto unregarded corners.

I was glad to find that I was wanted, whilst always acting as one coming in from the outside and going back there once the job was done; not belonging for long to any group, however lofty its intentions. I believed that most of the activities, the public committee work in particular, could be useful. It is misguided for most British intellectuals to dismiss such democratic devices.

I would have found it difficult to bear the lonely business of gambling for years, at the cost of other commitments and probably to the family's cost, on a belief in the value of a big literary work in hand. I had a capacity to work hard, and staying power, but my mind focussed narrowly rather than widely. Few speed changes; a medium-sized tractor not a swish saloon. Nor could I knock off commissions of momentary interest and importance whilst keeping a larger piece of work steadily moving. 'The immediate is the enemy of the lasting', if this is your cast of mind.

I admired those who did not need regular responses from others, who expressed self-sufficiency in their whole manner. Mine was a common condition and bred multiple devices for putting off the moment at which I sat before that blank sheet of paper. I did this not only by undertaking reviews, lectures, some broadcasting, committees, but also by performing repetitive patterns, from too often sharpening pencils to clearing each day's mail, however trivial, before anything else was settled down to. Another image, to match that of the delta, lodged in my mind: that of a hen distracted by every casual handful of grain thrown its way. Fret and stir. Thoreau in *Walden* fits: 'Our life is frittered away by detail. Simplify. Simplify.'

Yet I learned something from these many excursions, and enjoyed much in them. Especially from the committees; they showed important decencies in the British public-spirited character, well below simple pushiness or pomposity; and I needed to learn about those. The Orlick spirit and the conspiracy-theory spirit come easily to people with my background. Still: I was putting off taking sufficient intellectual and emotional stock of where I might best go. I was putting off the real test, which was to learn how to work steadily at two activities: writing something substantial and true to what talents I might have, whilst at the same time justifying my wages as a teacher. Instead, I tried to pay proper dues to the long-term teaching whilst also accepting the short-term engagements; and more or less shelved the long-term commitment to writing.

So there was a loss. Not of great books, just of a book or two more central to my experience than the – usually workmanlike – things I did produce. My greatest surprise was the realisation, quite late, that I was living like one who assumed there would be numberless tomorrows, endless opportunities for adjustment. I was living like a man with three lives; there would always be a time to change tack; next week, next month, next year.

4

These were some of the changes which flowed from the publication of *The Uses of Literacy*. They produced gains and losses, but it is in the nature of such intangible matters that the person directly affected cannot be sure his balance sheet is the same as that of an observer. I feel somewhat surer about two gains, one emotional, the other professional and practical.

In spite of what I have said about fret and stir, the recognition given to the book, even after some excess has been allowed for because of its timely appearance, did make me feel more secure. Looking round at people who had more powerful minds or greater imaginative gifts, I felt chuffed that I had managed to make as much as apparently I had from the talents I possessed, and from a start in the social and educational rear.

The professional gain from *The Uses of Literacy* came because it appeared as we were thinking of trying to leave the eleven years, night-after-night, sequence of extra-mural classes and the increasing succession of weekend schools, all of which interfered with family life. I had a very good chance of becoming the head of a university extra-mural department, but that is a largely administrative job. There was also the slight possibility of 'going internal', moving into a university's English department.

I was by then a senior extra-mural tutor, almost forty, and hence expensive. This was the late Fifties, well after the immediate post-war boom in university jobs and before the Sixties expansion and the creation of the new universities (that began about 1962). If I was to move into an internal department, *The Uses of Literacy* was the best recommendation. But few heads of English departments were likely to appoint an extra-mural tutor, even though he had written a well received book; that book was, after all, well off the main academic lines of publication for specialists in English.

In late 1957 I applied for a lectureship at the University of Leicester. The head of department was at that time seeking a practising creative writer and found one in the poet and critic G. S. Fraser who was ready, after more than ten years of its excitements and worries, to leave the London freelance literary scene.

Some time in late 1958 the same department advertised for a senior lecturer. At that time such posts were hardly ever available. The Leicester department had one professor, the vacant senior lectureship and a handful of lecturers and assistant lecturers. This post was certain to attract large numbers of well qualified candidates. And it seemed wrong-headed, since I had not long before failed to gain a lectureship in that department, to seek the senior lectureship. But a 'phone call indicated that an application would be welcome; and I was appointed.

For the children's education, mid-1959 was a reasonable time to move. Our departure ran true to form. Mary's father's rather limited and sometimes unreasoned integrity had given him the strong belief that it was sharp practice to sell a house for more than you had actually paid for it, no matter how long ago. He never assimilated the concept of continuing inflation, even of a very minor kind. I had a not altogether clear idea that he was mistaken, though I should certainly have known he was. But I shared Harry's reluctance to exploit others; which is why we have still never held stocks. We had been in the Hull house for eight years and made some major structural improvements. We were finally persuaded by our solicitor to add about £150 to the price we had paid eight years before, so as to at least acknowledge the improvements, and told a couple who had heard we were leaving that they could have it at that price. They, both lecturers at the local college of education, accepted eagerly. Then they came back, said they were a little short of ready money, and so would we drop the price about £100 and that off the down payment (the whole cost was already less than £2000); it seemed niggling to refuse.

The liveable Leicester house we found cost about £3500. We discovered from the deeds that the sellers had paid less than £2000 for it only three or four years before. They were within their rights; and after a very slightly rueful week or two we thought no more about it. Not virtue, just a matter of finding your own balance in attitudes, learning what it is comfortable to live with.

I began this chapter with an image for the shape of my professional life after the publication of *The Uses of Literacy*; the picture of a single river breaking into many subsidiary streams. Yet the dispersal was in forms of activity, not in types of interest. The delta has had only four or five branches, and they all interconnect.

Their common source is a sense of the importance of the right of each of us to speak about how we see life, the world; and so the right to have access to the means by which that capacity to speak may be gained. The right, also, to try to reach out and speak to others, not to have that impulse inhibited by social barriers, maintained by those in power politically or able to exercise power in other ways.

So the main currents of my interests have been: the right of wider access to higher education, the need for wider access also to the arts as the most scrupulous explorations we can make of our personalities and relationships, and of the nature of our societies; and, as a support to all this, the best uses of mass communications.

All democratic societies, and especially the wide-open clamant consumer democracies such as ours, need many more people who try to think hard about the value of the lives they are offered and then describe, straightforwardly, what they find. As Chekhov did, speaking with love and anger to his own people: 'You live badly, my friends; it is shameful to live like that. . . .'

✤

CHAPTER 2

MILD MIDLANDS:
LEICESTER 1959–64

I was appointed to the Leicester University Senior Lectureship, in 1959, in characteristically mild Leicester fashion: because of a stroll in a park. Victoria Park, on the edge of which the university sits, is a medium-sized inner-city space, on a short hill overlooking the medium-sized city's centre less than half a mile away. Almost everything in Leicester fits its chosen mode; nothing dramatic, everything as it should be to a reasonable person.

The head of the English department, Arthur Humphreys, was intrigued by my candidature and teased away at the questions it raised long after a more cautious man would have decided to tell the interviewing board that, 'in all the circumstances' and with no disrespect to Mr H's unusual record, 'x' from the very good other applicants seemed the right man.

After that morning session Humphreys asked George Fraser, partly to reassure him about my possible arrival, to walk round the park. Hoggart's the most interesting candidate, he said, but he'd be a gamble. He'd come in October and in December I'm to leave for a term at the Folger Library in Washington; he'd be in charge. He's lectured a few times a week in the Hull internal department but never been a full-time member. Could he cope with the time-tabling, the examination preparations, fighting our corner in faculty and university committees, sorting out problems with students and sometimes staff? It's certainly a gamble, Fraser said, but so was my appointment. If you still want Hoggart, after the interviews, you should say so.

That afternoon, one member of the board either decided to play devil's advocate or genuinely doubted whether a tutor from an extra-mural department, even a senior tutor, would be scholarly enough for an internal senior lectureship. I resisted on behalf of the extra-mural world, especially when he questioned the academic soundness of introducing great European writers, *in translation*, to a course on the novel.

They offered me the job. The Vice-Chancellor in particular, and perhaps most of the others, trusted Arthur Humphreys's hunches and respected his devotion to his department and the fledgling university. I started in Autumn 1959. The students, like almost all the staff, were friendly. For most students, and they were from a great variety of backgrounds, it was still a matter of surprise that they had managed to enter this wide-horizoned world.

I

Leicester and Leicestershire, with the old Rutland, are quintessential middle-England. Belloc was wrong, the Midlands are not sodden and unkind – at least, not the East Midlands. They are above everything mild and friendly. Perhaps Belloc had in mind parts of the West Midlands. Auden's heart may have 'stamped on / The view from Birmingham to Wolverhampton' but Belloc's Sussex-loving soul would be repelled by all those satanic factories, slag-heaps and stacks of rusting disused machinery along the rail-tracks. For two years, from 1962 to 1964, after leaving Leicester's university for Birmingham's I commuted between the two. The rattling, smelly diesel units, always too cold or too hot and shabby after their first six months, fitted perfectly the nondescript land-scape over which they tracked. Near Nuneaton a large sign announced JUDKIN'S WASHED GRANITE. That fitted perfectly too; the name, the trade, the bald notice. Did Judkin live near the works or had he, like many middle-range bosses round here, found somewhere pleasant and fresh up in the Charnwood Forest?

As you come nearer Leicester from the west, the landscape changes to the gently rolling, and remains comely all the way east past Leicester, and some distance from north to south: to the Vale of Belvoir, across to Lincolnshire and Grantham, down to Melton Mowbray and across again to Stamford, a beautiful but dead town, grey in stone and seemingly in spirit, a place which long ago turned its back on modernities; a feudal relic from which most young people have to escape since the embalmed beauty says nothing to them.

Depending on what you expect from where you live, there are several effective sizes for a city. Leicester's three hundred thousand is one of the best sizes for those who dislike massiveness and anonymity, but want some artistic and intellectual life, respectable shopping and a reliable train service to a capital or metropolitan areas which are not so near that better-off executives will use your place and its nearby villages as a dormitory, but are near enough for an affordable day-return to the big place. It is possible, on that middle scale between the small and ill-provided and the huge and inchoate cities, to retain a sense of a coherent community in which different groups are not corralled from each other but to some extent mix in the market, the cinemas, the theatre, the bigger classless shops, some of the recreational and good-heartedly purposive clubs and societies.

Leicester, the archetype of such cities, is homely, decent, manageable, able to be held in the hand. It is clean, since by the time it began to acquire considerable industry, gas and then electric power had arrived. Such heavy industry as it has did not, even before the Clean Air Act, place a pall over the city; and the coalfields are a few miles away. It is diversified and so has avoided the great slumps which can affect cities with only a few industries and those interdependent and, with many smaller industries, suppliers of parts and specialised services, dependent in turn on the bigger. Leicester makes shoes, knitwear, polishes – like itself middle-range things, but necessary and useful. It is slightly hilly but you hardly notice that as you walk in the centre or drive down the 'boulevards' which radiate from town, their verges wide, their semis clean, well back from the exhaust fumes. Leicester is hardly ever dramatic and never apocalyptic; Dostoevsky would have left for a more startling climate.

Of course, there are big housing estates, some of them dreary and anonymous in the usual manner, but no huge slum areas like my own native district Hunslet, in Leeds, and its counterparts in Manchester, Liverpool, Sheffield. Near the railway-station there was – it may have been cleaned up by now – a poor lodging area catering to working-class transients. I once went down there to pass on some good news to a woman living in one room with several young children and no wage-earner; she had asked for help and given an address among those latish-nineteenth-century houses. I failed to find her. The house she had named and those on either side, all smelling of boiled bacon and cabbage, were full of Irish labourers preparing their evening meals. They were working on the M1, the first motorway, and would move with it. Every one of them denied any knowledge of the woman and slammed the door in my face. They were not going to give anything away to a chap who looked like that and spoke like that; he was probably an official nark.

Truer to the generally helpful and relaxed manner of a more secure Leicester were the events surrounding the setting-up of an inner-city Youth Club, in the early Sixties. It had been inspired by the Albemarle Report and I was asked to serve on its committee. The chairwoman was Joan Goddard, of the well known polish family and, with her husband, a strong upholder of the characteristic Leicester virtues. The inspirer and first director was Ray Gosling, now a popular broadcaster but then just finishing or prematurely dropping out from his university course. The club, in a bleak non-residential area just off the centre, had predictable birth-pains. Gosling told the committee early on that the police were frightening away just the people the club was meant to attract. In particular, they made frequent obstreperous raids in search of drugs. No doubt some of those who came to the club were using drugs; that knowledge was part of the point of the experiment, which now looked like foundering.

'I will ask Robert if he will meet the committee,' Joan Goddard said. Robert turned up at the next meeting, splendid in his accoutrements – the Chief Constable, Robert Mark, later the Commissioner of the Metropolitan Police. Elfed Thomas, the city's Director of Education – known as Well-fed Thomas for his amiable plumpness – was given to advising visitors, usually in one of his favourite aphorisms, not to commit a parking offence: 'Our Chief Constable is a sea-green incorruptible.' On this occasion he proved to be an extremely flexible incorruptible, with the flexibility that probity and conviction can give. He listened to our story, thought for a few seconds, and said: 'All right. I see your point. I'll put a ring-fence round the club at four hundred yards and my men will only cross it if there is clearly a threat to public order. But if we catch any of your people into drugs outside that fence then we'll jump on them; hard.' That helped settle the club's unsteady legs.

Spread in and around the inner city, like most of Leicester institutions, were Vaughan College, for long one of the finest adult education centres in Britain, the home of the Leicester Poetry Society and several similar initiatives; and – except for a few years' gap – the professional theatre or, more accurately, succession of theatres all well supported by town and gown; and the Literary and Philosophical Society. Provision for these kinds of interests was strong, continuous and, to a degree I had not seen in other cities, still in part assumed to belong not simply to the cultivated among the prosperous middle class but also to young people from all around and to a range of autodidacts of all ages. Leicester was a perfect place to be the home of a certain kind of university, one both international, as any university must be, and also genuinely local but not parochial.

Leicester was also, at that time, still a very large county town, the haunt at suitable times – for shopping other than in London, for solicitors and the right county clubs – of the eastern shire people, ineluctable Tories from the fat counties; from round Melton Mowbray, which gave its name to those tasty pork pies, invented for eating on or near the saddle; and from Oundle and other beautifully preserved eighteenth-century ironstone small towns and villages. Such places smell too much of a prosperous and not greatly literate rural upper-middle class (or, now, commuting senior executives) to be liveable in unless you close eyes, ears and mind to the narrowness of most of the residents' horizons. A pity, since the natural horizons are calm and courteous. But such people know and order their world. Driving through Oundle at about eleven one night, going home after talking to a WEA group in Lincolnshire at my brother Tom's invitation, I was flagged down without cause by the local policeman. What was I doing at that time of night? Was I, he clearly thought, one of those thieves who break into country houses, steal a few treasured heirlooms, and then rush for the new motorway or trunk road? 'We don't like cars going *late* through Oundle,' he said.

Once settled in, we were able to see a lot of this countryside.

Tom and his family had gone to live in Bourne, a shortish ride east
into Lincolnshire; he had become headmaster of a new secondary
modern school serving a large and backward rural area – so rural
that you constantly met pheasants neurotically scurrying over the
roads. So rural and feudal that the local lord still paid the boys
of the villages to act as beaters at his shoots. One boy at Tom's
school was slightly peppered with shot, and carefully recom-
pensed. He wrote humorously about it in the school magazine.
That wouldn't do at all. The Earl's secretary was soon on the
'phone to say that his lordship, who had a direct line to the
school's governors, disapproved. This in the early Sixties. O God!
O Lincolnshire!

It was, I think, Edith Wharton who wrote warmly about the
littleness of England, the patchworking and the variety in so small
a space. Standing in the railway station at Stuttgart, watching the
trains pull out for the great European cities, or in the airport at
Minneapolis as the destination boards click over, gives a sense of
space not to be found in England. One can enjoy both and wonder
at both, at the way humans respond to their different sorts of
spaces and make them all into home landscapes. Leicestershire
and the old Rutland encapsulated one of the most representative
kinds of English experience and reality.

All that in a panorama which was still, though one of the
most humanely gentle landscapes of Europe, given over to the
squirearchy, the hunting squirearchy. They came into Leicester,
the women more often than the men, in their well made tweeds
and aggressive felt hats, and sat taking tea in the lounge of the
Grand Hotel; or went to fixed points in Joseph Johnson's stores,
fitting out their teenage daughters with the regulation camel coats
and their sons with the public schools' mandatory grey flannel
trousers and navy-blue blazers – the mothers' silver-plated voices
making the nearby display stands tremble.

Hunting was, for many of these people, the main occupation
(after, for the newly half-accepted, anxious to keep up, the pursuit
of money). The men with hard, broad, florid faces. The women
with hard faces too, but beginning to be lined by the dietetic and
cosmetic effort not to become as jowly as their men after reaching
forty-five, or to slide into looking heavily horsey.

We lived in Leicester itself, less than a mile from the city centre, four hundred yards over the park from the university, within easy walking distance of the three schools the children joined (no comprehensives in the town then; two went to grammar schools, and the third to a gentle Church of England junior school two hundred yards away). We had five years there, from 1959 to 1964, during the last two of which I commuted to Birmingham so as not to disturb the children's education at the wrong time.

We had found a pleasant, turn-of-the-century, double-fronted, middle-class house with a small walled garden. It was in a short street of extremely mixed housing, some small artisan terracing, a large, splendid, Ernest Gimson detached house on a nearby corner (occupied by the Professor of Philosophy), a doctor's house at the other end – he was a nationally known supporter of euthanasia – and, slotted in the gaps, a few modern semis, in one of which lived the bachelor head of Leicester's thriving department of sociology. The immediate area, about a quarter of a mile square, was socially mixed; and when groups of students began to settle in some of the working-class terraces, that added a new and ever so slightly Bohemian element.

Only a few weeks after we had moved in, Mary's father fell ill. Advanced cancer of the prostate was soon diagnosed and he took to his bed in their front room downstairs. No question of taking him to hospital; he would be nursed at home until the end. Mary went to Stalybridge every week to help an entirely uncomplaining mother. The end came in four months and we buried him on 10 January 1960; he had seen the children – his only grandchildren, as he was their only grandfather – as often as could be managed in those last months, but he never saw our Leicester house. A tiny matter, that; but he would very much have liked to see it, the first house in a new kind of life for his daughter and only child and her family. Compared with his own decades of dedicated teaching in the town of his birth, left only for teacher training college in Chester and for front-line infantry service in Flanders, his daughter's life was proving bewilderingly mobile and ascendant. After the funeral, Doris came to stay with us but refused to move in permanently. She was entirely at home only in Stalybridge; her house was easily coped with; she knew everyone around; she continued to feed herself properly. Until her death at the beginning of 1970 she visited us often, for long stretches, and was at ease with the mixture of people, of a kind she had not known before, who came into our Leicester and Birmingham houses. We took quiet holidays each summer with her. Her lights were strong, steady, sensible, and we all admired that.

Once settled in house and schools the children, becoming more independent by the month, got to know all the rabbit-tracks of their age and kind: down into town on Saturday afternoon to buy the latest single, or to Leicester City's match, or to pop concerts in the De Montfort Hall; again, all within walkable reach if they wanted to put the bus fare to some other use. So were the Public Baths which we often visited early on Saturdays with Philip Collins. He had directed Vaughan College for some years and took my place in the English department when I left for Birmingham; his reputation as a Victorian scholar was already beginning to be well established. We came back from the Baths to a big bacon and egg breakfast. Now and again we went boating on the Soar a few miles out but so ineptly that, on the occasion we hired a cabin cruiser, we cut all the lines of the Leicestershire Fishing Club; and half an hour later four of the five of us fell into the water as we tried to get under a crowded bridge.

Leicester life was also interspersed by a sequence of trips away: to the Royal Shakespeare Company at Stratford; up north to see sister Molly, Aunts Ethel and Annie, to stay in Stalybridge or with old friends in Dewsbury; and to see Tom. At this time too there were invitations to lecture at summer schools in Germany, and to those we tacked roaming holidays.

We had bought our first television set in late 1957 on returning from America, not long after commercial television started. But television only became a regular part of the family's routines in the Leicester years. The appearance of *That Was The Week That Was*, in late 1962, marked the moment at which, like millions of others, we realised that the box in the corner could offer, was prepared to offer, a funny and slightly subversive angle on our lives, especially to our sense of where we fitted in to the various authorities in London. I talked about those years later to Hugh Carleton Greene. Had he realised, as Director-General of the BBC, what he was opening up – at the most serious, a reflection of the divisions within British society; at the most ribald some very enjoyable snook-cocking at the powers-that-were? As to the first he was rather uncomprehending, but he understood the snook-cocking. He did not seem to have thought greatly about the nature of society or about broadcasting's relationships to it. He was a tough journalist with a powerful objection to anyone who tried to stop him telling things as he saw them; more important, he was a middle-class, public-school educated, at times bloody-minded, eccentric of a kind the English regularly throw up. He was part of at least one Establishment; he went, for example, to Ascot in the regulation formal dress for the occasion. But he hated the habits and especially the old-boy mutual protectiveness practised by the great Establishments of state and church; and so he gave the young satire team their heads and stood by them when they were attacked. A television interviewer mused to him one day, as two or three of us waited to go on air, that he would soon be questioning the Secretary of State for Education and was wondering whether he could fairly point out that her daughter had just been enrolled at an independent school. Greene's reply was immediate and unqualified: 'How can you imagine *not* asking that question?'

After the unsocial regime of extra-mural life, with hardly ever a weekday evening and not many weekends off, Leicester offered what seemed like a plethora of social occasions. George Fraser may have given up the excitements of London literary life, but he thrived on parties wherever he was. The Frasers created the nearest thing in the area to a literary salon – of congenial university staff, people from the town whom catholic George had met in classes and at readings; and, as often as not, visitors from elsewhere whom he had cajoled into talking to the Poetry Society. This period saw the beginning of provincial England's acceptance of wine for general circulation at evening parties, instead of coffee. Plonk of a usually inferior kind could be had for a few bob a bottle; so you brought your own, and soon learned to avoid Lutomer Riesling, Emu, Mateus Rosé and Liebfraumilch; as you might today pass by Piat d'Or. Those were the most companionable literary get-togethers we have known.

2

It is not surprising that the main Leicester University building, the original heart of the University College and its small-scale but domesticated social life, have figured in several modern novels: in early Larkin (he was assistant librarian there), in *Lucky Jim* (Amis was a friend of Larkin, and visited), and in Bradbury's *Eating People is Wrong* (he had been a student in the English Department). The main block had been built as what used to be called a lunatic asylum, but to a more human scale and style than the northern asylums, frowning on their sooty hills outside the bigger cities. The flower-beds at the front had a drilled municipal air; one could, on dull days especially, easily imagine the patients wandering there, lost and disconnected; but when students were spread out on the grass after the June examinations all was as pleasant as an impressionist park on a summer Sunday.

The college had been founded in 1918, became a university college in 1950 and a university in 1957. It suffered less than Hull and some other small new universities from the wish to assert its academic standing against Oxbridge and the great and long-established Redbricks. True, the staff at Leicester were expected to wear gowns when lecturing, but so they were at much bigger and solider places such as Birmingham; an odd habit, it seems now, and given up after 1968 if not before.

Leicester's greatest single act of independent good sense was the decision not to have a twig of Royalty, or at least of the older aristocracy, as its senior honorific figure, the Chancellor. Instead, they invited the most distinguished academic person they could persuade; in my day it was Lord Adrian. That was also a shrewd political move since Adrian was one of the great Oxbridge personalities of his time, and when he decided to make Leicester a special interest he at once brought it into almost a special relationship with what most of the university world still thought of as the heart of things. But above all Leicester's decision here was inspired because it said: in our development we put the promotion of scholarship above titles and dignities by birth.

Most of us have a cast-list of *dramatis personae* in our heads, of figures, faces, and above all, for me, voices of people with whom we carry on intermittent but lasting dialogues. They are our intellectual or imaginative mentors, or our moral mentors, or something of all three. We spread them like markers around the frontiers of our minds, or they position themselves there, even if we do not want that, a gallery of onlookers towards whom we often feel ambiguous. They are on guard across different parts of our personalities. We respect them, at least in parts (the parts we feel least sure about in ourselves), though we may not approve of some aspects of their own characters. But in the admired parts they become bench-marks for things we would like to do well ourselves. They do some things better than we do, and we know it. They write better or act better or meet challenges better or choose better or know how and when to refuse or shut up better. Often we find them severe, as if clothed in black, as they stand looking at us. On the other hand they may also be teaching us how to relax and stop caring, or caring-and-not-caring, about the wrong things, in the wrong ways.

At Leicester I soon, but not entirely clearly at first, realised that George Fraser had become, in a qualified way, one of my onlookers. That is always a choice by both sides, though rarely made explicit. He was watching me for signs that I might be succumbing to the temptation to become a public figure, to become a public rather than a private face and voice. He respected me as a writer, though not a regular enough writer, for that was to him – as to me – the greatest of callings, not lightly to be deserted for however worthy a public cause. That way lay propaganda and shrillness, not the honest careful voice. I like to think that when he took up this stance he hadn't actually detected that weakness in me but was just making sure. The success of *The Uses of Literacy*, the part I played in the 1960 *Lady Chatterley's Lover* prosecution, and the stir about the Pilkington Report on broadcasting of 1962 might well, he seems to have suspected, made me change into a big bow-wow. He was suspicious of all signs of the bureaucratic mind; that was like imaginative death, frost-bite, gangrene, creeping out from the insecure but all too often bossy areas of the personality.

So I, and I expect others, knew that George could be a kind of litmus paper who would detect even a marginal dishonesty of the imagination. If he did, he would give a sharp little laugh and produce a phrase – in a dry and slightly sly Aberdonian accent – which cut you down, impaled you, as it was meant to. You became aware of him watching you in that spirit, though affectionately, if he cared for you. If he did not care for you, if he had written you off as an imagination-less person, he would not have much bothered to watch. He was keeping his preferred image of you well rubbed down and polished.

All this sounds too disciplinarian; but watchfulness can also be generous. I once wrote a piece on Parson Kilvert, whom I especially admired for his access to his own vulnerability. I wondered if it had turned out sentimental, for the tightrope was tricky. A day or two after it was published came a postcard in George's spidery scrawl: 'That was very good; you had the balance right and the reasons for the affection come out without mawkishness.'

He was in some ways insecure. Without the all-enveloping care of his wife, Paddy, over three-and-a-half decades, he would have been many times lost. He was no good at doing-things-about-the-house or with the administrative business which all families need. His literary absorption was able to flourish because Paddy provided a protective hedge around him.

She also knew when to call in outside help. On one occasion George was badly shaken and our roles reversed; Paddy asked me to call in and try to comfort him. A senior member of another department had suggested George's appointment had proved a mistake (his time-keeping was not impeccable but, having once arrived, he taught with complete concentration and regardless of time). If you have painfully built up such poise as you can whilst all the while trying to be honest before your own weaknesses, you may not have adequate defences if you are hit below the belt; you have no carapace such as, for instance, salesmen or politicians have to develop if they are to survive at all. You have always laid yourself open, so if someone comes at you with more harshness than the cause warrants you are almost defenceless.

George's fragility was one of the qualities which informed his generosity towards other people, especially young people; and the struggling and wounded of any age. He was hospitable to dropouts and to students making a muck of things because they wanted to make their lives 'meaningful', as the fashionable word was then. He was less interested in the student who was working calculatedly towards getting a First. He had no calculation in himself and did not warm to it in others. He caught the combination in an early poem: 'My simple heart bred in provincial tenderness / And my cold mind which takes the world for theme.' That is too harsh on himself. His mind was not cold; it was tough. His imagination could be, was, tender and even sentimental; his mind was dry and severe when he felt it had to be, if the main things he believed in were threatened.

I had first met him in 1948, in Great Ormond Street, in the Frasers' flat opposite the Hospital for Sick Children. I was working on my book on Auden. Someone had said: 'You must meet Fraser; he'll be helpful; he'll help anyone he decides is serious about modern poetry.' They were packing for Japan and the cultural attaché-ship, and the place was all huge boxes. George asked Paddy for a pound and we went to the local pub. For the next hour he devoted his whole attention to the obscure extra-mural lecturer from the north who had written for advice. There was no hint of the literary-man-in-the-swim giving his inside knowledge to an outsider. Many years after the book had appeared, and in response to my remarking that it was by then far outclassed, he put his finger on what he saw as its worth; that it was a young man's book about the living author who had most fired his imagination; that it did not greatly matter if other books had surpassed it as literary criticism, because this one had to be written, was of a particular and unusual kind.

He liked to think of himself as a serious craftsman who was also a competent journalist able to meet deadlines. He regularly turned out pieces for the *Times Literary Supplement*, each well shaped and carefully argued, scarcely ever tired or repetitive. The paperback on Ezra Pound was an example of this workmanlike quality. At one point he was not keeping to his schedule on that and then one day – I expect Paddy discovered it – the deadline was only a week or so off. She put him in the attic with a succession of cups of coffee and packets of cigarettes, and he did the job in about a fortnight. There was a certain pride in having done it at such speed, and we had a party. I doubt if he would have written a better one if he had had six months. He had one kind of book on Pound locked inside him, but almost ready; once he was forced to unlock it the birth was rapid.

From Birmingham, after we had left Leicester, I assessed his MA students for several years. They had had the same precise attention as he gave to preparing an important long essay or lecture for a prestigious national institute, or for the Leicester Poetry Society. From his perspective, you respected anyone who came to you, or asked you to come to them, to talk about the thing that mattered most, writing. He was not by nature, but became, one of the sorts of people I especially admire, who work devotedly and long in the provinces and do not all the time at the backs of their minds wish they were elsewhere, in London, at 'the centre of things', who do not cluster in little groups of their own kind but go out and become part of their local communities.

That was the microscopic side of George Fraser's way of working. There was a broader side which was even more unusual. He still had the dream, probably from his Scottish education, of the duty to be a wide-ranging scholar-intellectual-artist; something of the Johnsonian man of letters. He assumed he and his colleagues should be interested in and knowledgeable about society and politics, and was irritated if they betrayed inadequate historical backgrounds. So his talk ranged exceptionally widely, and confidently.

His central quality is best summed up in a favourite word he took from Yeats's use of it: 'companionable'. An enduring snapshot is of him at one of the parties in their Guilford Road house, glass in hand, in a group, he talking cheerfully all the time. He felt you *should* belong to groups you liked.

I only once saw him out-talked. After C. P. Snow had spoken to a literary group one evening (round about the time of Leavis's attack on him) George and I took him into a pub in Granby Street. He was angry and hurt about the Leavis attack but talked of the need for 'magnanimity'. Soon an expansive and benign helpfulness took over and he began to address us as 'you boys' and to give advice as from one old hand to another – especially about how to get on to the 'American lecture circuit gravy train'. There was about him something Leavis may have found coarse-grained, like a tough businessman who had strayed into writing. There was generosity also, and a touch of surprised naïveté at realising how far he had come from his Leicester background. One knew better then why Lionel Trilling felt he had to tell Leavis he regretted the tone of his attack on Snow.

George Fraser loved women. Not as a sexual courtier but because he felt they held a quality essential also to a man's proper being. He loved his mother; in his marriage he was, with this side of himself, uxorious; he loved to have women around; he liked the way they smelt and the ways their imaginations worked; and they responded with equally straightforward warmth.

Another instance, which directly concerned me, showed both his generosity and his toughness. I gave the BBC Reith Lectures in the early 1970s. Richard Crossman, to the surprise of the literary editor, asked the *Sunday Times* to let him review the published version. Crossman's review was an act of revenge because he thought his assumed intellectual eminence had been questioned by me during a conversation ten years before. The following week's *Sunday Times* carried a letter from George saying the review was unjust, and exactly why. He knew from experience how deeply one could be hurt by such treatment.

On the other hand, years later, George reviewed a book I wrote about life as a cultural bureaucrat in UNESCO and – here was the guardian in full action – whilst being complimentary, decided to warn me that my own style had become a bit bureaucratic too. I don't think he was right, all in all; I think he was unconsciously looking for that before he began, so anxious was he that none of his friends should become exponents of Bafflegab. But no guardian pleases those guarded all the time, or he wouldn't be a good guardian.

George Fraser's expansive body expressed well the expansive side of his nature. From another angle the body was alien to him because inside it was a thin, lean personality looking out sharply at what he thought was the truth of things. When we heard of George's death I said to Mary: 'If you were allowed one word to describe George, what would it be?' 'Oh,' she said, after a moment, 'nimble.' That could not be bettered.

He died in January 1980 and was buried outside the town, at Oadby. Predictably, we all went back to Guilford Road for drinks and snacks, and moved through the rooms and hall, and sat on

the stairs; all very much like it had been at parties in the old days.
George would have approved.

3

The main quality of the Leicester English department in my time
was its general evenness of temper. There were mean glances
between colleagues from time to time; but in general the department conducted itself with an unusual respect for persons. Arthur
Humphreys was there in the centre for so long, working without
self-pride or irritability; and that held the whole department
steady. I never heard him make a smart crack or any judgment,
direct or implied, simply for effect; I never knew him make a
secret deal or use a sly device. He was the least 'knowing' of
individuals. He did not play the ends against the middle or use
selective flattery. He simply kept on being fair, which is a most
difficult and disciplined activity for anyone in a position of authority. Whatever undercurrents there might have been in the department's internal relationships, he was not caught up in them. By
his example and his presence – and he had what the more self-
conscious world calls a 'presence', but as if by default, by being
unaware of the possibility of 'presence' – his undeniable authority
helped keep disagreements within manageable but not evading
limits. He too steered straight and looked for no limelight.

The complexity of character of a good-natured person is much
more difficult to understand than the complexities of the deeply
corrupt. 'Goodness' is not a word one uses easily, but of all the
people I have known Arthur Humphreys was the only one who
made me want to reinstate that epithet.

Loyalty to his department and to his duties as head was part
of a larger loyalty; to the demands of his profession as an academic. He was a distinguished critic and editor, especially in
eighteenth-century studies and, later, on Shakespeare. But when I
remember him – which is often, since he is another touchstone –
the integrity and strength of his day-by-day professional behaviour
comes first to the front. Fresh from a British Council appointment
in Turkey, by then in his mid-thirties, he had come, in 1947, to
be head of the small English department of the small university

college. Over almost thirty years, he built up a large and distinguished department, and was himself always the first to teach, to examine, and to take on the drudgeries of routine administration. There are few heads of departments, and their hesitation is understandable, who give themselves roughly as much week-by-week teaching as their junior colleagues. They can fairly argue that larger matters call, especially faculty and university committees. Not boasting but recalling a simple fact, he once said: 'My working programme, for long spells, was a minimum of a seventy-hour week, not counting coffee or meal breaks or other respites, and all of it called for alert attention.' In the tiny gaps, he played the piano extremely well and wrote talented occasional verse. In everything, like George Fraser, he relied on the total devotion of his wife, Jean.

It was ironic but not surprising that his appointment was strongly resisted by some students of the department. Their hearts were bigger than their heads and that caused injustice to candidates from outside. They had no personal feeling against Arthur Humphreys but greatly respected the Senior Lecturer, who had been running the department and was a candidate for the chair. There followed some unpleasant weeks, since people who take up such causes out of the goodness of their hearts can be harshly insensitive to the person they wish to keep out, even though he has been caught in a battle not of his making. The affair naturally disturbed Arthur and Jean but, sooner than most observers thought possible, he had won the respect of the students and become friends with his internal rival. When the Senior Lecturer died some years later, his widow asked Arthur to speak at the burial service.

I was once given a lift by a man who had been a student of English at Leicester some years before, after escaping from Nazi Germany. He said Arthur Humphreys's way of running the department had made him feel able to trust people again. Once he had accumulated enough money, he honoured that experience with a grant for the department to buy works of art.

It follows, but is worth stressing, that if Arthur had so willed, if he had played the prima donna, given himself a lighter load, not given his best on university committees and so not been asked to serve on more and more, we might have had several more books of the scope of *The Augustan World*. There is always a price, and it is higher for the more conscientious. Other and very good books were written by Arthur, somehow; but there was not as big a written legacy as might have been. The less visible legacy was and is all around, in the department's strength, and in staff and students across Britain and the world who were affected for good by the care he gave them and the example he set.

More than one vice-chancellor had cause to be grateful for his loyalty to the most tenacious of British university principles: that we should run our own affairs, served by good administrative officers, rather than being managed by an 'Administration' which can come to think of itself as superior to the academics it hires and fires. That can mean continuous slog for those willing to face the implications; all those unhistrionic orderings and efforts at good judgment while some of their colleagues think only of their departments and of their, often histrionic, scholarly faces.

Arthur Humphreys also managed to tuck in service to some of the city's main artistic bodies, was as always willing to sit down month after month and help sort out problems and map futures; the provincial faithful servant again.

The Humphreys had a bewilderingly large circle of friends, not just academics and other professionals but people met in many kinds of situations. Arthur was one day run over crossing Victoria Park Road on his way to the university. The Asian driver was not only upset but very worried as to how the police might behave. Arthur assured him at once that the accident was entirely his fault. Questioned by the police, he refused to lay charges; he had been insufficiently attentive. The driver and the policeman became his friends.

A tiny incident in the record of his life he was writing in the last few weeks before his death captures his natural generosity. He describes being given his first weekly pocket money, at about eight years old; one penny. The decision what to spend it on was agonising. He saved for four weeks, and then bought penny buns for his mother and father, his brother and himself; un-self-regarding virtue set in early.

He knew what prescription he had written for himself. He spoke of 'those things one ought to do – teach with zest, write productively, know and entertain colleagues and students, administer soundly, take part in the outside world, and yet keep up life with family and friends and personal interests.'

Kind and unpushy people are easily assumed to be lacking in firmness or the capacity to take risks. The appointing of both George Fraser and myself showed that there was a determined gambler inside that apparently mildly flowing personality. When unpalatable decisions had to be made there was great firmness; not the firmness of the executive butcher who rather enjoys a display of ruthless determination, or the casual firmness of the person who ritualistically intones that you can't make an omelette without breaking eggs as he moves into brutal action.

He was never punitive or lacking in charity so that, when he did utter a criticism, it came with all the more force because of the disinterested judgment behind it. He had tremendous moral authority, the kind of dignity which is not founded in self-import- ance. Once sure, he did not vacillate. If you were tempted to mistake him for someone who was 'too nice to be firm' you had only to hear him say with finality, *apropos* a high-flying candidate: 'Yes, he is a very well qualified and attractive applicant in many ways. But in the end I do not think he would measure up to this particular job'; he then gave his reasons.

He was so unmalicious and accessible that the lions and lambs of academic life gathered round and sat quietly, for a time at least, in his benign shadow. He radiated a sense of decent avail- ability without seeming all things to all men. He made clear to me a phrase often heard but not so far fully understood: he 'brought out the best in people'. It can seem a soft old phrase until you see in action the quality it is pointing at. It meant he saw the best in you and trusted you to bring it out, to live it out, for your common ends. He was not taken in by surface shine or engagingness, but drew a large cheque on the bank of your potentialities and trusted you to rise above your weaknesses – laziness, egotism – so that the cheque would not bounce. He was loved by many and different people, not all of them very nice and certainly not people who all loved one another. We all behaved better towards each other in his company and to some extent lived up to his gamble on us; so we were indeed that bit better.

Arthur Humphreys's favourite words included, as well as 'zest' and 'alert' which we have met already, 'splendid . . .

enthusiastic . . . generous . . .', all spoken with a pleased lift to the voice; and 'quite captivating', with a slight laugh (as compared with the abrupt and boyish laugh at anything which tickled his fancy); and '*keen* anticipation', spoken to the end of his life with a youthful stress on the adjective. Most of his favourite words were warm and positive; dry, oblique, allusive tones were alien to him. It was all of a piece: the quick stride across the park to work, the sudden erupting laugh when something touched his funny-bone, and sometimes a giggle which made him look much as he must have looked back in Liverpool, in his teens. Then he would turn to his work again; he did not try to cap others' jokes.

He never sought the spectacular or stylish, but a remarkable personal style emerged over the years – 'a fine figure of a man' whose straightness shone out of him, an innate dignity. That lasted to the end, through the final weeks when, ravaged by cancer, he sat in their cottage on the Isle of Arran, looking out to sea, the cat always on his knees whilst he bent yet again to his still vast correspondence. I think I was the last member of his old department to see him alive. I gave him the proofs of the first volume of this sequence; it was open on the counterpane the afternoon he died.

He was buried in the island's hilly, windy graveyard. As is the Scottish custom, six of us were designated as holders of the ropes which let the coffin down. There had been a service in the packed little church – a handful from the mainland, the others from the island community, many of them Jean's farming relatives. I tried to say what he had meant to many of us a long way from there. Most of them would not know the detail I spoke of, but they knew it was all a tribute of love; and they came and said so and shook hands warmly after the committal. 'Most heart-warming,' he would have said, 'but so unexpected – and so undeserved.'

❦

CHAPTER 3

PICKED UP BY THE TIDE:
LADY CHATTERLEY'S LOVER
AND
THE PILKINGTON REPORT,
1960–2

Some time in 1980 I was asked to dinner at an Inn of Court, to one of the black tie occasions when members may bring guests. My host was a witty retired judge under whom I had served on an Arts Council committee about the funding of the National Theatre. Most of the senior legal people and their guests, gathered in the panelled ante-room, seemed to know one another. As the champagne circulated, my host began to introduce me to different groups. At the second group someone said, as though he found it hard to believe what he had heard, especially in that place: '*Hoggart*, did you say your name was? Weren't you . . . ?' My host cheerfully finished the sentence: 'That's right. *Lady Chatterley*.' Twenty years on, but the memory of what had obviously been to them a very strange trial – not necessarily of my part in it – had remained. Then the group uttered a brief prayer in memory of the dead: 'Poor Mervyn,' they said – as old soldiers might remember one of their comrades who had drawn the short straw and been sent on a dangerous mission into unknown territory.

I

The five years of living in Leicester contained the by now usual crop of outside lectures, committees, small publications. The Albemarle Report had produced the Youth Service Development Council and I served on that. After the Pilkington Committee had reported, the BBC asked me to rejoin their General Advisory Council and the British Council offered a place on their British Books Overseas Committee, chaired by C. P. Snow. It was interesting to compare the committee life in his books with the reality as he orchestrated it. His manner was genial but, with the council officials, rather self-consciously firm – a common quality in chairmen, as though they are establishing that they are not the agents of the body which has invited them into that chair.

Virtually all these activities were aspects of the interests I mentioned earlier: the importance of freedom to speak (and the way that, in Britain, many – often covert – practices work against it); the centrality of literature to expressing and defending that right; the power of class divisions to impede freedom; the crucial significance of 'the common reader', and the value of paperbacks and, possibly, mass communications for such readers.

These interests came to special public notice at the turn into the Sixties, in two events with which I became associated: the prosecution of Penguin Books for publishing the unexpurgated *Lady Chatterley's Lover*, and the Pilkington Report on the future of British broadcasting. In each I found myself, not entirely accurately, cast in a leading role; each can be seen as a telling indication of the nature of the continuing argument about freedom, class, and the tensions between public and private morality.

My being asked to appear for the defence in the *Lady Chatterley* case had had its origins three years before, when Allen Lane read *The Uses of Literacy*. From then on he was intermittently in touch. He needed to be in contact with people whose insights he respected, who seemed to know things he didn't know about intellectual, social or cultural life. He used these people as advisers, almost gurus. He tended to refer to them like a pupil before a teacher he did not quite understand but who, his instinct suggested, had hold of truths which might be important to him and Penguin Books.

I was not in the front row of people like that but, a generation behind, was added to the group's fringes. He conceived the idea, and I was not the first or only person he so fixed on, that I might make a Chief Editor. I did not realise this until one day he asked me to call in to his office just off Piccadilly to meet a long-serving and trusted colleague, Eunice Frost. They were sizing me up as a possible team-member. I wrote saying I preferred to stay in academic life.

He continued to write or telephone me from time to time. On one occasion, in the early Sixties, he arranged for one of the brightest and most attractive of his younger staff, Dieter Pevsner, and me to stay overnight at Silverback, his mini-mansion near Harmondsworth. After supper he left us, with adequate drink, so that we could discuss what might be the nature of a new series of Penguin Specials, aimed at catching the mood of the Sixties in the way their pre-war predecessors had caught the mood of the late Thirties.

At supper there had been cottage pie, luckily one of my favourite dishes (so long as illicit onion isn't added); and, it proved, one of Allen Lane's favourites. I don't think I had had it with Burgundy before, though. The dining table was a huge oval of splendidly polished mahogany. Lane and I faced each other from opposite ends. At one point I rested my elbow on the table, not very heavily. It immediately tipped so that his end went up and mine down, as would the most expensive and genteel and smoothly lubricated of see-saws. He was boyishly delighted. It allowed him to reveal that the table had been made for Edward VII's yacht and was ingeniously pivoted at the centre so that it remained level no matter how much the boat tossed. Presumably the monarch's guests were too well bred to put their elbows on the table, even when in smooth seas.

A few years later, in 1967, Lane became greatly exercised about the future of the remarkable institution he had created. He asked me yet again to go down for a talk. He was wondering whether some sort of trust or foundation of universities might be set up to take over Penguin. If the idea could be made workable he would sell his shares, worth three-quarters of a million or so, to the trust at two-thirds their market value. The proposal indicated both his innocence of the ways of universities and his high and, at bottom, non-commercial vision of Penguin.

Over lunch at the Ritz Lord Goodman, whom I knew slightly through work on the Culture Committee of the UK National Commission for UNESCO, sketched with typical easy lucidity the pros and cons of such a scheme. I had seen that ease at work some time before, when he had asked me to a working breakfast in his comfortable bachelor apartment in Portland Place. Once we had agreed about a letter which had to be sent somewhere about something, he picked up a speaking tube which connected him with his secretary's desk in the City, and dictated an exactly phrased letter. No hesitations, no second thoughts; nor, so far as I could tell, any further thoughts at all on that particular matter; it was done with. A lesson in how to do in a day two or three times as much as most of us manage.

At the Ritz lunch Lord Goodman offered to be host to a supper in his apartment for a representative group from the universities. For a number of reasons, the proposal did not get far; university authorities do not have the power to give all the assurances Lane wanted, especially as to the provision of further capital when long-term growth called for it to protect the future of his creation. I still wonder whether the universities were willing enough to try to alter their rules and habits.

To the 1990s, the trust scheme sounds bizarre; no one would nowadays approach the universities with such an offer. Their commercial acumen is not sufficiently respected, and their role in wider public decision-making or advising has been greatly reduced. It has inevitably been argued that they would have made Penguin into a dull, scholarly imprint. That was a risk. But no greater than the risk of what has now evolved under a new and different management: a Penguin imprint which, whilst it still produces some very good titles, is also willing to produce quite awful best-sellers. The *Boule de Suif* argument, that the whores can protect the virtuous women, doesn't suit artistic matters.

Those who write about Allen Lane's character always dip into a file of contrasting epithets: he was shy, sly, quixotic, ruthless, kind, mercurial, cunning, restless, unjust, generous, impish, naïve, open, elusive. I suppose I would have seen some of the harsher qualities if I had joined the firm; as it was, I saw the milder, kinder, more attractive.

I had been happy to talk to Allen Lane whenever he asked because the Penguin/Pelican idea had been part of my education, of my sense of what was needed by people like me, from just before my student days at Leeds, from almost six years as a soldier and a dozen years as an extra-mural lecturer. He had created a major democratic instrument; he had believed in greater access to the world of ideas for 'the people of England / Who have not spoken yet'; he had assumed that they had the capacity to judge those ideas in spite of the barriers which made access so difficult for so many.

Would he have put the matter that way? Probably not, though this does not mean that that sort of impulse was not behind his initiative. He was in this similar to Hugh Greene of the BBC – inspired by a rebellious resistance to restrictive aspects of the society into whose more comfortable reaches he had been born. The chief mentors he gathered round him, especially the Pelican Advisory Group – W. E. Williams, Krishna Menon, Peter Chalmers-Mitchell and the chief academic pilot, H. L. Beales – could make the analyses and then suggest how to reach readers who had hardly been reached before; but, and this was crucial, not by a fashionable intellectualism, nor by talking down or watering down, but by clear, firm speech. They all believed that it is important, in Forster's phrase, 'to connect', and that connecting starts in respect for both the subject and the readers. Allen Lane asked authors to write to the top of their bent for the Judes, the Leonard Basts, the Paul Morels and the Gordon Comstocks. They had to bank on people's potentialities – the most important of all rules of thumb in a democracy. In this, Allen Lane stood for more than commercial success. Today, when the very existence of a 'common reader' is denied, this splendid conviction needs to be assessed afresh.

He died in early 1970 and there was a memorial service at St Martin-in-the-Fields. I was asked to speak, but had just started work at UNESCO headquarters in Paris. The Director-General, René Maheu, was very reluctant to release his half-dozen colleagues on the top board, except for official missions abroad. But he had known Allen Lane in his young days, as French Cultural Attaché in London, and during the formation of UNESCO. I asked to be released. In their impulsiveness, their total commitment to their institutions and their ruthlessness, those two were brothers. 'Of course you must go,' Maheu said. 'He was a great man . . . and a very good friend of our organisation.'

There is a coda to the story. In late 1988, in Penguin's offices,

I remarked that H. L. Beales would be a hundred early the next
year. They had assumed him long dead and immediately proposed
to arrange a celebration on his birthday. He died a few weeks
short of his hundred.

2

The legal people I described at the beginning of this chapter were
remembering their former colleague, Mervyn Griffith-Jones, who
led for the Crown in the prosecution of Penguin Books for publishing an obscene libel, the unexpurgated *Lady Chatterley's Lover*.
The case ran from 20 October to 2 November 1960 – over thirty
years ago, so one might have expected that it would attract today
no more than a footnote in books on Lawrence or on censorship
in Britain. Instead, it has echoed loudly down the decades.

It was certainly a dramatic few days, to the informed public
imagination one of the most dramatic events even the Old Bailey
has seen; not melodramatic in the manner murder or treason
trials can be, but intellectually dramatic, more Ibsen than Grand
Guignol. It has been entered on the agreed if conventional list of
literary judgments as the moment at which the confused mesh of
British attitudes to class, to literature, to the intellectual life, and
to censorship, publicly clashed as rarely before – to the confusion
of more conservative attitudes. On the far side of that watershed
and largely as a consequence, the favoured story continues, we
had the Permissive Society. All of which is excessive and over-
simple, but has some truth.

The *Chatterley* trial was the second test case (the first was
not significant) of a law promoted by Roy Jenkins: the Obscene
Publications Act of 1959. This Act was meant to pension off the
Man on the Clapham Omnibus as the arbiter of obscenity. For
the first time in such trials in Britain expert witnesses could be
called to testify to a book's literary quality. A book was now to
be considered as a whole, rather than having its 'dirty bits'
extracted and held up to frighten the jury. Even if a book were
found to be obscene, its publication might be permitted as in the
public interest if it had been proved to have literary merit. These
were large liberating steps.

But the trial showed that the Man on the Clapham Omnibus was not so easily spirited away. He was alive and active in the Office of the Director of Public Prosecutions. One of many jokes at the time had a colleague asking the Senior Treasury Counsel, Griffith-Jones, how he decided whether or not to advise the DPP to prosecute. 'I put my feet up on the desk and start reading. If I get an erection, we prosecute.' That was as near the mark as most of the justifications for prosecution brought forward during the trial. The Man on the Clapham Omnibus was also still there, in court, in a judge's and a barrister's wigs. Judge Byrne caught in his summing-up the whole manner in which he and some others had approached the interpretation of the new law. Weakening any claims to literary quality made by 'expert witnesses', he suggested – probably remembering a succession of psychiatrists being brought on for the defence in the sorts of trial he was most used to – that you could find experts on anything these days. That is in a way true, but does not reduce a judge's responsibility to try to distinguish the weighty from the lightweight expert. More puzzlingly, or perhaps more cleverly, he dug a new ditch between 'obscenity' and 'literary merit', a ditch the jury were invited not to bridge. He said the jury could themselves define obscenity without outside assistance, since it is an 'objective' matter. So literary merit was dubious, the province of often unreliable experts, but obscenity, being objective, was entirely within the jury's judgment. If that dual argument had affected the jurors in the way which seemed intended the presentations by the line of defence witnesses, not only as to literary merit but about the relationships between obscenity and the exploration of human relationships in different sorts of literature (from Lawrence to sex-and-violence novels), would have been set aside. The Prosecuting Counsel took a similar line to the judge.

A letter from Penguin's solicitors asked if I would be willing to appear for the defence. I agreed, since I admired much in the book and, the abridged version being a filleted and tasteless thing, thought the unabridged version should be published. The sexual passages were tender and sometimes comical rather than objectionable – as compared with, for instance, the violent sex to be found in many paperbacks freely available even then. I knew Allen

Lane was anxious, again for more than commercial reasons, to complete his run of Lawrence's novels.

It was predictable that the prosecution would imply that the expert witnesses for the defence were long-haired dilettantes, against all censorship as a matter of faith and themselves probably no better morally than they should be. The defence produced a pattern of thirty-five witnesses so un-Bohemian that we felt like a stage army of earnest *Guardian* readers. There were eminent and elderly men of letters, none of whom would frighten a jury with farouche manners and beliefs; no Kenneth Tynans. There were equally elderly lady dons, impregnable in tweed costumes and sensible shoes. There were quietly spoken clergymen, teachers of various kinds and from various levels, and a beautiful, Catholic young woman. I appeared in a V-necked pullover and 'sports jacket' – fashionable uniform at the time among provincial academics (together, especially in seminars, with a pipe clutched by the bowl as point-making called for the arm to be waved). Presumably I was cast as the northern working-class provincial now a university teacher; a sort of muted 'eeh-bah-gum' figure fit for a short walk-on part in *Sons and Lovers*.

Faced with this procession, robbed of the chance to scare the jury with wild literary types, the prosecution prudently decided to call no witnesses who would claim that the book had scarcely any literary merit, but to make all the headway it could with the 'appeal to honest Joe' approach. One possible defence witness was greatly missed by those of us who, having given our evidence, were free to sit in court and enjoy the literary theatre. From where I sat I saw a prosecution lawyer pull from the shelf under his bench Eliot's *After Strange Gods*. Were they going to invoke Eliot's criticisms of Lawrence in that book? Dieter Pevsner whispered that all was under control. Eliot had said that if the prosecution drew on his book he was to be telephoned and would at once come to the Old Bailey and repudiate what he had said there. They did not. Apparently Eliot did go to the Old Bailey and wait in the corridor, on the off-chance.

The prosecution showed a level of class-bound, education-bound, profession-bound, cast-iron incomprehension about works of the imagination which was, even at that time, hardly credible. Griffith-Jones's early question to the jury, as to whether they thought it a book they would wish their wives or servants to read, is quoted in every discussion of the trial I know. That was inevitable; it crystallised the gulf between the Britain even of 1960 and the understanding of his time by a man brought up in a closed, archaic world. It was hard to believe that a clever lawyer, even if his assumptions about the desirably ordered life were those suggested by the question, should be so out of touch with the lives of most others as to make such a huge tactical error. Yet he was not alone. The debate about the acquittal in the House of Lords two weeks after the trial ended was, even by the standards of the day in that place, absurd.

I was asked to attend on the second day but was not called until shortly before the court rose. As I walked down the corridor to the entrance to the court, a solicitor for the defence said, 'You're on next. Things are not going well. Do dig in hard' – or words to that effect. Jeremy Hutchinson for the defence began by asking if I agreed that the book was, as the prosecution claimed, 'vicious'. I replied that it was highly virtuous and then, no more than half-realising I was putting up a very big kite indeed, 'if not puritanical'. The court rose a few minutes later. I walked away, realising more with each step that by the word 'puritanical' I had given an enormous hostage to the prosecution.

The following morning I was in the witness-box for an exceptionally long session. Griffith-Jones had had plenty of time to prepare to demolish this witness for the use of that big word. The exchange which followed has been regarded by many observers as the turning-point of the case. It did not feel like that; I could see only the trees immediately in front.

I have always disliked the Sergeant Buzfuz manner favoured by many barristers, that hectoring – are you *really* saying that? – contemptuous style calculated to make witnesses both feel small and lose their tempers. Griffith-Jones had that manner in its nastily smoothest form. It didn't make my blood boil when he spoke to me in that way; it made me cold and obdurate. He sneered about the word 'puritanical', professed ignorance of the meaning and asked me to define it. I did, briefly and reasonably clearly. His response showed he was losing his sense of advantage; he took refuge in banal sarcasm. He thanked me for the explanation but told me not to lecture the court, to remember that I was not at that moment teaching in – with a slight pause as if he had to recover the name of so insignificant a place from the depths of memory – *Leicester* University. He had given himself away. He saw himself as cross-examining someone who taught at a provincial and therefore inconsiderable place, for inconsiderable people.

Later that day the usher called on 'Edward Morgan Forster'. One felt like standing up in respect as that small bent figure in an old-style, but certainly clean, mackintosh walked slowly to the witness-box. I doubt if Judge Byrne knew of his work, but he courteously asked Forster if, not being young, he would like to sit. Equally courteously, Forster said he preferred to stand. There then came for me an extraordinary moment. Jeremy Hutchinson asked Forster to comment on the relevance of the word 'puritanical' to Lawrence's work. Forster paused to think and I held my breath. Then he said: 'I think the description is a correct one, though I understand that at first people would think it paradoxical.'

Some days later Allen Lane gave a celebratory party. Forster wrote asking me to have supper with him at the Reform Club afterwards. 'I shall have something light, perhaps an omelette,' he said as we sat down. 'But do have what you want. I recommend the lamb *chops*. They do good lamb *chops* here.' So I had lamb chops. We talked for a while about Griffith-Jones and his absurd manner. Then Forster said, with an ungenteel directness which is one mark of the highly literate middle class and recalled Bonamy Dobrée: 'Oh, the man's a shit. Let's talk about something interesting.'

There followed the usual concomitants of a brief notoriety, such as anonymous obscene letters and at least one packet of shit in the letter-box. In Singapore, examining for Dennis Enright, I heard a twelve-inch record dramatising the trial, with me luxuriating in an Albert and the Lion voice. At a party there a perfervid woman, constantly bending her very low-cut dress towards me, kept asking eagerly what it felt like to say 'fuck' to a judge. John Sparrow, then Warden of All Souls, Oxford, produced an engaging piece for *Encounter*, making fun of the defence witnesses. Almost incredibly, he asked me to give his prestigious annual Chichele Lectures. The Schools were crowded; clearly, this was not a conjunction to be missed. He led me, both of us in full academic dress, up the centre aisle of that crowded hall. I could almost swear his tail was lashing with pleasure at the perversity of the situation.

I was asked to appear in the defence of *Last Exit to Brooklyn* and of one other book whose name I do not recall. I did not wish to become a professional witness and refused both. Nor, though I am against most forms of censorship, do I greatly take to some of those most active in anti-censorship organisations.

Meanwhile, the family went on much as ever. The fourteen-year-old and twelve-year-old, to deflect embarrassment, made fun of my brief notoriety. The eight-year-old said he sided with me; four-letter-words were no worse than any others. He used them every day, like 'door' and 'coat'. After a couple of weeks Lady Chatterley was not mentioned.

Always we have to come back to certain questions. Why was the decision to prosecute taken? Why did the DPP think such a course proper and the outcome likely to be in his favour? Two major elements were in play, one about the magic – in this instance the black magic – of words, the other about frozen cultural assumptions.

It was felt deep down that if the word 'fuck' were allowed to escape into free print then more than a word would have been released. If that word had not appeared in the book, a prosecution would have been much less likely. There are some sexually explicit passages in *Lady Chatterley* which do not use the word. They do not shock the British psyche as much as that word does, when seen in print; it breaks some most important veils. It may be – it is – used in almost every sentence uttered by millions of workmen, as a lazy, brutish, male chauvinist intensifier; but that repetition reduces most of its oral force, so that it has to be repeated again, and again.

Yet for many who were in court throughout, it has been said, the awful word gradually lost its power to shock and the tenderness of the passages of love-making came through. Not for the judge and prosecutor. Griffith-Jones may have been theatrical, but he was not acting. The book appalled him – especially the passage about reverence for a man's balls – as it did Justice Byrne. For them, no argument about literary merit could compensate or justify. Presumably they had not appreciated on reading the book the power and beauty of at least one of the finest passages in all Lawrence's work. It is when Connie reacts against the 'queer, rabid curiosity' which Mrs Bolton's endless gossip arouses: 'One may hear the most private affairs of other people, but only in a spirit of respect for the struggling, battered thing which any human soul is, and in a spirit of fine, discriminative sympathy . . . It is the way our sympathy flows and recoils that really determines our lives.'

The other main element in the opposition to the book's appearance was the fact that it was to be a paperback and so available to anyone who had a few bob to spare. We are back with the lack of trust, the overweening sense that 'ordinary' people have to be protected from corruption by those who know better – a comical as well as a sombre thought when one remembers Griffith-Jones and Judge Byrne. But here again ordinary people proved more steady and robust than those who would protect them. We learned later that most jurors were in favour of acquittal after they had read the book, immediately before the trial began. So perhaps all the defence witnesses had little influence and at best reinforced rather than changed the jury's verdict.

Did the trial of *Lady Chatterley* 'liberate' literature? No. It allowed a flood of cheap and nasty pornography to come on to the market; that was an inescapable price in a democracy. I think, but neither I nor anyone who thinks differently can prove our arguments are right, that that miserable stuff did less harm than the exercising of censorship against Lawrence would have done.

The verdict did nothing to 'free' literature or open new avenues for literature to explore. Literature was not in prison. The exploration of sexuality does not need explicit words, and is often better done obliquely rather than directly, as Chekhov characteristically noted. The verdict on *Lady Chatterley* had no implications for the development of literature. In so far as it was a kind of victory, that victory was social and cultural, not artistic and intellectual. It was a tactical victory over old, tired but, even today, tenacious and strategically placed elements in British life.

But perhaps there is some movement. In 1990 the local professional theatre at Farnham, one of Surrey's Conservative-minded middle-class bastions, mounted a dramatisation of *Lady Chatterley's Lover*. There were nine minutes of full frontal nudity for the pair of them. Would the town be outraged? Hardly. One of our neighbours was advised to see it by a friend: 'Nothing shocking. All very tasteful.' Would the local police inspector be on the look-out for an erect penis, the sure and official sign of obscenity? That hardly mattered; the stage was so cold any penis would have been discouraged. One night it did pop upright for no apparent reason, to the discomfiture of Mellors. But Connie giggled, so John Thomas flopped immediately. The producer hovered anxiously at the back of the stalls afterwards and an elderly lady bore down on him. 'Thank you very much,' she said, 'I haven't seen one of those for years and I did so enjoy it.'

3

One Thursday in the early summer of 1962, at around midday, Simon Raven and I were waiting in a BBC hospitality room for a minister delayed at a cabinet meeting. We three – the old Etonian and Christ Church Tory grandee, the ex-Charterhouse and King's College novelist and rejector of all that upper-crust educational establishments stand for, and I – were to discuss the future of English education. The minister arrived, tossed his bowler hat on to a window-ledge, declared, 'I need a pee,' and was led out. Simon Raven picked up the hat, turned it over and announced: 'Thought so. Not from Lock. Cheapskate.'

I do not remember what kind of programme that bizarre trio produced. I remember better the minister's hiccup as we were introduced. Whether he knew Simon Raven's work I could not tell; he merely nodded briefly and turned to me. At, 'Do you know Mr Hoggart?' he gave a slight start, as one hearing an echo and not a particularly pleasant one.

That was the morning on which the Pilkington Report on the future of broadcasting was discussed by the Cabinet. It had been a heated discussion. We had not expected the Tory administration to like the report, though some members of the Cabinet were ready to accept it. More were not, and their anger was great.

'Who', asked Harold Macmillan, the Prime Minister (in what I imagine was an unengaged drawl; he was unlikely to become heated on such an issue), 'is responsible for this?' The answer from, I was told, Maxwell Fyfe, clearly a lawyer in the Griffith-Jones mould, was 'some lecturer in a provincial university'!

A scene to be treasured, that, because it conjures up once again the assumptions of the then ruling class and mirrors the cosy, squabbling littleness of much in British public and intellectual life; the extended family with all its snobberies and jobberies, and also its members' often irritated awareness of one another.

By the time the Pilkington Committee was assembled, in early 1960, I had written a few articles on broadcasting and its relations to cultural changes. The most recent was a long piece in the January 1960 issue of *Encounter*, 'The Uses of Television'. Not surprisingly, it contained strictures on the performance of commercial television since its start in the mid-Fifties. That is only worth mentioning now because a sequel illustrates yet again the living-in-each-other's-pockets character of British life, at least at that time. Sir Robert Fraser, the first Director-General of the Independent Television Authority, gave a lift after an official lunch one day to a senior civil servant. 'We know why that man Hoggart was put on the Pilkington Committee,' Fraser said. 'You've only to read that piece in *Encounter* to see why.' It would be pleasant to think that the interaction between public policy and an intellectual journal of relatively small circulation could be so swift and close; but as to the composing of the committee Sir Robert's antipodean ear misled him. The usual 'trawl' round interested ministries produced my name from the Minister of Education. Whatever his suspicions, this was the answer given to the Postmaster-General when he subsequently asked the official serving the committee to explain how I came to be appointed.

The rage of some members of the government against the report was slight in comparison with that of the commercial television bosses. One of them gave a party in his garden at which copies of the report were put to the flames. A very few newspapers and journals gave a fair account of the findings and proposals. Others threw every dirty word in their box of cliché abuse at us: 'nannying . . . élitist . . . patronising . . . grundyish . . . do-gooding . . .

superior . . . schoolmarmish' – all the usual dreary, underdeveloped litany of fear. The noisiest among the popular press had shares in commercial television, but omitted to mention this in their Islamic-fundamentalist-like fury.

The Labour Party thought itself in a spot. One imagines they would have liked to support a report which so clearly revealed the bad effect of profit-seeking on the pursuit of good broadcasting. But – and this was the trap they could not see the way out of – since most people watched commercial television rather than the BBC, wouldn't it be undemocratic to criticise their choice? I am not saying that they refused to stand up for the report because they feared to lose votes. I believe they did so because they had not thought about the issue to the point at which they could see through the apparent contradiction in which they found themselves.

Hugh Gaitskell, the Leader of the Opposition and so far as I know a man of integrity, appeared on television but could say little more than 'on the one hand, on the other . . .'. I followed and criticised him. Richard Crossman, the only MP to suggest a meeting after that television discussion, asked me to lunch at his Westminster house. He came in late, from a meeting of the Shadow Cabinet. 'I told Gaitskell I was giving you lunch,' he said. 'He said I was to kick your backside.' Homely, again.

We had a good discussion; Crossman had a sharp mind and liked argument. The report had said that the worst sin of broadcasting was not obscenity or being lowbrow, or vulgarity, or élitism, or any other of the usual charges, but 'triviality'; and that that could show in all types of programme, whatever their professed height of brow. We had at the backs of our minds Tawney, on triviality being 'worse for the soul than wickedness'. On that, Crossman said, with the turned-back-upon-ourselves smile we adopt when about to produce an epigram of which we are rather proud: 'As for me, I stand up for the common man's right to be trivial if he pleases.' Inverted snobbery, intellectual showing-off, unconscious belittling of less fortunate people. Still Crossman did, in 1971, write an article suggesting that the Pilkington solution for ITV was right.

Most social scientists treated the report with respect. A few of those who specialised in mass communications research took umbrage because the committee had not commissioned considerable sociological studies. There are several answers to that: even if such studies had been wholly germane to our purpose, we had not been given the funds or the time to commission them; there was, in any event, a considerable amount of published research in that area and we acquainted ourselves with that (it was inconclusive and still is). More important, such research was not central to our main brief and purpose. We were engaged to the best of our ability in a study in social philosophy. We were asking about the nature of good broadcasting in a democracy. We could not enforce our judgments scientifically; we could only say at the end, in Leavis's formulation: 'This is so, is it not?' Our readers could say 'Yes'; or 'No'.

Ours was no worse a situation than that of the quantitative research workers. Interesting though their work was, no amount of it could change 'Is's' to 'Oughts'; and no 'Oughts' would emerge automatically from the 'Is's'. At that point they too were in the 'This is so, is it not?' type of proffered judgment, a judgment of value which could be rejected by anyone so disposed, because not objectively verifiable. That is why we were able to say, in a sentence some broadcasters and commentators found difficult to assimilate but which went to the heart of the issue, that broadcasters had to recognise that, whether they willed it or not, they were 'in a constant and sensitive relationship with the moral condition of society'. This was not a moralising sentence; nor did it propose any particular form of morality or imply that broadcasters should deliberately promote any form; it simply stated the inescapable connection of the broadcasters with the society out there and with the nature of its life, its assumptions, choices, judgments. Some journalists found the idea deeply irritating and took refuge in derision. As late as 1986, an essay by a university lecturer tried to dismiss this section of the report as 'provincial puritanism' – imposed by me.

Sir Harry Pilkington, of the glass makers, was well over six feet tall, like a large stork or genial eagle, lean from sobriety, from an enthusiasm for tennis, and from riding an ancient push-bike across London to meetings. A good example of the old-style quango chairman, he was full of public spirit and now, well into middle age, able to devote time to national causes as well as to St Helens ('Pilkington *is* St Helens', people said), to his nonconformist church and to his roses. He led the committee by a well-practised shrewdness which was no worse a foundation for his role than great knowledge, in advance, of our subject. He readily told the press that, until he was asked to be chairman of the committee, he hadn't had much time for television and had no prior views on it; but he rapidly picked up the main elements.

In many ways he was a conventional, intelligent but not intellectual, hereditary British businessman. He was rarely ruffled; when that happened, it usually showed the gap between his world and that of the non-commercial talkative groups. One day I mentioned approvingly a Consumers' Association report. He responded with great irritation: CA was a nuisance, didn't understand the problems of industry, was technically shaky. Tiny moments such as that apart, he was good-humoured and equable to members, staff and witnesses.

He soon assessed the different uses of the members; he tended to use me as one of the trouble-shooters, carefully controlled from his chair. To him, I was a strange bird, of a sort he hadn't much met before, but one who could have a useful place in the committee's work so long as he wasn't allowed to tempt them to unrealities. He reined me in if he thought my questioning of witnesses was giving our thoughts away. There was a lunch with one of the big commercial TV companies in London, at which the placing was highly political, with executives set next to those committee members assumed to be suitable for ear-bending or as indicators of our thinking. The company chairman, opposite me, smoked a cigar so long I thought the ash might fall in my soup. I was put next to a journalist high up in their newspaper interests, and we began talking about principles of public service broadcasting. Pilkington decided that that could become dangerous. 'Richard,' he called across the table as we had reached the Stilton, 'are you a scooper or a slicer?' That meant, I realised after a second or two in which I assumed he really was interested in how I tackled cheese: 'Lay off that argument, he might think he can make use of you.' The senior newspaperman didn't manage that but, undaunted, offered me a few days later a very large sum for writing a small article. Later, an MP with commercial radio interests also tried to establish a special relationship.

Above all, Harry Pilkington was fair-minded and brave so that, when our conclusions began to look radical and likely to be unacceptable to the government, he did not flinch – once he had been carefully convinced – from making the radical decision.

The most unusual member of the committee was Joyce Grenfell, and those who wished to devalue the work from the start said she would be a token member only, representing the lightweight tastes of middle-class, middle-aged theatre-goers, a sort of Mrs Miniver one could easily ignore or placate. In fact, she had written radio criticism and was well acquainted with television. She also fitted well into that pattern in committee work which I described much earlier. If two or three members were gladiators, clarifying and fighting out the main issues, she was one of the leading Roman spectators. She followed each argument closely and would not let it end until she knew enough about it to make up her own mind.

This determination was fed by great seriousness combined with an excessive modesty because she had not been to university. That was an accident of her upper-class background and time and meant little; she was an autodidact. Her pertinacity and honesty led her to become the litmus paper of the committee's own sense and honesty; she was not an intellectual but she had uncommon intelligence.

We became friends, and she was one of those who believe in keeping friendships in good repair. In the second half of the Seventies, when we settled again in England after five years in Paris, she telephoned within a day or two of our return to say she and her husband Reggie would like to drive down to welcome us back. Mary has a bundle of little cards from her saying she was glad Richard had stopped smoking, or was being more careful about kicking off his shoes in committee or unbuttoning his collar and that, though he called himself agnostic, he was a Christian in spirit (she was a Christian Scientist, which told more about her generation, background and earnest good nature than about the quality of her mind). If she had thought that any members of the committee were drinking too much, she would have sailed in and mildly rebuked them, being tolerantly teetotal.

She was fiercely against the snobberies of many of her class but certain that I made too much of class divisions. After all, most people were kind and not superior when you got to know them, weren't they? She was a congenital upper-class jacket-straightener who shook hands across the gulf with the working-class Primitive Methodist jacket-straighteners of my childhood. She hated gossip for its own sake, since most gossip is at bottom unkind; but she loved funny stories and that helped lighten the work.

The committee secretary, Dennis Lawrence, was from a south-east London working-class home and grammar school; he had climbed very rapidly from the lower end of the civil service to the Administrative class, thence to Assistant and, later, Under-Secretary, by ability – and by exceptional integrity, even for a senior civil servant. His belief in the importance of getting broad-casting policy right was so strong that he stayed at that desk after Pilkington reported, putting at risk the improved career prospects for which wide experience is often a necessary preliminary. Chapter three of the report, on the purposes of broadcasting in a democracy, remains the finest statement in English of those issues. It was generally attributed to me. Dennis Lawrence and I discussed the issues, both during debates in the committee and together outside. But the written chapter was his, subject only to review by a drafting sub-committee chaired by Sir Harry. It left the draft virtually unchanged, as a true expression of the committee's corporate opinion.

Underlying the report was a set of principles for good broadcast-ing in a free society. The report does not list them one after the other nor all of them explicitly; but they are all there and easily winnowed from its pages. They are all, or should be if broadcast-ing has been set up properly, elements of the broadcasters' internal sense of professionalism, those things which should be central to the work if it is to be well done. At their heart is enthusiasm and respect for the medium and its possibilities, and respect for its audiences. Nothing else: in particular, no eye on what any govern-ment or the advertisers might want. This is strange language in the Nineties but still compelling, like a lost faith.

The elements were:

- So far as possible provision must be made for all, not just for those who are worth wooing for an ulterior end.
- We all at some time belong to a number of minorities or, better, of overlapping communities of interest; and sometimes belong to majorities.
- There is a qualitative difference between assessing on the one hand the size of an audience and on the other the intensity with which individuals respond to different programmes.
- Quality is determined by integrity before the subject and before the intended audience, not by height of brow.
- A licence fee, not direct funding by government or advertising revenue, is the cornerstone of broadcasting in the public interest, a safeguard against overweening political or commercial pressures.
- Good legislation for broadcasting is not restrictive but liberating. It says 'Thou shalt not' much less often than it says 'Thou shalt'.
- This approach requires broadcasters to provide, and at good times, living-space for programmes which do not or do not at the start attract large audiences.
- If, in the effort to increase audiences, producers make programmes they secretly or even unconsciously despise, they will quite soon despise the audiences they make them for; and eventually – some of them – come to despise themselves.
- Broadcasting should not hesitate to reflect 'The quarrel of this society with itself', even though politicians may not like the result.

It follows from all the above that broadcasters should be prepared and encouraged to take risks, to gamble on people's possibilities, to surprise us and themselves.

The Pilkington Report, it was said, unduly favoured the BBC. That was not in our minds, though certainly the final effect was far more favourable to the Corporation than to the commercial network. This was partly because its programmes were better and partly because it behaved better in opening itself to inspection, and argued its case better. Sir Arthur fforde and Hugh Greene, the Chairman and Director-General, were the BBC's Nervo and Knox. We found it a lot better than its enemies said, and worse than some of its friends said. It was facing competition for the first time and in such circumstances all big institutions do not explicitly rewrite their briefs; they reinterpret them so that the institution may survive. Even if some of its whites become blacks in the process, they are called a new kind of white. The BBC revealed itself as a tough and not always scrupulous fighter when threatened.

It saw itself, and to some extent still sees itself, as the upholder of the national consensus; 'the national instrument of broadcasting'. It was easy for commercial television to present itself as much more 'of the people', but the image was a mirage. Neither system had much sense of the reality of the British life they thought they were reflecting.

The initial structure of British broadcasting was established at an odd moment, in the last full decade of cultural paternalism. It lived within its origins for years, chiefly because it was protected; its democratisation was accelerated but not inspired by the arrival of commercial television.

These peculiar circumstances, and the character of the British inventive imagination, ensured that the BBC became at its best a unique expression of democratic communication. The philistinism of much of the press, and the widespread fear of appearing to be élitist, have prevented us from seeing what a valuable creation it was at heart; it was left to foreigners to recognise that. We let it be weakened, and weaken itself, by default.

By contrast with the BBC, the commercial television system's representatives showed arrogance before the Pilkington Committee. One titled ITA grandee dismissed criticism of their programmes' quality with: 'People get the television they deserve.' The relation between ITA and the companies, we were told, was that of 'friends and partners'; it should have been 'principals and agents' (or 'gamekeepers and poachers'). In general ITV witnesses looked at the committee as at a line of hens rocking gently on a bench. Their financial presentation was in the beginning so cavalier that our barrister member became extremely fierce; this was no way for a public corporation to treat a committee of enquiry set up by HMG for a task of great importance. They were playing ducks and drakes with the provisions of the Television Act (which defines their functions but not those of the BBC, which has a Royal Charter). Independent Television News was underfunded (that began to alter as soon as they were warned, by ITN's director and with our agreement, that we meant to expose the neglect). They were getting round the regulations on advertising, chiefly by creating a monstrous hybrid programme called an ADMAG – a type of programme so blatantly against the spirit of the Act that one wondered how on earth they had thought they could get away with it. We decided to take their advertising practice apart by a most severe cross-examining of their spokesmen; that session became known in television advertising circles as Black Friday.

The evidence showed that for most of the bosses in commercial television a franchise was just another way of multiplying their money, and in that no different from investment in junk food or property development. Almost all politicians took their word as to their good intentions, either because they simply had not thought about the best uses of broadcasting, or because they were fearful of seeming élitist by criticising an aggressively populist channel ('If people want game shows at peak time every evening, who are we to . . . ?') or because they were members of a commercial television company's board.

It was at first surprising that Sir Robert Fraser, who was neither a fool nor a knave, could not only tolerate all this but could defend it. Probably he saw the commercial television network, with all its grossnesses, as preferable to the British establishment from which, as an Australian, he had originally felt excluded. He had his sense of wry humour. He invented the cheeky, false title 'Independent Television' for his commercial network; most people rose to the bait and adopted his formulation. He liked to say rather piously that, because he respected people, he would hesitate to condemn anyone's taste; he seemed not to realise how what is called public taste is a manufactured and selective distortion.

There remain odd, some very odd, memories from the seventy-eight whole days and forty-three sub-committee meetings in Pilkington's two-year span. Such as the difference between the Welsh and the Scottish evidence, in Cardiff and Edinburgh. A large

Welsh lady, swathed in operatic purple, aggressively harangued us with the claim that if a Welsh-speaking television channel were not provided soon Welsh culture would die. A Scottish lord, asked if he felt the same about television's threat to Scotland, answered laconically and like the landowner he was: 'You can't put a ring-fence round a culture.'

A senior Treasury official, challenged on his department's right to give the BBC less than the proceeds of the licence fee if it was not officially a tax, told us more than once, again with an inturned smile but this time that of one revealing a single, small, arcane, linguistic element in the mystery of his profession, that we were perhaps not familiar with the important principle of 'avoiding hypothecation'.

The towering and anguished-looking Lord Reith spoke as though his words were being cut out of granite during a thunderstorm. Asked at the end of his evidence what he thought of the new competitive BBC, he simply but oracularly said: 'I fear, Sir, that it has *lost its way*.' I met him a few years later, when he was chairman of a committee set up by the Labour Party to enquire into the good and bad of advertising. Called to give evidence, I waited in the committee corridor at Westminster. He courteously came out to lead me in. As he did so he rested his hand on my shoulder, bending down from his six foot six or so towards my five foot six. He then, like a biblical prophet passing on a great duty, called me to the heights. 'We have asked you to speak to us,' he intoned, 'because we want you *to show us the way we should go*.'

Most impressive of all was T. S. Eliot, who asked to give evidence as the President of the Third Programme Defence Society. He was frail but beautifully turned out, indeed elegant, in a light summer suit and with a fine, fresh Panama hat rested carefully on his knees. Before he came in, I was deputed to invite him to give an opinion on the foolish, false comparison which had been made again and again: 'We aim to give the people what they want, not what we think is good for them.' The programme companies – Granada with most conviction and more convincingly than others – officially rejected that argument. But the tawdry standard was unfurled by shabby entrepreneurs and titled public figures alike in defence of whatever their commercial television transmitted; low populism masquerading as democracy. Eliot paused a moment on the question and then produced, in a voice with hints of Kensington, the Middle West and New England, a sentence so finely phrased that you could easily identify the semi-colon before the final assertion: 'Those who claim to give the public what the public want – (*pause*) – begin by underestimating public taste; they end by *debauching* it.' That fragment of uncollected, and unattributed, Eliot (it echoes a statement by Reith in the late Twenties) is naturally quoted verbatim in the report.

For the committee itself the high-point, and turning-point, was a weekend in a modest hotel in Hove. We had been sitting for several months and the evidence that something was radically wrong with the working of commercial television was by then unmistakable; and unmistakedly was the most important issue before us. It was time to think in quiet. By the Sunday we had decided that full restructuring of that network's way of operating was needed. The secretariat were asked to prepare various options which were radical in that way. We discussed those and – a sign that by now the committee had found a firm collective character – had no doubt the most radical proposal was the right one. Sir Harry then did as a chairman should at such a time. He told us that the proposal would not find favour with the government and might cause the report as a whole to be discredited. Did we think the proposal so right, so necessary for the better future of broadcasting, that we still wished to make it? Or did we wish to amend it into a proposal more likely to be acceptable to government? Without hesitation or dissent we said we wished to go for the radical proposal; also with no hesitation the chairman said: so be it.

Our proposal for the better future of commercial television was simple and beautiful: that the makers of programmes should not also be those who sold advertising. A branch of ITA could sell advertising and then pay programme companies to make programmes for the network; the better the programmes, by various criteria, the better the pay. So: competition, but for good broadcasting across the whole range of programmes. There was a fatal squint in the eye of the programme companies, which had made them behave badly. The requirement of the Act to make good programmes according to the widest definition of broadcasting in the public interest was conflicting with the temptation to increase advertising revenue by concentrating on programmes, especially at peak times, which narrowed range and quality in the search for maximum audiences. That squint could be removed; they could concentrate on making good programmes, and know they would be paid properly for them. It was and is the best solution.

Of course, it was not accepted. But all was not lost. British broadcasting would have been very different, much worse, had Pilkington not sat. The power of our proof that the Television Act was not working well led to amendments designed to make more nearly sure the companies honoured the full range of their brief. The Television Bill of 1964 reflected the government's and opposition's agreement with our report on parliament's proper expectation of the aims to which ITA's performance should be directed. From that time commercial television, screwed into virtue, seriously began to challenge the BBC across the whole range of programming; that was due to Pilkington. Memories are short. People now talk as though commercial television was behaving well from its inception. In fact, in its first eight or nine years, the pre-Pilkington years, it behaved like an Oxford Street barrow boy.

Our major recommendation, the separation of the collecting of advertising revenue from programme-making, was, as we expected, totally rejected. Yet it rose again in a somewhat different form in the Annan Report a dozen years later. Channel 4's grandfather was Pilkington.

The Pilkington Committee was one of the admirably disinterested quangos, proof that that curious British device could work well, in a different and sometimes a better way than a committee internal to the civil service or to a particular government, or than a special parliamentary committee of MPs, or than a committee whose members have been chosen for their known prior commitment to particular points of view.

Some months after the committee's work had ended, I spent a weekend in Malacca with a lecturer from the University of Singapore, a break from examining there. The hotel was old-fashioned Malaysian, catering for local and peripatetic businessmen. As we booked in, the clerk asked (as in England they might ask, 'Tea at 7 and *The Times*?'): 'Do you want a girl for the night?' He took my mumble for hesitation and added: 'Malay? Chinese? Indian? White?' My refusal brought only a shrug. I went upstairs to a hot and humid room and had a shower. Combing my hair before a long mirror, I looked at its maker's inscription. 'This mirror was made by Pilkington's of St Helens.' Harry's nonconformist eye was everywhere.

4

A Short Coda

The Pilkington Report brought about the chance of a longish talk with T. S. Eliot. In early 1963, Teachers' College of Columbia University in New York asked me to give their centenary lecture. I chose to talk about the reception of the Pilkington Report, as an example of the character of discussion about cultural issues in Britain. The lecture was called 'The Difficulties of Democratic Debate' and was published in their journal, the Teachers' College *Record*. Not a very widely circulated publication; but a few weeks later came a postcard from Eliot saying he had read and liked the essay and, some time when I was in London, would I care to call on him at Faber's. This was in September 1963.

I had three-quarters of an hour in his attic room. An electric fire was on and the window shut though it was a balmy day. After about twenty minutes he said if I was hot I should switch the fire off; he could do without it now but had needed it when he came in after lunch. I realised then, more sharply than before, that he was indeed a frail elderly man now; it was hard to readjust one's visual image of him, of that solid fifty-ish figure and firm, hawklike face which had stared out at us over so many years. The head was still finely boned, commanding; the face was lined and jowled and his body a little bent. He said that the asthma which had put him into hospital the winter before was not quite cleared; he broke off from time to time to cough. He spoke tenderly and touchingly about the care his wife had given him, how she had sought out the hospital – the Brompton – best

suited for him, and how right she had been; they had treated him
marvellously. When he was released they had gone to Bermuda,
where they could hope for a dry climate. But it had been rather
damp and so did not have as much healing effect as they had
hoped. Whilst he was talking of all this one had a sense of a man
quite wrapped around, for the first time in many years, with love
and affection; and very much aware of it. 'What seas what shores
what granite islands towards my timbers / And woodthrush calling
through the fog / My daughter.'

He began most courteously – and was extremely courteous
throughout – by saying he had wanted to meet me for a long time
and had much enjoyed my work, particularly *The Uses of Literacy*. (Years later, Mrs Eliot told Mary, after one of the annual T.
S. Eliot lectures at the University of Kent, that they had read out
of that book in bed.) He said again, as he had in his postcard,
how much he had liked the New York lecture and hoped it would
be published here. I told him the most relevant British journal
had just refused it. He seemed to think I might be hoping he
would suggest somewhere else, though I wasn't. That thought
made him add that he was in touch with and wrote for few
journals nowadays, perhaps most of all for the *New Daily*
(founded by Edward Martell in 1960, a right-wing paper). He
added that Martell was coming to see him that afternoon. This
was the first sombre hint that as he had grown older the part
of his character which made him a royalist, a classicist and a
conservative (a position he had earlier justified far better than
most people of that persuasion) might be leading him to ally
himself with people who were shallow in their right-wingery.

I remembered then a remark of his about *Notes Towards the
Definition of Culture*. I had been talking to a specialist in educational theory who shared many of Eliot's views on culture and
education. I said I didn't *like Notes Towards*; it stood for so much
I did not agree with in conservatism. Yet it was the hardest book
I knew, from that side of the cultural debate, to rebut – for
example, on the impediments of a meritocracy as compared with
those of inherited status. My colleague had passed on the remark.
Eliot had smiled and said it was one of the best reviews he had
had.

Another characteristic – which I now recognise well, being at much the same risk – was that he went on talking ever so slightly as if engaged on a monologue, and sometimes went round the same circuit twice. And there was a slight acerbity or tetchiness in some judgments on people. We talked for some time about the lack of good platforms for intellectual debate and he made sharp remarks about some of those who were prominent in the liberal journals; superficial, 'silly fellows'. He was sharp about the declared anti-Establishment attitudes of some of those, and particularly about the wreath a group of such people had sent to Stephen Ward's funeral; apparently there was a card on it saying Ward was a victim of the Establishment. He was especially mordant about Kenneth Tynan signing it. If the artistic 'or – whatever it is – dramatic director of the National Theatre isn't a member of the Establishment, then who on earth is? He's certainly more a member of the Establishment than I am.'

He began to talk about Leeds, very warmly; Headingley and Weetwood Lane, in particular, near where Valerie's parents lived. Not my part of Leeds, much posher; but Mary's Hall of Residence was up there so we had gone for many walks nearby. He spoke affectionately and at some length about his mother-in-law. She had said that one branch of our family had been near neighbours of hers. He mentioned the road but it meant nothing to me. Otherwise I would have assumed a possible connection with the distant member of our family who taught elocution, Harehills way. It is hard to think there was any link since our family were so firmly in the insalubrious working-class area of south Leeds, on the other side of the river and the town. He suggested we might meet, up there in Yorkshire, some time and that I certainly should look up his mother-in-law.

At this point we began to talk about writing. He said he would not write more poetry; but had something of a yearning to try another play. 'I can always get them mounted, you know,' he added, surprisingly and touchingly. He said very decidedly that he could hardly understand how people could write novels and carry on a normal life. They demanded so much from you, they required you to wrap yourself up so much in the characters, that he did not see how people who wrote them could have a usual kind of domestic existence. He couldn't have managed that. I asked him whether he was at least to some extent wrapped up in his plays when he was writing them. I was wondering whether the warmth of his remark about the demands of the novel might owe something to a feeling that he would find it very hard to write another play now that he was, so to speak, living in the present as a married man.

He said yes; he was caught up with his characters when writing a play. I asked whether different characters took it in turn to occupy his mind as they developed. He said: 'Oh no, they are all there together all the time; they are living there together – and they have to get on, you know.'

He mentioned more than once his affection for Bonamy Dobrée which had run over many years; we all knew of this in the English department at Leeds, and some had wondered if Bonamy had exaggerated the closeness, but he had not.

At one point Eliot said he had been struck by my interventions when he gave evidence to the Pilkington Committee: this was no doubt because I had been asked by the chairman to lead by inviting Eliot to comment on that 'Giving the people what the people want' chestnut. 'In fact,' he added with a bit of a smile and rather grandly, 'you were the only one I remembered – except the glass manufacturer.'

I began to wonder whether I ought to go; it's always difficult to estimate that moment. I thought I would make a move at about four, having arrived at a quarter past three. However, at about three minutes to four, as neat and nice as you like he got up and said he would 'have to release me' (a less genteel and slightly more flattering form of words than 'I mustn't detain you') since he had someone else coming. I wonder if that was Martell. Martell had just announced he would apply for one of the new area franchises in television. If it had crossed his mind to invite Eliot to join the board I guess he would have been refused, given Eliot's commitment to the highest standards in public service broadcasting.

As we parted he added, and seemed to be saying it with warmth and genuineness, that he hoped we would meet again, in Leeds or London. We did not, in either place, and he died two years later.

CHAPTER 4

GREAT HOPES FROM BIRMINGHAM
1962–70

The move to Birmingham, like that to Leicester, was marked by an academic stroll; one more instance of the casual humaneness of appointing practices in some universities at the time. After an informal lunch with the Dean of Arts and half-a-dozen professors in the Staff Club, I was asked to go over the road to the Vice-Chancellor's 'residence'. 'Let's take a turn round the garden,' he said. There, laconic in a manner which seemed particularly suited to a lean, lanky distinguished medic and Rhodes Scholar from New Zealand, he opened without preamble, 'Well, they seem to want you. Are you prepared to come?'

I

The journey to that garden had begun three or four months before, in early 1961. We had been at Leicester about eighteen months and were well settled. But ties with Hull were still strong so, that Easter vacation, we borrowed a friend's house near that university for a week. The quiet was broken by two letters forwarded from Leicester, each asking if I was interested in becoming a professor. Manchester University is large and distinguished, and its named Chair in English a famous one. But Mary did not wish to go back to live there, after years of schooling in the heart of the city. Her mother would have been near, but saw a lot of us wherever we were and enjoyed those frequent excursions.

The letter from Birmingham was trickier. To begin with, it did not ask directly if I was interested in occupying a new, second, chair in English there. It said it had advertised but had not found the right person. Would I care to meet a few senior members of the faculty over lunch to discuss their needs? I was impercipient enough not to realise they were really saying: 'Will you let us look you over, to see whether we would like to offer you the chair?' I went and talked; then someone must have made a 'phone call to the Vice-Chancellor and I duly appeared in his garden a quarter of an hour later.

I told the Vice-Chancellor I would think over the offer very carefully but should say at the start that I would hope for three conditions to be met. I did not wish to move in that autumn of 1961, because Arthur Humphreys was again due to spend the Spring term of 1962 at the Folger Library in Washington, and I had promised to mind the shop once more. 'That is a pity but I think we must respect your wish.' Though I could join the department in eighteen months, in the autumn of 1962, I would wish to continue living in Leicester for two more years, since a break in the children's education before 1964 would be particularly unsettling. 'I am sorry about that but assume you would be here for the greater part of each week – two or three days a week professors are not our style – and on those terms we can agree again.' Finally, and as to the post-graduate side of the job, I said I would not be greatly interested in gathering the usual disparate group of graduate students. I would like to set up a post-graduate centre in what I described as contemporary cultural studies. Here came the first instance of the freedom the rank of professor confers. The answer was: 'I cannot, of course, have a view on the precise subject. But you will be a professor and, if that is what you want to do, I do not think we would wish to dissuade you. But you would have to find the money for such a centre from outside.' The combination of soft-nosed permissiveness and hard-nosed practicality is also very English.

That was how we came to Birmingham; not, like Jane Austen's Mrs Elton, with 'no great hopes' but with good hopes, and they were largely fulfilled. Had the three conditions not been met, I would not have agreed. Not out of a wish to have all my own way, but because each condition was important, the first as the payment of a debt, the second on family grounds, the third because not to use a professor's position to try to advance the interests which had emerged in the writing of *The Uses of Literacy* would have been to throw away for the sake of a title what now seemed professionally most important.

We were reluctant to leave Leicester and grateful for the three-year stay of execution before we need actually move house. Arthur Humphreys at once did his best to persuade his colleagues to give me a chair there. I would then have stayed; and sought to start a centre for contemporary cultural studies. But this was just before the great expansion, chairs were rare, and there was opposition to having anyone jump the queue. I closed the agreement with Birmingham and after a year and a term more in the Leicester department began, in Autumn 1962, two years of commuting for five days a week; during which Leicester's pleasant social life continued.

Like Leicester's, Birmingham's university fitted and in some ways mirrored its town. It was large, several times larger than the two universities I had worked in until then. It was confident of its own strength; the tall tower at the heart of the grounds – modelled on that of Siena – had been intended by its late-nineteenth-century sponsors to assert that confidence. Anything you can do we can do better. But in that climate the tower was of a dead-looking brick and, in the townscape seen from a distance, looked like just another factory chimney though with quirks on, much as West Riding mill-owners went in for.

As was the way in those days, the university and the College of Advanced Technology (later, Aston University) – on the other, less solidly bourgeois, side of town – were not greatly involved with each other. The irony was that the university's own strength was founded more than anything else on its science and technology; at its heart it was a very superior College of Advanced Science, Technology and Medicine. The medical, scientific and technological professors had a solid, broad-clothed assurance I had hardly ever seen at Hull or Leicester. They were, and knew it, in the big league; and indeed a good number of them were FRSs. Most of them looked on the Arts Faculty with an uninvolved and uncomprehending tolerance, as a forceful eighteenth-century Germanic prince with a strong commercial sense and drive might have looked on a chamber orchestra he had inherited; though glad to know it was rather a good chamber orchestra by national or even international standards and as such things go.

When the Vice-Chancellorship became vacant those Powers would assume that one of their kind should be asked to take the helm. That happened once in my time there, in the late Sixties. Edward Boyle, an MP for a Birmingham constituency for many years, had just left parliament, and two or three of us at Birmingham, including a couple of scientists who recognised his outstanding qualities, suggested he might be considered as Vice-Chancellor. Boyle himself, but we were not told, was uneasy about becoming V.C. in the town where he had been MP; another medic was appointed. Soon afterwards, Leeds University had the great good sense to appoint Boyle.

The silent leaving to one side of the Boyle proposal was typical of Birmingham's government at that time. There was a Senate, of course, meeting on a few Wednesday afternoons each term and almost entirely composed of professors. But you soon learned that Senate's powers were informally qualified by the Committee of Principals and Deans, known as the pre-Senate Saturday morning mafia. There was a sense of power being exercised, not corruptly but for the good of the institution as they saw it, by large men behind closed doors, doors symbolically lined with thick padding so that little got out to indicate and little in to influence their deliberatings.

The demi-gods who sat under the would-be-Sienese tower were solid, steady, sure people; according to their lights, fair and just – and also, in any crisis which called on their humanity, immensely kind, as we had particular cause to discover in the middle of our time there.

It is plain that Leicester was for me, until I became used to Birmingham's scale, the easier place in which to work. Leicester's day-by-day practices were more familial, and always lubricated by Arthur Humphreys's kindness. By contrast, Birmingham did have a touch of the big bow-wow, the air of confident consequence and lack of some stylistic graces common in the bigger Redbricks. The Leicesters and Hulls and Keeles were minnows; Oxbridge was not quite as real, as firmly on solid industrial and commercial earth (but most at the big Redbricks would have happily answered a call to Oxbridge). That is the way Birmingham affected you much of the time, even though you knew well that in all faculties it had some very distinguished people, its library was splendid, and its students by-and-large of a slightly higher intellectual calibre than those at the smaller places. More, it was, once you had defined your own area and rabbit-tracks, as friendly as anywhere else; but it was big enough to need separate areas and separate tracks, and they overlapped much less than at the smaller places.

The Senate at Birmingham, of which I became a member as of right, encapsulated all the qualities I have described – probably most Senates did and do. It was large and inclined to the ponderous. The ponderosity was alleviated by one or two extremely exotic birds; a big place could afford a few of those. Here the outstanding example was a professor whose specialism was the Old Norse dialect of the Faeroe Islands, and there he went as often as possible. But lectures had to have their due so, at the beginning of each session, he put up a notice saying his lectures would be held late, on an unpopular day. That kept numbers low. After a week or two a further notice would announce a move to a smaller room. Legend had it that by the third or fourth week he was meeting his class in a telephone booth. At any rate, the class usually petered out in that first term. He then made his one annual appearance at Senate: to ask for a grant to visit the Faeroe Islands. Oblivious to the fed-up faces all around, he was given the grant and left the meeting.

The only occasion on which I recall him attending Senate more than once in a single session was after he had realised that he was nearing sixty-five and didn't want to retire. Appearing unexpectedly, like a small-part actor with strong self-regard who had come in an act ahead of time, he put down a motion that the retirement age should be raised to 67. Everyone recognised the cheek but a number were nearing retirement age too and wouldn't have minded a couple of years extra. A committee was set up and worked hard in the interstices of time for two terms. The arguments for extension were strong and we recommended that. The proposer then appeared yet again – three times in one session! – thanked us, and withdrew.

In the conduct of Senate's business there was – there is in all the universities I know – a base-layer of good sense and good intent, not harried by commercial or political considerations. It follows that sometimes the good sense becomes unrealistic until the Vice-Chancellor (it is one of his main jobs) reminds members, usually dryly, of the relevant facts of political or financial life, even for academics. A few persist in arguing only for the interests of their own corners, but all in all the discussions are fair-minded in a way which a comfortable assured income and assured employment will encourage in all but the incorrigible. Writers on university life like to assert, with the satisfaction which comes from identifying the Old Adam wherever we look, that university committees are at bottom as ruthless as those in Big Business or Big Politics. I have no experience of Big Business but some of Big Politics (with the UN) and I know that equivalence is an engaging nonsense. University committees are free from some distorting pressures. Some members do behave like market-shysters; but the general conduct is, as it should be, more disinterested than in places where money or politics rule.

Still, above what I called the base-layer, gravitas tends to be common. It is as though many people, having acquired the extraordinarily luminous title of professor, subcutaneously feel that in physiognomy and style they have to live up to their own favoured inner portraits. The hair lengthens well over the ears, a well thumbed pipe succeeds cigarettes, the voice takes on depth and the walk weight. I was talkative enough in Senate but rarely felt I looked the part. The woman who helped two half-days a week in the Birmingham house thought that too. 'He doesn't look like a professor,' she told Mary. 'Looks more as if he runs a pub.'

Of the few lecturers who by election were made members of Senate, some tended either to be slightly abrasive, to show they didn't feel under patronage, or tried to outdo the professors in gravitas. One lecturer seemed literally to put on weight from the day of his appointment. On one occasion he ended an argument for some minor change in the rules with the oracular coda: 'We have thought about these things' (or was it 'on these things'?), in a voice which mingled the regal and magisterial with that of a housewife insisting that her whites are whiter than white.

Birmingham's department of English had had for many decades a good reputation, mainly of a solidly scholarly rather than a lively literary kind. Ernest de Sélincourt and Allardyce Nicoll had presided there. The Shakespeare Institute drew fine post-graduate students from all over the world. The department and contiguous departments were big enough and hospitable enough to contain many types. In the Thirties a bundle – not a school or identifiable group – of gifted writers or writers-in-the-making emerged within town and gown: Walter Allen, R. D. Smith, Leslie Halward, John Hampson, Henry Reed, Henry Green. Louis MacNeice taught in the department of Classics; Auden's family home was not much more than a mile off, his father being the Medical Officer of Health for the city's Education Service and a lecturer on public health in the University's Medical School.

In the early 1960s the Vice-Chancellor and the head of department, Terence Spencer, were anxious to strengthen the more modern side and so, just before they proposed I join them, David Lodge arrived. In mid-1961 Spencer consulted me, as professor-designate, about the appointment of Malcolm Bradbury. So small are some British academic circles that Bradbury had succeeded me at Hull in 1959. He then arrived at Birmingham, just before I did. Lodge and Bradbury were launching their careers as novelists and critics, and soon became close friends. For the modernists it was a particularly good time to be there, cheerful and productive; and especially for Lodge and Bradbury. Long-standing strengths of the department – linguistics, Shakespearian studies, mediaeval literary and language studies, and studies in Romanticism and Victorian literature – continued to flourish. Post-graduate numbers were larger than the entire English departments of many other places.

Not long after I had settled in the department came a call asking whether I would be interested in a chair at the new university of Sussex. In other circumstances, I might certainly have been very interested indeed but by then I knew, at least after a minute or two, that I would refuse; it came too early, for the family and me professionally; and Birmingham had already become friendly.

A letter from Tom Driberg asking if I was interested in being Professor and Head of Department at Tripoli could be turned down even more quickly. But what was he doing acting as a contact man for King Idris?

We had soon discovered that a professor's life, at least in the Sixties, was very privileged. You were being paid to do something you enjoyed: to follow your intellectual interests and try to pass them on to others. If you found teaching a strain, against your nature, one part of your life was less happy than the other. But most liked talking to young people, and those who found lecturing painful usually enjoyed seminars or tutorials. The salary was not handsome but enough to live comfortably, especially in the provinces.

After you had passed a 'probationary period', which in many places was hardly noticed, you had security of tenure and so were shielded from fear of the sack and other pressures of the open market. This security, which is now not given to new entrants, was usually justified as a way of protecting academic freedom: the threat of being dismissed could not be used against those who said unpalatable things. For many years I supported this argument, especially since my own early years in academic life saw McCarthyism in America at its worst. We did not suffer that, but its virulence over there made us sit more tightly behind our own bulwarks.

But the usual justifications for unrestricted tenure were thin. If tenure had not existed would sacking have occurred when someone became a nuisance to the university authorities? I doubt it. The policy was an excessive and largely irrelevant insurance and, paradoxically, implicitly called in question that very freedom to make their own decisions which the universities are so proud of; it offered greater protection than the circumstances warranted, was a belt where strong braces – those of substantial self-government – already existed.

The sad reflection is that, even if we did live in an ideologically centralised society, many academics would accept its rules and do as they were told; not simply to protect their jobs but because they are natural runners with the tide, cannot imagine any action initiated by them which might interfere with their devotion to their subjects, and do not stand for any great general principles of intellectual freedom.

That is the way the world goes and in this the people who are gifted enough to be appointed to university posts do not in general have a stronger hold on the right to the unfettered pursuit of truth than some of the less gifted outside. For most in Britain, the defence of tenure was the invoking of a democratic rallying cry to defend an unexamined, excessive, comfortable perquisite. We should not accept a formal protection which most others do not have and which implicitly calls into question the democratic assumptions we profess.

2

House-hunting in Birmingham, in 1964, had underlined how we were gradually going up in the world; but not always to heights with whose styles we felt at home. Our preferred areas, for easy access to both the university and schools to fit the children's ages, were in the middle-class arc around the campus: Edgbaston, Harborne and Moseley. The search produced a fascinating cultural cameo of provincial middle-class and middle-executive life at that time. The doors were usually opened by middle-aged ladies in twin-sets of powder blue or similarly coded colours, no doubt from Rackhams, the Selfridges/Harrods of Birmingham. Their voices were genteel, with none of the Brummie nasal twang. One of them, in a house we fancied, answered a question about bus-routes with: 'Oh, we do not think of buses. We are all two-car families in this part of Moseley now.' Most haunting were the children's bedrooms, the overlapping pop-star posters seeming both lonely and public gestures, the children away at boarding schools.

In the recesses of a surprising number of such homes one came across a raffish element. The owner would swing open a door to exhibit the great size of a built-in wardrobe, and out would fall a profusion of operatic gear, amateur dramatic costumes, voluntary association uniforms, Country and Western, Civil War and pantomime outfits. Inside so many Englishmen is a woman trying to get out; inside many an Englishwoman is a little girl wanting to play at nurses, Carmen, Mrs Miniver. This is W. E. Williams's Doomsday Book of English Leisure in all its abundance and frequent kinkiness.

In some 'backstairs' areas (today, simply the kitchens, but I introduce the old phrase since it is redolent of places some among even servant-less professional families in the Sixties clearly went into only when they had to, and cared little about), in those parts one occasionally came across squalor like that of a seedy boarding house, or of some Parisian *chambres de bonne* within elegant *maisons particulières*. Some of my elderly relatives, remembering days 'in service' or as daily helps, used to say, 'Some posh people live like pigs when they aren't on show'; we drew our respectable skirts even more closely around us. By contrast, prick-neat kitchens, shining like colour supplement ads, more often appeared lower down that middle-class scale. There, the homes were prosperous but still striving; the casual, careless style, which did not bother about what the neighbours might think, had not been acquired and almost certainly would never be.

Eventually we found a large, architecturally odd-looking but wonderfully accommodating place a quarter of a mile from the university, comparatively cheap because it was on a forty-year lease and had some time before been converted to two flats, only one now occupied and by the vendor. Made into one premise again it had, if you counted in two or three cellars and three attics, twenty rooms, two bathrooms and three lavatories; none of it was smart but, altogether, it was perfect for a family with teenagers. Once his boss had discovered that the tipsy Irish fitter who installed the central heating had connected the hot with the cold water and vice versa and put that right the house warmed up, and for the first time we knew the sybaritic delights of a home in which there were no cold corners, no early morning chill in the bedrooms, no ever-present suspicion of damp in the loos. The half-acre of garden had a splendid cedar of Lebanon round which foxes played; and those other newly urbanised creatures, the magpies, squawked like fishwives in the branches. There was also a large coach-house with a bare upstairs space where the coachman had lived (his lavatory was in the corner of the side-yard, near the cold tap for washing the coach and himself). The first owner, in the latter part of the nineteenth century, had been a manufacturer of nails, nuts and bolts, and the like; probably a devout Unitarian and upright citizen of the sort who made Birmingham able to boast in those days of being the best governed city in Europe. They did themselves well, too, those Birmingham industrialists; it would have been assumed that four, five or six staff were needed to run the place.

Leeds, Sheffield, Manchester – those larger cities all have hill-walking country not far from their boundaries. Except for the Lickey Hills just to the south, Birmingham has not. The day, in 1969, that I was asked to be a candidate for an Assistant Director-Generalship at UNESCO in Paris, Mary and I walked all after-noon on those hills, weighing things up. The Lickeys are a small tasting for what lies further west; the Malverns and Worcester-shire, Herefordshire, Shropshire and the Marches. Softish country-side, somewhere between the uncompromising grandness of the Pennines and the slightly suburban amiabilities of Sussex; and in some ways more attractive than either.

Simon saw less than his siblings of these places, and of the novel pleasures of the large house and garden. During our first year in the Birmingham house he worked in a school in Uganda and then, having decided he would be the first of the family to aim for Oxbridge, got himself into Cambridge. The other two had transfers from their Leicester grammar schools to King Edward's, just down the road, made new friends and helped keep the house and garden occupied; and musical, with Pat Boone and Clarence Frogman Henry giving way to the Beatles in the latter half of the decade. Grandma stayed with us frequently and was as easy with mini-skirts and the sound of music as she had long been with the variety of visitors.

Birmingham was by far the biggest city we had lived in; there were about 1.2 million in its conurbation at our time. Leeds had had about half a million; manageable, if messy. Hull and Leicester in their different ways were even more manageable, less divided in great differentiated chunks, less finally unknowable, less chal-lenging. But here was this great galumphing place – rightly proud of much in its nineteenth-century civic and industrial achieve-ments, still keeping some magnificent Victorian-Gothic piles, but prone to taking itself up by the physical (not mental) roots every half-century, living by great psychic waves, not so much purse-proud as given to the ethic of 'I can get it for you wholesale' (the Birmingham equivalent of 'It fell off the back of a lorry, love'). Hearing that my fog-lamps had been stolen whilst the car was in the park at Snow Hill Station, a decorator at work in the house, without a prior word and as a matter of course, brought two new ones the following day. I tried to refuse but he did not understand. 'Give me a pound each and we'll say no more. I don't like to think of you being ripped off.' In the end I yielded to his code of ethics, at least in appearance, paid and put the lamps on the garage shelf; and threw them away, rusty and unused, twenty years later.

In our day, Birmingham was still very prosperous, chiefly from the flourishing motor-car industry and its ancillaries. In spite of this it behaved, collectively and publicly, very nervously, like a bruiser with an exceptionally thin skin. No wonder that from the Sixties and onwards it has bred one of the most active ranges of alternative styles of living, voluntary bodies out to pierce air-holes in the great thick carapace, immigrant styles second only to London in their variety, a semi-Bohemian student quarter, and inner-city 'villages' which insist on their difference, their reality and distinction.

Over it all was the appalling central redevelopment; that regular half-century taking apart had, in the Fifties, surrendered totally to an outlook which, sometimes evident, sometimes submerged, had always threatened Birmingham. It expressed the push into seeing people as unavoidable but small elements in the repeated assertings of the city's massiveness, a readiness to disregard human-sized needs in the thrust towards finally proving its place as the Big One. By that redevelopment, centred on the Bull Ring Rotunda, a gasometer with windows, the citizens of Birmingham were reduced to matchstick figures who spent most of their city-centre time in interweaving underpasses, lined with 'artistic embel-lishments' of so crude a social-realist kind that they would have been more at home in the industrial cities of the Don Basin. The upper world of fresh air was left to the motorised traffic which was now able to swish through what had been the heart of a reasonably walkable city. It would be hard to find a more damning instance of the limits of party-run local government in England. The Nineties are being declared the age of Birmingham's cultural and artistic renaissance. They may well bring it off this time, with all that energy.

The City Library and Art Gallery had long been of an international standard; the City orchestra and the theatres were of good provincial English standard. There were dozens of artistic and cultural offerings, far more to see and do than any single family could handle; picking and choosing became a bore. University people were less involved than those at Leicester; one went to fewer and fewer events and spent most spare time with university friends.

My own main involvement with the city was as a member of the board of the Repertory Theatre, respected over much of the world since the great and often invoked days of Barry Jackson, and still one of the best English nurseries of talent.

The Vice-Chancellor had been invited to become chairman of the board in the year I was appointed to a chair, accepted the unaccustomed commission, and swiftly took the opportunity to acquire backing from a more literary type. The board meetings were a mixture of exciting initiatives, since the Rep. could take risks and was often invited to do so by impresarios, and of aggressive small-mindedness from some board members.

This brew came together memorably quite early in my time. The director announced he had been offered from the London agent a new play by Anouilh, one not yet seen in Britain, and that he was anxious to take up the offer. He outlined the case for accepting and was then immediately asked by a councillor to outline the plot. As that was being done, the councillor's Chaplinesque moustache twitched more and more. Suddenly he interrupted, in a vocal mixture one soon became accustomed to in the public life of those parts – orotund public phraseology carried on the Midlands urban moan. 'Am I to understand', he asked, with a Chadbandish look around the other members, 'that this *French* play is one of those so-called *kitchen-sink* affairs?' The director, who enjoyed tweaking their tails, sometimes past the point of discretion, replied that he supposed it could be called that. 'Then, Mr Chairman, I wish to register my strong dissent. To me the kitchen sink is a place of *honour and dignity* and I for one will not be party to impugning it. Nor should this city's world-famous Repertory Theatre be associated with such an activity. I move that this offer be rejected.'

The Vice-Chancellor, to whom this was no trickier than many

a moment in Senate, asked the director to obtain copies; he, the director and two other members were to read it. He said he was sure that, so as not to risk losing the play by delay, if our opinion was favourable the board would allow the director to take up the offer without further reference to them. The outraged councillor was not entirely happy but so it was agreed. We never saw the English script. When the director telephoned for it he was told that another well known Rep. – Nottingham, I think – had closed the deal at once.

3

As soon as we had properly settled in the Birmingham house and department, the claims of the promised Centre for Contemporary Cultural Studies came to the front; they began with the need to find the funds the university could not provide. Seven-year, tax-deductible covenants to charitable bodies were easier to acquire then than now. In the early Sixties income tax for the very wealthy reached 19/6 (97.5p) in the pound. 'It only costs me sixpence in the pound to be generous. The Inland Revenue pays well over ninety per cent,' said Allen Lane as he agreed to set us up.

It was inevitable that some people would say he gave the money as a covert thank-you for my evidence in the *Lady Chatterley's Lover* case. I am sure I would have asked Allen Lane for funds even if I had not appeared in his defence three years before; I knew him well enough to be sure the idea would interest him. His reply to my letter was predictable. He would 'take Bill Williams's advice'; would I meet him at five-thirty a few days later at Williams's office in St James's Square.

As we sat down, Williams produced a bottle of hock from a well stocked cupboard incorporated into his desk. Allen Lane asked me to outline the proposal. Williams told him he should support it. 'What did you say you wanted?' Lane asked. 'Two thousand four hundred a year for seven years.' A look of enjoyable cunning lit his rather heavy-cherub's face for a moment. 'What if I give you half and you get the rest by asking someone to match Allen Lane's covenant?' 'I'm asking for the minimum needed to set us up. If you give it, I'll ask others for more so we have room for manoeuvre.' He gave a quick smile. Williams intervened: 'Oh, give him what he asks, Allen. You've made a fortune by riding cultural change without understanding it.' Taking a piece of paper from his jacket pocket, Lane said, 'All right. You'll have the agreement next week. Where shall I send it?' He made a note and the meeting ended. The agreement arrived within a week.

Chatto and the *Observer* each added a little, so that within a month I had £2500 a year for seven years and a once-for-all £500. That allowed for the appointment of a fairly senior research fellow and a secretary; there was some left over to start buying books and pay travelling expenses to visiting speakers. The university did not ask for anything towards the costs of accommodation, light, heat, postage or any other administrative expense. It was all very simple, unbusinesslike and, by today's standards in university administration, impermissible.

Quite soon, foundations gave money for specific projects, notably the Rowntree Memorial Trust, whose grant allowed us to produce a substantial study of the press, *Paper Voices*. There followed a range of publications, large and small. We would not accept money for work defined from outside unless the definition and purpose agreed with our own; we never allowed our aim to be deflected so as to secure a grant. If we had, we could have had many more grants.

I advertised the research post and some good candidates applied. But I had met Stuart Hall a few times and been very impressed by his grasp of this still inchoate area of work. The thought grew of inviting him to leave teaching in London. I finally asked him, and he agreed readily. The two of us announced the opening of the centre for Spring 1964, and invited graduates to apply for entry the following October.

For me at least, that was one of the best ideas I have had. Stuart, who had come to Britain from Jamaica as a Rhodes Scholar, was brilliant and particularly at home with theoretical issues, one of my weak spots. He was a Marxist and I a centre socialist; so differences of emphasis reflected differences in our casts of mind. But all was in the open and discussed. Neither of us doubted the importance of the work or, more, the value of different approaches to it. In the seven years we worked closely together I do not remember a cross word; we were always very good friends.

Most of the students, and members of staff looking on, recognised and respected the nature of the partnership. A good test of the steadiness of an individual's sense of self is the frequency with which 'I' appears in his conversation; Stuart Hall used it less than anyone I have known. His intellectual energy went into ideas, not self-presentation. He was a charismatic and compelling pro-pounder of theoretical structures and could be spell-binding on public platforms. Yet all that was, for me and I think for him, secondary to the firm and proper, the intellectually objective, establishing of the centre and its area of work.

Most of the Arts Faculty staff seemed to wish the scheme success or, if they didn't, kept their counsel. To my knowledge only one showed malice. He told colleagues in the Senior Common Room that Hoggart was inventing 'a nice line in cheap hats'. It took a few minutes to see what he meant: that higher degrees from the centre would be easily given. Stuart Hall and I decided that for the first few years we would offer no doctorates, only masters' degrees, and would appoint the most severe external assessors we could find, all from departments of English; if they were not particularly interested in cultural studies, no matter. Within a very few years we had won the Faculty Prize for the best MA twice, and two of our first three or four external judges had asked why we had not changed the candidates' applications into ones for PhDs; one assessor recommended an MA to his publisher. That was hard on the first candidates, perhaps too hard. But it stopped malicious remarks about our standards.

A professor from a new university said cultural studies were all very well but he needed every hour of available time to introduce students to 'the subject', the established curriculum in English Studies; as though that was not itself a cultural construct but a prescription from heaven. Another head of department said he wished us well, but had we considered that in encouraging clever young graduates to study a field outside those normal within English departments, we might be spoiling their chances of being appointed to posts in universities or polytechnics. We had con-sidered that and hoped enough English departments within higher education would be willing to adjust the definition of their disci-pline in the way we were proposing. So it turned out, especially but not only in the polytechnics; some universities, mostly among the new foundations, appointed our graduates. Virtually all our students from abroad were very quickly given good posts when they got back.

Had we wanted to follow the easy 'nothing but Firsts from Oxbridge to be interviewed' method, we could still – within a year or two of opening – have filled our places with first-rate candidates several times over. We did not do that, so interviewing became a protracted effort, but well worth while. We did agree to short attachments of new, very bright, 'fast track' BBC trainees. I can recall without effort the names of half a dozen students from the first seven years of the centre's existence, up to my leaving, who are now well known. There are others like them from the subsequent twenty years. It was inevitable, given that most students likely to apply knew that I was 'on the Left' and, even more, knew that Stuart was a rising theorist of the further Left, that many of our applicants were already of that persuasion. We did not let that sway us, if we knew of it, at interview; and were careful not to proselytise in any of the centre's activities. I do not imagine all the major powers within the university's government believed this, especially after the new Vice-Chancellor, Hunter, arrived. When the 1968 upheavals occurred, and they were brief but fairly disruptive at Birmingham, some of the Top Brass simply assumed that the centre's graduates were the main group behind the disturbances, and probably their initiators. Our people did play a big part once the troubles began. They had grounds, given the way much in the university was being run, and they were taking fashionable political stands; but they were more argumentative than aggressive.

I had given my inaugural lecture as a professor in early 1963, eighteen months before the centre opened. I explained what I was trying to do by setting up the centre and deliberately pitched the case high so that, having put striking goods in the shop window, we would have to work hard to live up to the prospectus.

Taking literature classes with adult volunteers outside the universities had pushed me, and some others in that and other disciplines, to question the agreed university boundaries of the subjects. Adults asked, usually by implication: what does this study really mean to me as a person, and to my life in the everyday world; how does it connect with that life outside books? These are not ingenuous or jejune questions. It would have been easy to give bogus definitions of relevance, ranging from the British version of the politically committed to the spiritually inflated. Instead, one burrowed and worried away at what seemed sound definitions.

In the inaugural lecture I set out to make the case for widening the boundaries of English as it was offered at universities. There had, after all, been an impressive Culture and Society debate in the nineteenth century, one in which important writers – notably Coleridge and Wordsworth – had played a major part. That effort had to some extent been carried through to the twentieth century by Eliot, Lawrence, the Leavises, Orwell and others. But in most departments of English this great debate had little place. There were valuable books on what was sometimes called Literature, Life and Thought but they tended to be, as that title suggests, a more or less discrete setting of elements side by side, in the hope that they would spontaneously interact. 'Life' and 'Thought' were usually inorganic to the texture of the works and so of the cultures studied. Similarly, most work from Social Science departments on the sociology of literature and art, though it could be interesting and useful, was external to the nature and the experience of literature itself, for the writer or the reader.

So my own preoccupation was and remains: to try to develop the closest and most sensitive reading possible of any literary work in the belief that, read in and for itself, the work might throw a unique light on the culture within which it had been written. But it was not read *so that* such insights could be gleaned; it was read as a created artistic object. Only by being approached in that way could large, value-laden words often casually bandied about in departments of English – words such as 'significant', 'meaningful', 'illuminating' – carry weight; and by then you hardly needed them.

It followed that, at the heart of such a claim, lay a belief in the power of language itself as the most important indicator of a hold on values. The meanings, the weights, of those words and the sense of common assumptions would vary in different periods. Some tones would be available, some not, in each period, and so their meanings would differ from period to period. But all was not historically relative: some words, some weights, would echo down the years and speak to several generations in much the same way.

The centre was to study in particular contemporary rather than earlier culture because few people in English departments had looked at it, and most of those in ways we wished to question; because I had been led to examine it as a result of the uncloistered teaching within adult education and because both Stuart Hall and I were by nature interested in main aspects and objects of popular culture: magazines, cartoons, films, radio, T. V., advertising. We had learned a lot from F. R. and Q. D. Leavis but could not accept much in their positions, literary and social. For myself, I had always wanted to make connections – between the daily lives and habits of people and the material they read or looked at; and between their responses to that material and what might be their responses to less ephemeral experiences. On that, I had learned as much from essays by Orwell and insights by C. S. Lewis as from the Leavises.

In all this we were of course saying 'there's nothing like leather', nothing like literature to give a sense of the texture of experience. We were not quarrelling with history or sociology or political philosophy. We deliberately looked for graduate applicants in those and related disciplines, and our seminar speakers were more often than not from disciplines other than English studies. We were saying that literature is not 'evidence' about a culture if by that one means something which can easily be 'read off' as if from outside, by counting the references to this or that, by noting explicit statements of intent or of conviction, by a series of fact-hunting, 'objective' but exterior, raids on it. We were saying that to yield its true insights the literature had to be attended to disinterestedly; one had to get below the surface level, sometimes below the level the author had thought he or she was working at; one had to try to interpret tone, to hear stresses hidden from the author, to detect assumptions concealed behind what might be the public language of the time, to distinguish where the imagination had flowered and was penetrating further than at the times when the writer was in full control.

It followed that the methods of literary analysis could be applied not only to academically received literature or, if you go wider, to popular literature. They can be applied to all other forms of popular culture, and give insights no other method gives. But always, and again, you have first to read these things in and for themselves: then, the literary critic's ear for language, for tone, for stress, for selection, for inclusion and omission, for the power of images and symbols, for all the elements of the rhetoric of persuasion, all these can be relevant and revealing. Much television, in particular, gives itself to, needs, this kind of study. It is in important senses a medium of its own, with a 'language' of its own, and one has to be aware of that. It is an industry, and each of its products is much mucked about with by many different people. Yet it is also in some ways a work of the imagination and can be studied as that.

All the above describes only one area of what are now called 'cultural studies'. I have put it in my own, largely untheoretical, terms. I admire and sometimes use a language of theory which captures concepts irreplaceably. I mistrust the way some people use abstractions as props or crutches, substitutes for thought, ways of showing others and assuring themselves that they belong to an inner group. I suspect anyone who peppers his papers with 'heuristic', 'hegemony', 'hierarchy', 'paradigm', 'problematic', 'reification', 'homology' and the like. One can sometimes work through almost unintelligible and certainly rebarbative papers only to realise at the end that, though what they say is sensible and in some ways perceptive, it could have been said almost entirely without that apparatus of in-group theoretical language.

One English critic, friendly but slightly regretful, described my way of going on as 'deceptively descriptive to the point of casualness'. I expect he wished to find an explicit pattern of hypotheses, a set of linked generalisations which the individual descriptions supported (as one commonly finds in French writings). But it was a French sociologist, J. -C. Passeron, who, in the introduction to the French edition of *The Uses of Literacy*, suggested — to my surprise — that his countrymen look again at their predilection for theoretical structures and learn something from this English commitment to 'phenomenological' detail. He did not think my procedure 'casual' but, rather, 'extraordinarily precise'. He even found 'an underlying organisation that amounts to an ethno-graphic inventory.'

If you look long enough at a group of similar things, if you hold back from the first and second and third general comment which comes to mind (whether those comments are small talk or large theory), then occasionally a new unifying idea forms, more useful than what preceded it, able to become a tool of enquiry. Others may have reached similar ideas by that or different, more structured, routes.

My own early ideas of this sort, ideas now much written about theoretically by others and reached independently by different routes than mine, include, in looking at the ways of working-class people: the manner in which resistance and resilience to new things (cars, videos, television, houses owned not rented) and then their adoption, adaptation, modification and absorption if they prove interesting and useful, if they chime with existing cultural assumptions – how all this works.

Working-class people are then seen as less passive than is often assumed; and not likely to be quickly 'made middle class' by acquiring what are labelled middle-class objects. They will buy television on the never-never because it seems a marvellous addition to family entertainment, and will not wait – as the planners assumed – until they can afford it. It was the middle classes who waited. There are similar class differences in the use of video recorders.

The study of the popular press, of its effects (it is not uncritically accepted; but, still, a saving cynicism is not critical literacy) and, more important, of the extent to which it accurately reflects work-ing-class attitudes (rather than partial and often unpleasant aspects of them) can also be redefined by the modification-with-adaptation approach.

That approach prevents us from assuming that people are simply swept along by each new fashion; and it can dissolve hard analytic categories which have ceased to be useful. This is especially true of categories in discussions about art – 'highbrow', 'lowbrow', 'élitist', 'middlebrow', and all the other intellectual small change.

But the predilection for, the holding on to, modification-with-adaptation, can also hinder people from being open to what could be valuable new experiences – in leisure, art, relationships and much else – which cannot be quickly adapted to long-standing attitudes and tastes.

The most successful entrepreneurs for the mass market recognise much of all this, and in particular that you cannot take taste too far too fast; if you try, people will react against you. You have to latch on to an existing taste, convince people that a new object fits that taste and might even transmute it by extending it, but in acceptable directions. That is the point, not before, at which taste may begin to be changed. And may sometimes be debased, because underneath the emphasis now is so much on successive consumption for its own sake; as though a habitual pleasure is a dubious, out-of-date, pleasure.

Take, as a brilliant adaptation by commerce, the invention of 'Mushy Peas'. Traditional working-class life gave a special niche to dried peas put in a bowl overnight with a tablespoon of bicarbonate of soda. By morning they had swollen and become soft. Boiled then with a touch of salt and pepper and perhaps a sprig of mint, they produced a flavour which anyone from the early twentieth-century working class can never forget, a flavour quite different from and not in competition with that of fresh garden peas; as tinned salmon is a different thing from fresh salmon, not a cheap substitute. But dried peas belonged to old-style grocers and market stalls; and who nowadays wants to go to the trouble of soaking them overnight? Then along comes an exceptionally clever merchandising spirit who has peas prepared in what seems the old way but puts them in attractive tins, labelled 'Mushy Peas', and in various forms, including 'fish-and-chip-shop style' (fish-and-chip shops often sold mushy peas on the side). 'Curry-style' will come next. They now go on the shelves of supermarkets at a price towards which the cost of the peas themselves is only a small part, and sell very well. They offer a taste which brings back childhood to millions of people, but present it in the most modern of marketing manners.

The above has taken attention from the direct story of the Cultural Studies Centre itself. The day-to-day work of the centre was largely in Stuart Hall's hands; I had other duties, teaching as a professor in the department and serving on committees at department, faculty and university level. We evolved a good working pattern in which he saw to almost all the practical working of the centre and I pushed its case and protected it as necessary in the councils of the university. That kept marauders at bay and helped us to more facilities, notably accommodation, as we grew. We both played our parts in the academic life of the centre, but Stuart progressively shaped the pattern of intellectual work. So we continued agreeably until the end of the decade; the university became used to us, and only the incorrigible still looked askance ('What! Hoggart's little outfit asking for yet more rooms,' one of them said to the Bursar).

My going, in January 1970, to UNESCO naturally caused the stress to fall even more on Stuart's interests, less on mine. Small intellectual communities are living organisms. They take on, until the first departure, defection or revolt, the colourings and dispositions of the founder or founders. Stuart recognised the value of my approach as I did his, and we were without competitiveness towards each other. It was inevitable that when I went the atmosphere would change, that he would be not only the main element but the dead-centre of it.

Of course, I would have preferred more of my style in some things to have been kept; it was soon challenged. At a centre meeting of staff and students one PhD candidate argued that the centre should only admit those who were already committed to the far-left wing politically. 'We are', she said in effect, 'a Red Cell and have no time to educate people who are not already this far down the line.' Reading that in Paris, I remembered a student who has become a very respected author in cultural studies. When interviewing him, Stuart and I did not know or ask his politics, or if he had any. We thought him very bright, interested in an important part of the field and likely to contribute effectively. This would not have done for the champion of the Red Cell. 'We have no time', she had continued, 'for the Matthew Arnoldian liberal humanist line of Hoggart!'

I went to UNESCO for three years, a long time to have leave of absence. The university must have thought it a worthwhile piece of public service and agreed readily. Stuart Hall took charge of the centre as Acting Director, with sustained support from Michael Green, who had moved over from the main English department. In the second half of my second year in Paris, the Director-General asked me to stay for five years rather than three, until his own retirement, and so as to see through a complete three-year programme of my own devising. Mary and I talked and walked again; and decided the DG's wish ought to be respected.

I flew to Birmingham and told them what I was thinking, adding I would resign from my post there. They indicated that my leave could be extended until we got back. This would have left Stuart Hall doing the Director's job, with neither the title nor the salary, for two more years. I thought it likely I would find another job somewhere in Britain when I finally came back, and wanted Stuart to have the post, not simply to be holding on for even longer than he had originally and readily agreed. So I resigned. I found Stuart's letter on all this eighteen years later; it expresses exactly his good spirit, and the nature of our relationship.

The Vice-Chancellor, perhaps influenced by a peculiar letter in a weekly journal which claimed the centre was promoting left-wing propaganda, decided not to confirm the continuance of the centre's existence, and so the appointment of a new Director, until a committee, containing distinguished academics from elsewhere, had enquired into the centre's record and ways of working.

The committee reported very favourably, though making two criticisms, both of which seemed sensible: that some centre members were too fond of the jargons (not the proper technical terms) which abound in subjects cognate to Cultural Studies and had emerged in Cultural Studies themselves; and that the centre was placing too much emphasis on group work, to the neglect of the individual work essential in the early stages of post-graduate studies.

The case for letting the centre go on had been made, and eventually Stuart Hall was appointed Director. They also decided to fill my other post, as a professor in the department of English, and started looking in late 1972 or early 1973. The wheels turned so slowly that that post was filled only in Spring 1975, within a couple of weeks of my own return to England.

Towards the end of the Seventies Stuart left for a chair in sociology at the Open University. For the first time in its decade

and a half of life the centre was without either of its founders;
but that had been a good long spell, long enough to set it up
firmly. Stuart's going virtually coincided with the start of the
series of increasingly severe cuts in university funding and the
centre, along with all such small units, was under particular threat.
Demands for admission were growing all the time but there was
no hope of more staff. 'Retrenchment', 'rationalisation', 'concentration' and 'economies of scale' were the words emerging from
the planning committees which now seemed in permanent session.
A few people in the English department would not have minded
if the centre had disappeared elsewhere, either because they had
never felt at ease with such an odd bird in the nest of traditional
English studies, or because they resented its popularity with some
of the brightest undergraduates and graduates.

Luckily, the faculty of Social Science was more hospitable, was
reshaping itself and had at least two members of staff with
interests similar to those of the centre. It was finally decided that
the centre would be 'viable' if it changed faculties and was joined
by those two members. The change was made in January 1988.
Members of the new host-faculty were very welcoming and did
all they could to make sure that the centre's work continues.
There is much to be said for the new arrangement. It is sad,
though, to think some members of the English department had
not been persuaded that such a group's proper home was with
them, that cultural studies did not represent a departure from the
true stream of English studies but a new and natural extension of
it.

4

Birmingham University decided to give Auden an Honorary Doctorate at the summer graduation ceremonies of 1967. We offered
to put him up and give the statutory party in his honour.

I had already met him a few times, though never for very long.
In January 1958 he had sent a long letter – prompted by an
'understanding and generous' essay I had written about his work
– very warm about *The Uses of Literacy*, and full of vivid general-

isations on class habits. He proposed then that I visit him in Oxford, where he was at the time Professor of Poetry.

The sitting room in the apartment just outside Christ Church was, as I had expected, cluttered, even squalid. I had not expected the pile of papers on his working table to be surmounted by tins of pilchards and bottles of red vermouth.

Then there was a pleasant, talkative supper at Janet Adam Smith's in Holland Park. The longest meeting before the Birmingham visit had been in the early Sixties, in Berlin, when he had a visiting professorship and I was over for a few days to lecture at the Free University.

The British Council representative gave us lunch and Auden complimented his wife on knowing how best to cook trout. Afterwards he and I walked in the Tiergarten and he talked almost without stop – telling often moving stories, some of which he told again in Birmingham (many other people were told them too). That was the sum of our acquaintance before the Birmingham visit.

We had assumed he would arrive the day before the ceremony and leave the day after; two nights. In the event he stayed three or four nights, talking most of the time and giving no hint of when he would feel like going. The night before he did leave he told us he had an engagement, in Stratford, the next day. We enjoyed the visit, especially after we had become used to repeatedly replenishing the food – he was a very hearty eater – the gin and the white and red vermouth. He seemed at ease, in the well-run-in manner of one who spends a lot of time in other people's homes, especially those of academics across America and Britain; he was a uniquely well house-trained guest. He said you had a duty when on parade to be friendly, and that he had had years of experience in a hard school, the American campus round. At the party he was, true to form, thoroughly available and talkative.

The most striking, and sympathetic, sign of his skill as a guest concerned his love of crossword puzzles. He set out to do the crossword in our *Sunday Times* and began by putting a sheet of transparent paper over it and making a copy in bold pencil. He then read the clues off the newspaper and filled in his own copy.

He pointed out, with a touch of pride, that in this way you did not spoil the crossword for your hosts.

We were slightly surprised by his general equability and readiness to accommodate because we had heard from several people that he could be a prickly guest, and pernickety about his food. We had neither of those difficulties. He went to bed quite early and piled on even more blankets than we, warned in advance, had provided; he added the rug from the floor. He got up at a respectable time, not unreasonably early as we had been warned. He did not want to be called or brought a cup of tea, just to get up in his own time, and thump his way downstairs in his unchanging, shabby and old-fashioned clothes. His suit was shiny and needed pressing; his shirts lacked ironing – enough to make a housewife wince at the neglected effect, and get out the iron; which Mary did.

He would eat everything put in front of him and with relish. He had a full-scale English breakfast each day; at home, he said, it was coffee and toast. He obviously liked food very much ('Lyons Corner Houses – best food in London,' he said suddenly, talking in the kitchen); he was interested in everything to do with the preparation and cooking of food, and almost ingenuously proud of some things he could grow in his garden in Kirchstetten. He talked with great enthusiasm about mange-tout 'which grow particularly well in Austria and should do well in England'. Very useful for lots of purposes and you could, of course, eat it all. He offered detailed instructions on how to bake sweet-corn on the cob. He had a good deal of lore in domestic matters and a sort of fussy good sense, rather like a sensible housewife who values the old ways but is consciously open to new equipment. He spoke particularly strongly in favour of blenders; no kitchen was complete without one. He told Mary she should not be suspicious of new machines but decide which were useful and buy them.

He was anxious to help with the washing-up, but we only let him do it once. He insisted the cutlery be done first, which we knew was correct. We also thought one didn't put knife handles into really hot detergent water. He did. He gathered knives and forks into his very large hands and threw them into the sink – which meant that the person actually washing up had to jump back quickly or be spattered with hot soapy water. A curious sloppiness, after all the talk about precise kitchen procedures.

He was particularly exact about the way he liked his dry Martinis. The first one I gave him must have been a shock; half gin, half dry vermouth at room temperature. He said he liked them in the American fashion, five parts gin to one vermouth, the gin very cold, the vermouth less so. On the second day he taught Simon how to make them, so from then on there was a jug on the go all the time. Auden said it was the best pick-you-up ever invented and just the thing before the evening begins. He added that the two greatest American inventions were the dry Martini and the hamburger. He started on the dry Martinis precisely at six, but had only wine at dinner and after. I had noticed at Janet Adam Smith's and did so again at our house that he assumed he need not be invited to have another drink. Once the wine was on the table he started to drink and, when his glass was empty, filled it again.

He was startled by the changes in Birmingham centre. He said no city was more striking in the changes it had made in itself, not even New York. New York City rebuilt more, but you could always discern the old city behind or beneath. In Birmingham they seemed simply to have cleared away the whole thing and started again.

We went round his family house in Lordswood Road, now a Nurses' Home. It looked shabby and uncared-for on the outside. Inside, it was bright and fresh in the way nurses' accommodation provided by hospital authorities usually is. He stood in what had been his own bedroom, looking towards the Lickey Hills. He was clearly moved by the view. Then he turned and said he was slightly outraged by the change. The fresh, public-authority-style wallpaper, the bright suburban accoutrements and the little personal touches – a zipped teddy-bear container for the occupant's nightdress – all seemed to create a style he neither understood nor liked.

He was keen to walk around and look at the places he had known, especially around Harborne. It was as though this return, a rare event but now for him to be given an honorary degree at the university his father had taught at, had a powerful meaning which he wished to do justice to. He said the family used to walk virtually everywhere; down from Lordswood Road up to the family church and familiar points roundabout. He was touched also at seeing the church again and particularly glad, at first, to sit in the garden of the pub.

It was a Friday night and the place full of young people spilling all over the gardens and sitting round on the walls. He seemed startled and a little disconcerted. In his day it had been virtually a country pub, and also he had not known about the enormous increase in pub drinking among young people in Britain through the affluent Sixties. He finally said he supposed it was the result of prosperity, but that his reaction to it proved he did not really like the effects of a prosperous open society, whatever the correctness of his democratic principles.

He talked several times, suddenly and without cues, about quite intimate details of his friendships and family: the break with Benjamin Britten, his affection for Eliot (and pain in preparing an obituary whilst Eliot was still alive, but very ill), Edmund Wilson (nice, but a screwball towards the end), and Lionel Trilling.

He mused about his parents. You always feel the union of your parents is inevitable, a fact of nature, he said; until a certain age. He had realised at such an age that, viewed neutrally, his parents shouldn't have married. His mother was in some ways the more demanding and dominant and his father very anxious to make her happy; on the whole his father had been run around by his mother. He was implying that they had nourished each other's weaknesses, so that if someone had looked at them objectively they might have said it was wrong for two such people to marry. However, he added (sounding almost like a little boy, since this thought comes to most of us at seven or eight years old), if they hadn't married I wouldn't have existed. At another point he remarked that someone had said that most marriages settle down over the years into affairs of quiet affection rather than passion. In his experience there was often little affection, even quiet affection, and still a great deal of passion.

Standing on the pavement outside the Harborne house he spoke again about his father's death; at Repton, where his brother lived. Auden had gone in and realised that his father was near the end. 'You know you are dying, father?' His father had nodded as if he understood and accepted. 'Do you have any pain?' 'No.' He had had a good death. Towards the end he had moved outside and away, was no longer in touch with them or his past life or anything. Someone else who had heard that story at, I think, second-hand thought it rather callous. It did not sound like that as Auden told it, but direct, grave, loving, an invitation to his father to settle himself down for the passage.

He repeated something he had said in the letter to me of nine years before: that he hated to be a creditor. I told him about the credit system by 'checks' (money advanced so that something necessary could be bought, and paid off week by week, with sizeable interest) among working-class people, especially in the north. He was fascinated, and went on to reiterate that his responsible middle-class origins demanded you bought nothing until you could afford it, and then handled it carefully because the money for it had had to be earned. If that style had been forced on working-class people before the war, I suggested, their whole way of life would have seized up, like a car engine running dry of lubricant. To change it you would have had both to provide a regular topping-up of oil and to inculcate a more calculated method of driving. I suppose so, he said, before moving to another subject.

He was, in short, often strikingly opinionated and did not seem in this to be putting on a conversational act; he really did have strong and often very odd opinions, or at least opinions more decided than the case always seemed to warrant. This was bound up with his didactic spirit, his moments of ruthless 'common sense' and his middle-class eye on economy. He lectured Mary at length – the verb is only slightly too strong – on why it is usually cheaper to go by taxis as you need them than to have a car standing around from year to year, depreciating and running up big overheads. This common argument is only true if you do very little travelling, haven't a family and do not go for long and distant holidays. It has that unexpected inversion, the surprising twist, of which Auden was so fond.

In much the same spirit, he refused to use a seat belt – how did you escape in an accident? – and anyway he trusted me. Until he really did trust me he fussed at corners. He twice said he found head-rests amusing and could not see the point of them; clearly, whip-lash must be an invention of the manufacturers. He talked in the same manner about smoking, which he did almost without a break. If people say it will make you die sooner, he said – sounding like a truculent teenager – ask them if they want to live forever.

So the opinions rolled on: about the justifications for public schools, the sexy posters on the London underground, the provinciality of European cities as compared with New York, the virtues of Austria (opera, wine and the German language), how pleasant it was to live in Kirchstetten. He was not pleased that they had renamed Hinterholtz, his street, Audenstrasse. He would have been even less pleased by the riotously rustic announcement now placed above the street's name: (wooden gnomes, as bookends for wooden books), 'Zu den Dichterheimen d. Lyriker W. H. Auden'.

I wondered whether his frequent unhesitant decisiveness might be related to his living a sort of solitary life for a long time. He had spent many years with Chester Kallman but still seemed like a cat that walked alone, as though that relationship did not have much personal-critical give and take, much modifying influence on opinions that threaten to harden; as though important areas of his mind were out of bounds to anyone else. There was a self-ruling habitude about many of his actions and opinions. He would be drinking steadily after supper and then at ten o'clock, quite abruptly, announce he was off to bed and be mounting the stairs in thirty seconds.

He enjoyed talking about writers, not only to Mary and me but to the children – in particular, to Paul about Graham Greene and to Nicola about Tolkien. He was proud of a sweater embossed by an admirer in America with 'I love Gimli' in relief across the chest. As we were preparing for the drinks party, we heard him call, 'Nicola, Nicola'; she came into the hall to find him thumping downstairs in that sweater. He looked like a vast, retired rugby player run much to seed, his breasts very evident. He wore the sweater for the party; it was rather ugly.

I had invited to the party an old acquaintance who had done his doctoral thesis on Auden, and guided him towards the surrounding group. When he had the poet's eye, he felt unsure how to sustain a conversation with the great man, and looked down shyly. 'Ah,' said Auden, 'I see you're looking at my slippers' (old carpet slippers with holes in, which he wore almost all the time). 'The fact is I'm a martyr to corns.' Corns do appear once in his poetry, in 'A Change of Air'; the mixed style in action.

He suspected any poem of his which became an anthology piece, such as 'The Shield of Achilles', and would not read that kind of poem to an audience. At the degree ceremony he was asked to respond on behalf of the honorary graduates. He chose one of his more recent, difficult, meditative poems and read with the greatest care. No; he did not exactly read, but spoke. He had learned the poem by heart with the exact intonations and accents he wanted. You attended to the poem, not to Auden, so to say; in fact, it was best to close your eyes so as to take it in better, even though that meant blotting out the extraordinary face – the map of Asia, the Gladstone bag, the Pennine crag of a face. There was no public presentation or pushing forward of the poem, no internal announcement: 'Here I am. A real, poetic poem – read by a real poet.' He was rapt in it and you had to listen as closely as he spoke. If you did, you could have an exceptional experience. The huge audience in the Great Hall would have contained few who had even heard of Auden. They would have understood better 'The Shield of Achilles'. But he had done right, by his poetic lights.

Immediately after the ceremony, at a short reception, a great many people, especially former members of the Medical School, came up smiling and spoke of his father with great affection. He was deeply touched, hugely and warmly responsive. Many of them seemed over eighty or even ninety, all looking in extraordinarily good health, apple-cheeked and bright-eyed.

There was a grand lunch with the Chancellor, Anthony Eden, by then the Earl of Avon, presiding. Auden was put between him and the Countess. Before going in, he said he'd be tempted to ask: 'Well, what do you think about Suez now, then?' or 'What's your view on the Arab-Israeli war?' In fact, he said afterwards, they had been charming and he had enjoyed talking to them.

I did not see Auden again. By the beginning of 1970 we were in Paris and he died in 1973; I heard the news some days later, after returning from a mission abroad. A few years later still, I heard how his remaining books and papers had been dumped on the St Mark's Place pavement after the landlord had gained possession of the flat. Sad, but also apt; and a conclusion which might have appealed to Auden. He had deliberately left the English 'literary happy family' for the metropolitan anonymity of New York; to the end, New York lived up to its image and style for him.

5

Though work at Birmingham was quite heavy, other things, if they seemed to justify it, had to be fitted in; especially if they had particular relevance such as the Royal Shakespeare Company. But service on the Board of Governors there proved at best a marginal case, interesting chiefly for the light it threw on rubber-stamping committees and their links with social climbing.

Meetings were alternatively in Stratford and London, preceded by a good lunch and followed by an early tea. The body was large, had a sprinkling of titles and, it soon became clear, little coherence. Business proper began soon after lunch and was usually over in half an hour. There had been a meeting of the executive in the morning, and they had sewn up the responses to whatever issues were in play. A couple of us soon said it hardly seemed worthwhile to spend the better part of a day going to London or Stratford for a half-hour of nodding-through. There were, we said, ways of engaging a large board, even if you did not want it to take executive decisions. For example, it could at each meeting be given a paper on some current issue of general policy and asked for its views. The chairman of the RSC, a leading figure in the Midlands motor industry, was also chairman of the executive. He entirely failed to take the point and simply assured us we would have our turn on the executive in due time.

At tea, the Secretary to the company, presumably tipped off, sat next to me. He too was puzzled at our criticism. He seemed to think one should be pleased simply to be asked to join the board, whether or not it proved useful in helping the company. 'Many people write asking to be appointed,' he said, 'people with titles who regard membership as a further feather in their caps.'

I know now he was right and that self-proposing extends to knighthoods and honorary degrees.

One of the most worthwhile invitations came early in 1969. OECD, the Paris-based Organisation for Economic Co-operation and Development and very much a club of the rich nations, would by invitation make a study in depth of aspects of any one of their member states. It might be asked to report on the coal industry of Belgium or the transport system of Italy. The organisation must have been startled to receive a request from the French government for its educational system to be reviewed. Clearly, the events of 1968 had profoundly shaken French confidence in that area.

OECD's practice was neat and precise. A committee would be very small and have a chairman of undeniable international standing in the subject to be examined. Whilst supporting him in every way needed, OECD would leave him to choose three other members and then get on with the job.

The chairman of our committee was Charles Frankel, Professor of Philosophy at Columbia University; I had first met him a dozen years before, on his home-ground in New York, and intermittently afterwards, usually at UNESCO. He had served as Secretary for Health, Education and Welfare in Kennedy's Presidency. He invited Henri Jannes, Professor of Sociology at the Free University of Brussels, and Torsten Husén, Professor at Stockholm and known for his massive longitudinal studies of educational development, and me, to join him. In professional educational terms, I was the least qualified of the four.

We soon got to know and like each other, and that could not have been taken for granted. We were all busy, and keen to make the fullest use of the time we could spare for meetings; no one sought to show off or flannel, and no one pushed an interested prior position. Frankel quickly gave us each an area (mine was the university system), within which to gather and order the material, to discuss it with the others, to write a draft chapter, present that and then rewrite. He conducted the whole operation smoothly, showed great diplomatic skill with senior French functionaries and politicians, and finally made sure that there was intellectual and verbal coherence between the parts of the report.

He was the cool and confident conductor of a very specialist quartet.

Edgar Faure, interviewed in his large apartment overlooking the Bois, was lyrically Cartesian about the beauty of his *loi d'orientation* for university reform; under three main heads, inevitably – 'Primo . . . Secundo . . .' Others were naturally less enthusiastic.

Our report had some critical passages about French practice at different levels. The French politicians and officials received it with no sign of ruffled feathers. One might well have expected them to take umbrage; perhaps the British would have done so in their place. But then the French had already shown their new, post-1968, educational openness by asking for the enquiry.

Elements of the events of 1968 in France, which had inspired the OECD report, surfaced from time to time. Round about 1980, I assessed a doctorate at Grenoble. The internal assessor was a professor of sociology there and said to be a hero of 'the events' and a dramatic performer in the lecture theatre. He made a late entry, clanking with beads, his hair in a long Indian-style tuft and tied with braid; there was a caftan, as had been almost obligatory ten years before. He said he assumed I was the English professor. Yes 'Thought so. Guessed it.' How? 'Only an English professor would have a haircut like that. And a parting! No style.'

The OECD report was not presented to the French government until early 1970, by which time I was working in Paris after the most hectic six months of our lives. It had proved to be a strange summer, that of 1969. Some time in August Grandma, who had no telephone, sent us a postcard; she used postcards a lot because they cost less to send than letters, or perhaps they didn't any longer, but she carried on with the belief and habit. She used envelopes for family letters, but for hurried news, however momentous, she still took out of a top sideboard drawer one of the postcards she bought in packs of half a dozen from the nearby sub-post office. This news was as momentous as could be, though she played it down. She had had a lump on a breast for some time and it had broken the skin almost a year before; she had not wanted to bother us by 'bringing it up' and had treated it all that time with Savlon, a favoured antiseptic cream. She had finally gone to the doctor she had known for decades; he had at once said she should be examined by the local hospital. Could Mary go to the hospital with her? The growth proved to be malignant and she agreed, with much remonstrating about the lack of a need for any fuss, to have a mastectomy; at eighty. Apparently the prognosis was good.

Just at that time came three unexpected telephone calls. The first asked whether I would go to the office of the Agent-General for Queensland to discuss the possibility of becoming the Vice-Chancellor of that state's university. We would have been delighted to visit Queensland but did not wish to settle there, so that was the end of that. Second came a call from New York University asking if I would go over and discuss the Albert Schweitzer Chair with them. That was extremely tempting: a chair with an international reputation, a salary large enough to allow you to recruit good research assistance, to mount important seminars, to buy all the books that could possibly be needed, to live in or very near Manhattan and to get over to the UK at least once every semester. I made a couple of 'phone calls to people who knew about the chair and they were encouraging. I suspected New York had over-estimated my abilities but, if there had been no hindrance, I would have accepted and done my best. But after a couple of days thinking it over we knew I could not accept. It was too far away from Grandma, especially since we were uneasy about the prognosis.

The third call was from the Ministry of Overseas Development. Some time before, the MOD had taken over responsibility for United Nations Affairs from the Ministry of Education. Since I had served on the Culture Committee of the UK National Commission for UNESCO and spent a couple of days at one or two UNESCO conferences, I was 'known to the UNESCO desk' in the MOD.

It was a typically casual-seeming proposal – 'just fishing, you know . . . no commitment on either side . . . thought we'd like to sound you out . . . one idea among several . . .' There was soon to be a vacancy for one of the five posts of Assistant Director-General at UNESCO Headquarters; it was felt that Britain should field a candidate, 'fly a kite'. Not much chance, they said, there'll be very strong opposition from other continents, but we'd like to run up the flag and, well, you never know . . .

It was in some but not all ways tempting, especially since my few days at Headquarters' conferences had produced their full ration of pompous gobbledegook and even more pompous notions. They had also produced one or two unexpectedly stirring declarations about UNESCO's importance, especially to the Third World (a phrase still less tendentious or evasive than others on offer). Paris was not far and there were daily flights to and from Manchester, so we consulted Mary's mother. She was anxious for us to go, chiefly to relieve herself of the sense that she might be 'standing in our way'. Mary said she would fly back each weekend if that were needed; we had our walk on the Lickey Hills, and I eventually told the MOD that I was willing to stand.

Then family life went on, life in the department and the centre went on, Grandma went on. Or so it seemed. But in late November she began to worsen and came to us. By early January we buried her; by late January we were on the move again.

CHAPTER 5

❧

EXPANSION AND PERMISSIVENESS: THE UNIVERSITY LIBERATED?

On a Saturday morning in the early Sixties one of the children brought the midday post into our Leicester kitchen. A letter asked whether I was willing to be considered for the Vice-Chancellorship of the proposed University of Essex: a very tentative approach from the Academic Planning Committee, merely suggesting that I might care to be interviewed. It was a bold proposal to a senior lecturer with limited experience of internal teaching, no experience as a dean and little as acting head of a department. The children wanted to know why we were showing surprise. One of them got the measure at once: 'It's like the Leicester buses . . . they can't get conductors now. They're having to use Pakistanis.'

I would have taken the job if invited. The committee let me down in the usual British saving-your-face manner. I'd been the runner-up, they said, but anyone so inexperienced with high-level administration would have been a big gamble, and I was probably more useful criticising the university system from outside than being diplomatic as a V-C. The Lyndon Johnsonian principle reversed: better on the outside pissing in.

Only in 1991 did I hear a surprising modification of that incident. Edward Boyle, I was told, had said I had been the preferred candidate but that the government had 'advised' against on the ground that I was that difficult or suspect Pilkington Committee member. I find this hard to believe; but Edward Boyle was not a fanciful gossip.

.

I

The new University of Essex was one among many. In the early 1960s most governments, especially in the developed world, decided to put very much larger amounts of money into higher education than ever before. The process went on until the oil crisis of the early Seventies reduced the money available; even before that, further growth had been discouraged by the student troubles of the late Sixties (themselves inspired partly by the expansion, partly by the prosperity which had set it off, partly by a few charismatic writers on the evils of open capitalist societies, and partly by the Vietnam war). Some governments abruptly cut short the increase in funds; a few, such as France, went back to the academic drawing-board and produced new, qualified and, they hoped, safer designs.

What is now most notable about expansion in the quiet, early 1960s, is the sameness of many assumptions behind the activity. True, in Britain, the Sussex and York sites would not be confused; each is a monument to the differences between Vice-Chancellors and the architects they chose. Below that obvious level, they were social brothers. Not an acre and a cow but two hundred acres, out of town, and lots of student residences.

Similarly, there were two or three powerful shared assumptions about why large expansion was needed. First and most powerful was the feeling that the Second (or Third, according to your choice of definition) Industrial Revolution needed vastly more technically trained people – technically trained from modest to highly advanced levels – than had ever been needed before. This was not an entirely novel feeling. In Britain it happens roughly every half-century, sometimes emerging as the hardships of the immediate aftermath of war pass, more often inspired by the feeling that Germany is once again getting ahead of us in yet more of those things we have always prided ourselves on doing better than any other country.

There was another, a more visionary, assumption behind the decision to expand, at least in the countries I know and certainly in some British educators. In the Eighties (and even more in the Nineties) this assumption gradually began to seem less well founded, seemed increasingly an inapplicable relic of the paternalistic, 'cossetting' thinking which had produced free libraries, university extra-mural departments, the Workers' Educational Association and the Open University. It was, in short, 'idealistic', this assumption that many more people had a right to higher education than received it and, even more important, that they were entitled to that education not only because they would then become more effective units in a highly trained and competitive work-force, but because a better education might help them become more informed and able to make good judgments within an open democracy.

Before that impulse could reassert itself a new prosperity, finally freed from the constraints of the war's aftermath and more widely shared than anything we had known before that war, had to have clearly arrived. In Britain, the publication in 1963 of the Robbins Report on Higher Education was the marker. It echoed exactly the mood of the day in its sense of social and educational concern, its assurance that that mood was widely shared and that it could and should be afforded. One of the luckiest of recent quangos, it was going exactly where the body of thoughtful opinion was going. I was one of the many asked to give evidence to the committee; it was clear that they wanted from me as strong a claim as I could make for wider access to higher education for people who so far had not had it. One aspect of this claim needs stressing. The case was not that many more should have higher education, even though standards might fall and more mean worse; it was that there were many people outside the universities who were at least as clever as many within, so more need not mean worse.

Once again Britain surprised herself by her audacity and goodwill, as she does from time to time. She then gambles on the power generated by greater opportunities not to use up the stock but to breed yet more. The most precise expression of that spirit in the Sixties was the founding of the Open University; but that was a close-run thing.

If we go back to the end of the war the best example is the remarkable and largely unacknowledged Emergency Teachers' Training Scheme, by which ex-servicemen and women who wished to become teachers could qualify in a one-year course.

Their training had to be skimped. If you went out for a pee in the middle of a lecture, the students said, you'd come back to find you'd missed one whole unit of training – The Romantics or Problems of Delinquency. Their enthusiasm made up for a lot, many went on to further qualifications by evening work, and the schools did not suffer anything like as much as they would have done if the schemes had not been devised. My brother Tom went through it in 1947–8 and became an admirable member of his profession until he retired in 1982.

The increased provision in the Sixties for higher education within traditional institutions was less unsettling, so more easily digestible by government, than the founding of the Open University. Britain was at last facing the fact that her numbers entering full-time higher education were smaller than those of most developed countries, and that the difference could not be justified on the old divisive grounds. Less firmly, she was also recognising the distortions in entry, the great extent to which your class of birth decided whether you would be educated beyond the compulsory age of sixteen.

Once she had decided, Britain did well, did humanely, made her plans better than most. Maintenance grants, which had started in '57, six years before Robbins reported, were not very generous but neither were they mean. Most students could manage on them. They did much to encourage the demand for university entrance which began to be met in the early Sixties.

Students who continued to live at home were given less, but again could manage unless their parents demanded over-much for bed and board. Apart from wealthy students with generous parents – and there were few of those in the universities I worked in – the most prosperous were children of working-class parents, with no siblings, living at home and, in the traditional working-class manner, expected to make no contribution to costs. One such lad drove from Wolverhampton to the Birmingham English department each day in his own car; an old car, but he could afford to insure, service and run it.

Before maintenance grants were introduced most students, other than those who went to Oxbridge, enrolled at their local universities, as I did at Leeds. The advantages were both obvious and half-hidden: public money was saved on lodgings grants and on the capital cost of student residences; and the students, going back home each night to different areas of the city, increased the sense among many people who would never set foot in so grand a place that there was, up the road, an institution with a national or even international reputation and one which could give their son/daughter/nephew/niece/grandchild a head-start. Students did not seem to have been imposed upon, or to be poshly parasitic upon, socially superior to, the local communities; town-and-gown resentments were slight.

The movement of students to other towns and cities which maintenance grants made possible also had its advantages. There is room for a university most of whose students come from many miles away and live in university residences or in digs round about. But universities of that kind should make special efforts to have links with the local communities which house them, and few do enough of that.

But again: even if all the universities most of whose students come from elsewhere did improve links with their local communities, we would do well to have some other universities most of whose students come from a few miles round about, whose premises are in or near the town centre, whose doors are open to adults who can slip in easily after work – universities which, no matter how well known they may be internationally, are also felt to be part of the educational life of their region.

Some polytechnics fulfil that role and most universities have been happy to let them; but there is, once more, room for both, especially since most polytechnics do not have as wide a range of departments as universities. As for a city-centre university institution specifically designed to cater for mature students in the evenings, rather than for 18–21-year-olds in the daytime, it is typical that we should still have only one of those – Birkbeck College in the heart of London, a 'school' of London University over seventy years old, but without successors. Today, when one recognises that many of the great number of applications to the Open University have to be turned away, and recognises too the high quality of that university's degrees, the tendency still to think that there are few adults who can rise to the demands of university work indicates once again a characteristic myopia – still widespread, even though most universities have in the last few years thought more about the needs of the people outside their walls.

The opportunity provided by maintenance grants for students to live away from home has had effects as striking, though not as large nor as broad socially, as those brought by the movements of servicemen and women in wartime. So far as I know, neither of those migrations has been thoroughly studied. Even now families none of whose members has ever been to university will regard, say, Stamford or Colne or Trowbridge as the centre of the world, and would be startled to think of one of their kind moving to a similar but better job elsewhere rather than looking for something similar in or near their home towns. All this is common enough in most countries other than North America. It is widely under pressure as the nature of work changes; but as always change is slow and resistance strong.

Some of the yeast has been provided by the peripatetic students. Their inter-marryings will help ensure that the process continues, the widening of a sense of English space, of the variety of its manners, of the idea of movement led by job and profession; all this could on balance be a gain.

University authorities have often thought life in a residential community should be a 'gentling' process for those, perhaps the majority in provincial universities nowadays, whose style of life has not been above and rarely lower than that of the lower middle class. It is in the nature of the departmental and faculty groupings of modern universities that the Oxbridge collegiate system, long assumed to be the main 'civilising' element in university education, was not felt to sit easily within them. Most of us thought it rather comical that the first Vice-Chancellor of the University of York tried to establish a collegiate system somewhat similar to that of Oxbridge. 'The oldest new university in Europe' was the routine joke. York doesn't really work like Oxbridge; it couldn't. But socially it works well, and two of our children have good memories of it.

There were deeply responsible conferences about the exact kind and level of provision which should be made in halls of residence. I attended a weekend meeting at which one Vice-Chancellor reported that he had ordered that the curtains be of the best quality and named a price per yard we would not have thought of paying for our own curtains. He had two grounds: that good quality proves cheaper in the long run (which is true, but most of us can't afford such shrewdness), and that most students would not have had the opportunity to take that lesson, to see how long and how well good materials last. He also thought – less convincingly, since a few drunken students might well wreck a place equipped to the standard of a five-star hotel – that to live with well made things rather than with the cheap and often nasty reduced the inclination to unsociable behaviour. In all this his decisions came from his view of the socially educative as well as the educational role of the university.

University 'halls of residence' and 'student residences' (these were more like groupings of bed-sitters than traditional halls) were generally of a markedly higher standard than those of poly-technics or, even more, of colleges or institutes of higher education. These institutions were furnished by local government not by the University Grants Committee, and furnished less well. That difference in itself indicated the assumption that those who went to university should be provided for at a higher social level than others.

Even though the universities built in the Sixties more residences than ever before, rapid expansion made the proportion of students who had to find lodgings outside increase quickly also. Nor did everyone wish to go into a university hall. They were freer in lodgings, and especially in self-contained accommodation. If they shared with others they could pay substantially less than the university charged. In the bigger towns there emerged a students' quarter, as in Birmingham. Cheap takeaways of several different ethnic kinds multiplied, wine-bars and launderettes, second-hand furniture stores, self-service grocers specialising in ready-meals, tinned goods and plonk; and the newsagents' notice-boards were full of second-hand offers by new graduates on the way out.

All this pulls people like me in different directions. We wanted and still want more people to have the chance to go to university, and once there to be as well provided for as their less numerous predecessors. But the cost of keeping up that level of physical provision was enormous; and little was done to improve the physical provision for other parts of higher education. University provision was lavish (later, conference lettings in vacations were said to provide some justification for the high level of furnishing). The increases were too fast, and certain to produce a backlash when times became tough. Assumptions about the level of physical provision were no more carefully examined than those about subjects.

Yet, to their credit, the universities adapted so as to hold on above all to their expensive face-to-face tradition in teaching, particularly through seminars and tutorials. In provincial universities this had been assumed to require a ratio of staff to students of about 1 to 7 or 8. The new and soon tightening funds didn't allow for that, but staff willingness to increase their hours of teaching usually made up. Again, this was an admirable holding on to what was thought to be one of the most important elements of British university life. Until 'permissiveness' made the concept seem unacceptable, there was a similar readiness to hold on to the idea that for every student a member of staff should have 'pastoral responsibility', be a 'moral tutor'. The value of this does not need justifying to anyone who has seen it in action. Most students liked having someone they could talk to, especially in the first year away from home, when they had to manage their own money or live with an entirely new and at the start haphazard group, and cope with sexual pressures from colleagues.

It would have been easy to have been more casual, to have let in numbers so large that individuals could not be given the historic level of care, academic or pastoral; and been ready for many to drop out at the end of the first year. At the height of the expansionist phase a French friend at the Sorbonne had classes of four hundred in the first year; he expected, he had to expect, a loss of forty per cent at the end of that year, or work would have become insupportable. I like Eric James's opinion – he was first Vice-Chancellor of York University – that, given the tight British system for entry, if we went much beyond our usual twelve or thirteen per cent of losses we were at fault. We would not then be discovering that more really did mean worse but be failing to live up to our good level of provision, a level which should have allowed us to maintain the sort of attention which more than anything else kept failures low. We would have let the students down, let ourselves down, and all the more because to get that far had probably demanded some sacrifice from many of them and their parents, and was for all of us a most unusual process to go through.

After expansion, self-government by the academics also went on much as before, with the willing ones (such as Arthur Humphreys at Leicester) taking far more than their fair share of the committee work and putting further and further back the date at which they would settle to their next major publication. They were worlds away from the French professor our OECD committee interviewed in 1969. In the new era for French universities would he be willing, we asked, to take some share in the running of his university? He raised his voice almost to a scream: 'I was appointed to take my courses,' he said, and repeated, 'Mes cours, mes cours. C'est tous.' He of course hated Faure's *loi d'orientation* though not, one suspected, for creditable reasons such as those given by Pierre Salmon, who called it 'a pseudo reform'.

Did so quick an expansion mean that some were appointed to university posts who would not have gained them earlier? Yes: in some subjects the search had to go very much wider than before. The level is never absolute; it varies according to available opportunities; but neither is it casual. In most subjects, the barrel of talent was not being scraped. There had for long been many extremely intelligent people fit to join university staffs but unable to get in during those narrower days, especially if they came from the wrong institutions according to the usual ratings. The risk of dilution was greatest where expansion coincided with the appearance of a new or newish discipline – one of the social sciences, perhaps – which meant that almost a whole department had to be appointed in a short period.

It is not disingenuous to say, and I am not alone in saying this kind of thing, that if the chair at Birmingham had come up twenty to twenty-five years later, and I then at the age I was in 1962, I would probably not have been appointed. Today, many exceptionally brilliant graduates have no chance of a university post.

By the middle to late Sixties, Britain had its dreaming-spire universities, its solid Redbricks, a handful of old-new universities such as Hull and Leicester, and the new-new universities like Sussex and Kent and Lancaster and Warwick (which should have been the University of Coventry if the Shakespearean-Baedeker spirit had been willing to relax its hold). The university map had been transformed within less than a decade, without a noticeable drop in general standards and without cruel student losses through early indigestion.

In four areas other needs were not seen, other opportunities not taken. With a few exceptions, especially among the new universities and notably Sussex – which set out to 'redraw the map of learning' – few saw that here was an opportunity not only to maintain work of a kind they had habitually offered but also to think of new forms of curriculum, new definitions of their subjects, or at least modifications of them. To do such things is difficult in a period when staff and funds are fixed; few people ever want to be moved over. Now there was an opportunity.

But there was little rethinking of boundaries. Most departments in most universities simply offered to greater numbers of students the mixture as before; members of staff made finer and finer subdividings of the field they ploughed. When I had arrived at Leicester in 1959 each of us was expected to take some first-year lectures, and our specialist areas were assumed to allow us in teaching to move across at least one or two centuries. By the end of the decade young lecturers were quite likely to say that their field had a spread of fifty years, and they expected to concentrate on that, even in their undergraduate teaching; they would do more, but be slightly miffed. In research that is understandable and right; as a guide for undergraduate teaching it is a regrettable narrowing; everyone should do some first-year teaching. Edward Boyle's favourite definition of a university is worth keeping in mind: 'A place in which teaching is conducted in the atmosphere of research.'

In most English departments the inadequacy of these responses was obvious: when those departments were small they could say to themselves, if they ever said anything about the futures of their students, that some would become dons themselves and most of the others teachers, in grammar schools or comprehensive sixth-forms. What would all those who now began to emerge from these larger departments do? If the question was asked, and this was rare, there was some talk about new opportunities, an increasing demand for humanities graduates, good generalists – from industry, commerce and communications. As a result many undergraduates, finding within the universities little sense of how life there might connect with the rest of their experience, or about its relevance outside the walls, began increasingly to regard university life as a marking-time, time off before you had to enter the harsh world, a phase you could expect to pass through without making much of an effort; not an experience with great meaning, other than perhaps economic, for life afterwards. Ironically, the decade that had opened university life to many more than ever before produced a generation many of whose members had the just-taking-for-granted approach one had formerly associated with some in Oxbridge.

One could say much the same about the failure of academic staff to reconsider methods of teaching, and in particular to recognise the limited value of the one-hour lecture. It remained for the Open University, above all, to think about these things, about the planning of texts which supported teaching in the right way and therefore about the inter-relations between these specially produced texts and face-to-face teaching.

The atmosphere is all-embracing. When the Open University was making an appointment to a chair in English, its senate decided that the first and main criterion should be that the candidate had a reputation for work of the sort which would have merited a chair at a traditional university. So the OU's own publications, inspired by the special nature of their work, were made to seem secondary. The external assessors, Raymond Williams and I, refused this narrowing. The man appointed was, it proved, fitted in both senses.

On the other hand, there was often a gain from simple linear expansion in student numbers in each department, and so in staff. Some departments had been too small to have a good-sized postgraduate body, and their staffs too much occupied with day-by-day teaching to develop their own specialisms enough. One of the good results of expansion was that more departments than ever before in provincial universities could provide even better nourished undergraduate teaching and more specialised postgraduate areas. Very slowly the word got round, among grammar schools above all, that 'x' was at Cokeville and developing a good school of this or that kind of specialist studies.

Most university teachers were disinclined to think harder about the narrow social range among the students they had been used to receiving and now, on the whole, still received, though in greater numbers. The culture of a majority of working-class people and of certain parts of the upper middle class – especially in their views of what is best for girls – were still hardly touched by thoughts of a university education. Too often the first group thought eighteen-year-olds should be earning their keep; the second group still felt their girls of that age should be preparing to marry the right kind of man. If society formed, socially, a pyramid and if the universities had taken from the top 5 per cent or so at its tip, they now widened downwards to 8 to 10 per cent. This range of attitudes produces the 'to him that hath shall be given' pattern in response to almost all new social benefits in Britain: those who know the value of the new provision make best use of it, can use up most of its always limited spaces.

Then there are those students, those potential students, of whom the universities had habitually thought little: the 'mature' students, those who have come late to recognising the value of further education, either because circumstances worked against them or because they could not when they were teenagers see the value of higher education. Most university extra-mural departments have done a very good job indeed since they were founded well over a century ago. Being funded by the Ministry or Department of Education, not by the University Grants Committee, they have been protected from raids by the big internal departments but also left in a corner, a sort of sop to the community, higher education's red flannel.

Their work has not much affected internal procedures, not made internal heads of departments sit up and say: 'There's a lesson here. Lots of adults seem to want and to be able to cope with higher education at our level.' If they had thought more about the particular needs of adults, they might have opened their doors more in the evenings, required staff to teach either by day or in the evening, and some of the time in local centres a few miles away. Academically, the needs of adult students may not be very different from those of 18–21-year-olds, once they have gained entry and been able to marry their working patterns to their studies. Domestically, they do have a harder time of it than younger, full-time people.

I have said that a fair number of eighteen-year-olds now come to university in a disconnected way. But those who take a year off and then come back are more committed to their work, have realised what they are missing and now made a choice of their own, not one urged on them by teachers or parents, or adopted as the habit of their generation. But re-entry is no easier for them than is entry for full-time mature students; there are few grants once you have broken the sequence.

The next step seems easy. Let those who decide to go away in their first year, but are not sure whether they will wish to come back, have the assurance of re-entry. Fill the spaces thus created not with eighteen-year-olds but with mature students whose grants would be found from the money freed by those who have chosen, at least for a while, to go out into the world. There would be administrative difficulties in such a scheme, but it has a fine and telling simplicity. It recognises two facts about university life, and about students and potential students, two facts each of which does credit to the people concerned; and it brings the two needs together. It has an almost symbolic rightness.

Oxford and Cambridge are magnificent places of learning. It is all the greater pity that the pattern of their student admissions is so warped socially. They will claim, usually fiercely nowadays because they feel themselves under attack, that the period of expansion together with other changes already under way within society have made them as open as possible to able children from all backgrounds; or at the least that they have made enormous efforts to this end, and been hampered only by external social and educational forces. I do not doubt their good intentions, or undervalue the progress achieved. But all in all the figures show that progress has been very much slower than they like to claim. For certain social groups, for pupils from certain schools and types of school, entry is still very much easier than for others.

It is true that many comprehensive schools do not think of Oxbridge as a goal for even their brightest pupils; nor do their pupils and parents. These forces are not weakened easily; Oxford and Cambridge will remain for a very long time places which very clever children from any background can often enter. Entry will remain much easier for clever children from comfortable and aware backgrounds; and many less clever children from a variety of privileged backgrounds will continue to be accepted. Both kinds and those in between are likely to assume, and to find, that their Oxbridge period has great value in the market outside. To regret this is not to be afflicted with the sin of envy, but to point to several compounded kinds of injustice.

The French Grandes Écoles are often cited as better models for the higher education of the most intelligent young people than our patchy system provides. Like any deeply rooted social creation, they are not easily transferable. Even a careful English imitation would turn out differently; which means, happily, that we *can* learn from them if we know how to adapt. This could be difficult but would be important if we suspect that to make Oxbridge into undergraduate and graduate universities for meritocrats only would bring the worst of both worlds so far as the effects on the undergraduates were concerned. Meritocrats given superior Oxbridge polish and social assumptions would be a bar to democracy in Britain at least as effective as the present muddled situation, and even less attractive. Apparatchiks expecting the privileges of party members but in the English manner would be misbegotten creations.

The expansionist mood brought also lateral, geographic, growth; instant growth, by which universities made links with colleges and institutes in their areas and agreed to validate their degrees. That produced many more graduates, and greater variety in the subjects offered. But often these degrees were validated in subjects and at a level which the university assessors would not have accepted in their own institutions. This was not, except by a very few, a cynical manoeuvre. Most university people did want to help the colleges near them; they simply assumed, only half-consciously, that degrees gained outside could be approved more easily than their own.

There also arose the further and related question of what to do about the colleges of advanced technology. Some of them were very distinguished, more distinguished in their own fields than some of the smaller universities. Should they not become universities, perhaps technological universities? But by that time the thought of yet another dozen or so universities properly so called disconcerted a lot of people.

Here another recurrent English spirit asserted itself: not the spirit which can on occasion make bold and liberated moves, but that which revels in fudge, compromise and semantic sleight of hand.

So we had from 1966, and from a Labour government, the spavined binary system by which the new polytechnics were, in relation to the universities, separate but equal; or almost equal, since they had to have their degrees validated by an exterior body, the Council for National Academic Awards, founded in 1964 (it proved to be, academically, both firm and open). Immediately and whatever had been said to deny the charge, the polytechnics were regarded as the Second Division. Naturally, it was thought rude to say so. As usual, Edward Boyle recognised it honestly. Looking from the window of his Vice-Chancellorial office in Leeds towards the newly named polytechnic, he pointed out that a sunken motorway divided them. 'Properly symbolic,' he said.

From the start we saw conflicting attitudes, some polytechnics keeping close to their communities in courses offered and students sought, others speeding up 'academic drift' as much as possible so that they became, as soon as possible, as like universities as possible – acquiring the right to grant professorships, trying to loosen ties with their validating bodies and local education authorities. It was all inevitable, since the binary system ran so much with the grain of the English insistence on class-distinctions; self-respecting people in the polytechnics would not tolerate their ranking for long. The best polytechnic departments improved their already high standing, and could have cocked more of a snook at the universities.

The 'polys' are now nationally funded and perhaps the wish to be called universities would have eventually subsided, though I doubt that. But, as I write, the government proposes to abolish the binary system. That is the right decision. The binary divide has been a twenty-odd years long social, cultural and academic hiccup in British higher education.

Many British university teachers have not noticed these things. It would be better if they had argued, resisted if they could not accept the above interpretations (which are not new), if they had shown they are alive to the situation of the universities in relation to society and its changes, and are willing on the right grounds to defend their best elements. An early warning signal was the passing, from 1963, of University Grants Committee funding via the Department of Education and Science instead of direct from the Treasury.

The universities rather grandly brushed aside Shirley Williams's thirteen points of 1976, a good list which among other matters stressed the need for more opportunities for adult students.

No wonder so many university teachers slid into the political climate of the Eighties with no sense of impending danger; when that danger came they saw the trees not the wood. They complained bitterly about the reduction in funds but little about the new government's restrictive view of society, of education and of the future for both, of which that reduction was only one symptom.

But when all the faults have been listed, it needs to be said that the British system of higher education is in many respects more humane and – towards those it does admit – more effective than almost any other. That does not need stressing. It is already adequately stressed by people most of whom will not also recognise its shortcomings.

2

Not long after I arrived at Birmingham University, in 1962, a circular plaza was opened in the middle of the campus with the Staff Club, the Health Centre and a few shops round its perimeter. I never visited the barber so didn't know whether or not he was practising the condoms-stuck-round-the-edges-of-the-mirrors and 'Do you need anything for the weekend, Sir?' routine.

He was, and someone told the authorities; or perhaps an amateur stringer first told a newspaper. Such an item was at that time worth front-page tabloid treatment – 'Contraceptives for Sale on

University Campus Scandal'. Almost immediately the barber was told to go.

Not many years afterwards, in 1966 or '67, I visited the university Health Centre on behalf of a girl who had become pregnant, was sure she did not want to marry the student who had brought that about, but not sure whether she wanted an abortion. She had asked me, because I was her 'pastoral tutor', to have a first word with the Medical Officer. When my turn came at the reception counter, I noticed a box of what looked like packeted pills on the right-hand side, placed in much the way supermarkets put sweets near their tills to tempt impulse buyers. A sudden thought – were those packets of The Pill, which I'd heard of but never seen? Yes, said the nurse-receptionist. Are they available to anyone? Not quite; they have to be having a serious relationship. How do you discover it's serious? We take their word for it.

The two parts of the above story bracket the date of arrival of what was called 'permissiveness'; more accurately, of a major change in sexual habits among many young people, with the more sophisticated in the forefront.

A short jump forward, to Paris in 1972, fits in here since it illuminates differences between British and French attitudes not so much towards sex as towards Authority, Them Outside. The student decided to have the baby and take sole charge of it. She became a teacher and for a few years I heard no more. One day came a letter: she enjoyed teaching and now felt ready to apply for a headship. One was advertised in a small East Anglian town; would I provide a confidential reference? She added that her son was growing up well and she had not so far married. I drafted a very warm reference, for she was an intelligent girl as well as responsible and brave. I referred to her pregnancy as a student and of her single-minded decision, as an instance of her admirable qualities.

My secretary was a very determined and independent French girl of Périgordian country gentry stock and, almost predictably, left-wing. She broke off typing the reference, came in and told me she would not prepare such a letter.

That the girl had had a baby outside marriage was no concern of the Authorities, she said; one told them no more than one had to by regulations, and certainly no personal facts such as that. I told her I did not wish to reveal to the governors of the school aspects of the applicant's private life (my secretary was also unused to the idea of local governors, and startled to think that they had the power to choose a headmistress). But if the governors appointed the girl and she appeared with a child they would almost certainly ask where the father was; if the girl had not told her story beforehand they might well take umbrage and even think of dismissing her. That would not be uncharacteristic in a fairly remote English township. I thought the girl had asked me for a reference in the knowledge that I could present her story in a sympathetic way. My secretary was not convinced, so we compromised. One of us wrote to the girl asking about her attitude to her child being mentioned in a confidential reference. She wrote back to confirm what I had assumed: she knew the facts could not be kept secret and so had best be told within her application. She did get the job; which reflects more credit on the governors than might have been assumed.

I am setting out here to describe the emergence of the period usually described in the rat-trap phrase 'the Permissive Society', a phrase which conceals and confuses much more than it illuminates. It suggests that young people suddenly became sexually promiscuous, declared their freedom from constraint and contingency.

Certainly no one in the early Sixties would have assumed that within a few years men and women would be sharing rooms at university, not so much because it was positively permitted in writing as because the universities had ceased to feel they had the right to intervene in such decisions. By the time I arrived at Goldsmiths' College in the mid-Seventies, Domestic Bursars were likely to say that, though they recognised that their institutions no longer had a moral say in these matters, they would quite like to know who was where so that they could charge something to unnotified lodgers who used a hall of residence's services for long periods but paid nothing. The Goldsmiths' Bursar said he could estimate roughly how many such squatters were in each hall by the amount of toilet paper used. There had, some time earlier, been long discussions between student officers and college authorities not about the right of a man or woman to stay the night on college property with someone of the opposite sex – that was assumed to be no business of the authorities – but about the length of time any one of them might stay without being liable to pay rent. I found in the minutes of the talks the cop-out phrase that they could stay 'a reasonable time'. What was 'reasonable'? 'Oh, we decided about a week.'

Later, a distressed wife rang to say her husband had disappeared but, she now believed, was sharing a room in one of our halls with a girl he had taught in the sixth form. Not surprisingly, since no one had told her about 'permissiveness', she assumed we could accuse him of using our premises immorally and advise him to go back to his wife and children. We did talk to him and he did leave, but whether he went back to his family I do not know.

Most attention in the press was given to presumed changes in sexual habits, but if a sort of 'permissiveness' (and the word becomes increasingly inadequate as one goes further into the subject) had developed, then sex was only one aspect of it. A more coherent definition would look at much else which marked the turn into the Sixties. In the universities, and students were one of the groups which led the way, it would include an assessment of the effect on manners of expansion itself. That growth brought a greater, though still strongly qualified, sense of social openness, of possibility; it to some extent lessened the sense of closedness and privilege. There was some change in the climate of residual deference, notably signalled by the BBC's satire shows in the early Sixties. The immediate trigger for those may have been the eccentric natural permissiveness of the Director-General, Hugh Greene; but he was responding, not necessarily consciously, to a wave which had already begun to form.

Surprisingly, and for a change, the British were in the first years, and in manners if not in range of intellectual debate, ahead of most of continental Europe. Their stylistic changes followed the changes of attitude. One of our sons was noisily objected to on the railway station at Cologne, by a middle-aged German couple, because of his long, Beatle-like hair; clearly, chaos was on the way. German social structures were more fiercely resistant than British, and eventually produced a more violent counter-resistance.

The language of the day among students told its own story:

words like 'real', 'genuine', 'truly significant', 'participant', 'dialogue', 'engaged' and 'committed' were common currency. Some
of those pointed also to the impulses behind the student troubles
of the late Sixties. In the beginning they shared a climate. 'Self-
definition' rather than external precept became dominant, and not
only in sexual matters after the appearance of the pill. But self-
definition in an increasingly relativist world can weigh heavily,
like carrying a large log, alone, across a featureless wilderness.

In the unholy duo, sex and drugs, as they presented themselves
to popular commentators, there seemed little of the second at
Birmingham. In many American campuses in the Sixties the smell
of grass hung over the snack-bars and lounges all day. I only once
met that smell heavily in Birmingham, at a post-graduate party
where we stumbled into the wrong room, into a haze of smoke
below which figures lay on mattresses. No doubt there was drug-
taking I did not see, but I do not think it was as preoccupying to
most students as the changes in sexual habits and their responses
to them.

The change in sexual practices was certainly the biggest single
indicator of social change at the time. It was the students or
former students who, increasingly in the late Sixties and early
Seventies, took their boy- and girl-friends home and announced
to their parents, in the face of varying degrees of dismay or a
nervous accepting, that they proposed to share a bed, as they had
been doing for months at university. At that time few lower-
middle-class or working-class young women or men, not part of
a higher education group, would have dared to propose this to
their parents, let alone try to justify it in argument. The attitude
filtered down from the educated-liberated or the merely liberated
and then took firm and fast hold, so that now council housing
estates are in this little different from Kensington and Earls Court
bed-sit areas, or student communities – except, and it's an
unhappy but predictable statistic, that council estates have far
more one-parent families, the one parent usually a woman. Management of the pill by the girl or tolerance of the condom by the
man is much weaker in those areas, and it is the girls who pay
the long-term price in most cases.

What was the main impulse towards this change in sexual
habits, especially among girls? The major agent was the arrival

of the oral contraceptive managed by the woman, the pill. The key date is 1960, when the US Food and Drug Administration approved it; it took only a year to reach Britain. I first heard of its being used here from a colleague at Birmingham University in about 1962. He had come into Snow Hill Station late one evening from a day's committee work in London. A girl who looked about fourteen years old had accosted him. He had shaken his head, but before giving up she had said, 'Come on. I'm on the pill. You can do it without a Frenchie.'

The fear of pregnancy, which for centuries had been the biggest inhibition on girls tempted, either by boys or by their own dispositions, to frequent sexual practice, had now virtually gone. The girl was in charge. Did that lead to promiscuity among them? Apart from a very few, I think not. It may have led the boys to be more insistent both because pregnancy was so much less likely and because they enjoyed sex more when they were free of the insensitivity of the condom. For most girls it was a new responsibility and a heavy one, since the choice, the decision and the consequences – and there were new consequences – fell on them more than on the boys.

The new freedom did not tempt most girls to sleep around. The new rules were different but rules or, more accurately, guiding pressures, there certainly were. If, as they were again and again told, the old prohibition on sex before and outside marriage rested not so much on virtue as on the fear of pregnancy, did they not have to consider other new rules of conduct now that that fear was largely eliminated? Was it really sinful to go to bed with a boy so long as you *really* liked him, so long as it seemed a natural extension of an attraction which now didn't have to lead to marriage (that looked too much like calculation), but was certainly not a crude, rutting instinct.

They were led to feel that they had to write their own code of conduct, and this became for most a form of prudence or of idealism, or more likely a mixture of both, rather than a recipe for looseness. It was very different from the wife- and husband-swapping of bored late-Thirties executives one heard much about in the Seventies. The weight of responsible choice could be enormous. The most painful cry I heard in those years came from a girl who was, though at university, not ready for a sexual relationship even with a boy she might like very much. She had to resist strong pressure from her friends in hall, not saying 'sleep around as much as you like' but rather 'What's wrong with you? Doesn't anyone want to be your steady and share your bed?' She said, 'I wish I lived in Jane Austen's day. At least you knew what the rules were then.'

The Americans had a phrase for it: 'serial monogamy', sleeping with only one man or woman at a time, but having a succession of 'steady' relationships, each of which soon led to the bed but few to the altar. Infidelity could be recognised but was not regarded as the breaking of an external moral injunction; it was a betrayal of a private contract or compact. If the partnership broke up because one of the two fell out of love, found someone else to be 'serial' with, that was not, in principle, a betrayal and could not, in principle, be objected to. Yet it could hurt as much as a broken engagement in the old days; only now you had no words of principle or emotional judgment with which to identify and assess it; you could only regret it, painfully, as painfully as your great-aunt (or great-uncle) did when they were thrown over.

Young men felt the burden of choice too, especially if they were socially shy, sexually immature at entry to university, or badly inhibited by nature or from some unhappy earlier experience, possibly within the family. I had a pastoral role towards one such student at Birmingham and did what I could, but that was little, especially in circumstances so severe. He went in and out of hospital, seemed to grow more assured, had a mild relapse and was put in the small residential Health Centre on the campus. I went across most evenings before walking home, feeling almost useless but hoping even trivial conversation might help. For a few days he seemed neither up nor down but remained in a sort of limbo; until what proved to be the last evening I saw him. Early next day, I had a 'phone call; he had thrown himself in the path of a train on the line just below his window. A disturbed youth might have done that in any decade; but the form of his stress, the language of his expressions of inadequacy, were typical of that time and that sort of place. Young men and young women could both be pushed too far too soon.

The heaviest weight fell, as I have said, on the girls. They would set up with a boy, usually in a small flat somewhere outside the university. In most instances the girl did the cooking and the washing so the boy had not only a near-replacement for his mother but a sex-partner as well. More often than not, this extra work was assumed as her responsibility by the girl and especially if she did have a hope of marriage. I can recall a string of girls who went on like this for months, only to have the boy leave them when he found another, or when their university time came to an end. I knew more than one instance in which the girl did after all become pregnant, in spite of the pill. One pair were delighted, married at once and are now bringing up their family in Canada, he teaching at a university. Others were messy businesses with the boys as unwilling to cope with the problems raised by the pregnancy as they had been to do their share of the housekeeping.

So, did permissiveness entirely break the 'pastoral' and 'moral' role of university teachers? The words, the title, soon fell out of use, as did the habit of asking us to get in touch with parents when severe difficulties arose. We were still asked to telephone the Local Education Authority if there were problems over individual grants. Many students still came to see tutors about difficult personal problems. But the atmosphere had changed; there was no longer a touch of deference, but more a disposition to use your Christian name as an indication of equality.

What did this relationship mean to us, the tutors; or to me, since on such a matter no one can claim to speak for others? I did no more in these pastoral duties than colleagues; and we discussed the problems of students whom two or three of us knew well. I do not remember any discussion of the curious nature of our own role, our own inner responses.

You do care, yet it is like care in a caul; caring and not caring – not in the way you care about your own children in trouble. You are a sort of neutered uncle; at the deepest level uninvolved, you hope you are 'professional'; and, above that level, you are very concerned. Misbehaviour does not bring the added distress of hurt pride in you because in these instances a reflection of your own weaknesses is not coming back at you. You would be hurt in that way, to that depth, if an incident revealed what they thought of you personally, how far they had seen into your own weaknesses. That particular moment of revelation happens rarely since, when they come to you for advice in trouble, you are by that act on a small pedestal, though fairly easily dislodged. Yet, again and finally, in a certain and not negligible way you do care.

'Permissiveness' produced a backlash of the predictable but unhelpful kind; a sex-obsessed backlash. In this the Festival of Light joined hands with the National Viewers' and Listeners' Association. The business of censorship, of the due limits of free speech, is far more complex than the out-and-out liberals will admit. Yet you can usually debate with them, rarely with the out-and-out censors. I once 'shared a platform' with Mrs Whitehouse and said that in thinking about television's possible effects, I would be less concerned about a play by Dennis Potter than about *This is Your Life*. In one way I meant that seriously, and would be willing to make the case. There was no opportunity then, since Mrs Whitehouse believed I was talking the most perverse nonsense.

In the universities the Sixties came to an end with the student troubles. I use that phrase rather than 'student rebellions' or 'student riots' because it best suggests the very English nature of most such events here, their less violent and extreme form than was common on the Continent or in America.

They seem to have had their origins in two converging streams, one public, political and evident, the other a part of less evident but no less powerful changes within society. That second change was, once again, inspired by greater prosperity and the associated movement which had given rise to great expansion in the universities. Large numbers of students in the Sixties, many of them the first in their families though not often from the working class, were able to assume that they would get jobs on graduating; and, paradoxically, felt trapped on a conveyor belt of society's making, as if too much had been taken for granted about them and their aspirations.

So the typical mood did not lead to thinking about jobs, of climbing on to a cushy professional bus. The reaction against much in their society, and in their universities seen as over-passive reflectors of that society, was at heart a reaction against conspicuous consumption, a puritan resistance to the emerging consumer society more than a grasping at anarchic liberty. Conversely, they were also reacting against the Protestant Ethic of work as a primary virtue, and against orderliness and acceptance of the status quo in its commitment to the dictates of a commercial society. They were reacting to 'getting on', climbing over the backs of others, keeping their noses clean so they could gain the benefits of continuing prosperity and a good pension at the end. All that was individualistic and competitive, and they rejected it. They sought freedom from the institutions of society – whether open and commercial, or closed, monolithic and authoritarian – so as to reach a more natural state, one of non-self-seeking community. Specifically, they wished to see the university as a moral community.

In the late Sixties I asked a student in his final year to see me so that I could tell him, as was the habit – it had happened to me thirty years before – that he stood a good chance of getting a First and might like to pace himself with that in mind. He thanked me but said a First did not interest him; he was more interested in his friendships and in the beliefs he shared with his friends, and those did not include competing for Firsts, isolated rock-climbing away from the others. His was at its best a friendly generation.

The most evident of the factors which led to the events of the late Sixties were: the Cold War, the nuclear threat and the conflict in Vietnam (which, in England, culminated in the Grosvenor Square demonstration of 1968). Some violence, many sit-ins of varying degrees of severity and destructiveness, took place but none bore comparison with, to take only one example, the events of 1968 in Paris, which almost brought down a government.

Among the students themselves there were also two main groups. The political activists on the far left looked for some very radical breaking of the mould, especially of the 'military-industrial complex'. At the extreme they had a very limited definition of freedom of speech and could not reasonably be called democratic. They were at the front of such disturbances as we had in Britain, and usually expected to go to jail, and some did; it was partly a self-fulfilling prophecy. The much larger but quieter group were those I have described as quietist, perhaps into flower-power, non-pushy.

To a considerable extent the two groups shared a vocabulary:

to the words I listed in talking about 'permissiveness' could be added 'authentic', 'to experience' (as in 'to experience a *real* sense of communication – or commitment') and 'relevance', whose meaning might range from a crude socially purposive idea of the nature of teaching and learning to a substantial critique of the universities' unquestioning relations with some of the more questionable drives of society. 'Confrontation', 'direct confrontation', 'repressive tolerance' and the rest – often evasive cant – belonged to the political group of students.

In the British troubles Essex blew up more than most and so did the London School of Economics and, in a different manner, Oxford and Cambridge. Birmingham was so much in the sober unspeculative middle that some of us wondered whether it would react at all. It did not have the rawness and special thrust of Essex, the political self-consciousness and sophistication of LSE, or Oxbridge's feeling that, if there was to be a party they would be at it in a special way. But Birmingham was a good indication of trends; if Birmingham blew up, those trends were exceptionally powerful.

It did blow up, rather late and not violently but on a surprisingly large scale. At the peak a meeting in the Great Hall was said to have four thousand students, though that may have been an over-estimate; but the hall was packed. The prime movers were a lecturer in sociology and a handful of students, some from our centre. Some faculties, such as engineering and medicine, stayed almost clear. Birmingham's was a very English disturbance: it focussed, rightly, on the enclosed way the university was run, on its failure to respond to questions about other ways of running a university or about its links with government, industry and commerce. As a result it brought into play for a few heady days most of the student body, including the quietist group. The case had been put in a way which captured their kind of idealism. And some just enjoyed the lark or came to the meetings out of simple curiosity. Birmingham's was not, at bottom, a very political upset in any wide sense; but it was uproarious whilst it lasted.

The huge and on the whole good-natured meeting in the Great Hall illustrated all this; and illustrated also a further catalyst: the inability of the new Vice-Chancellor, Hunter, to comprehend what was happening. Some other Vice-Chancellors cheerfully told the students how much they were on their side; others spent hours over coffee discussing with the student leaders, trying to moderate their grievances (at the best that cooled the temperature, at the worst it achieved virtually nothing; all depended on the cunning of the Vice-Chancellor and the degree of intransigence of six or seven students and members of staff). Other V-Cs became huffy and retired to their tents, as Birmingham's did when his building was occupied. His advisers finally persuaded him to speak to the proposed meeting in the Great Hall. More used to being a Dean of Medicine in Scotland and to the old-fashioned authority that conferred, he was ill-at-ease on the platform, by turns patronising and hedging. The good nature of the audience was being sorely tried.

In the end one or two of us, from the middle of the hall, urged him to give straight answers to the questions; they were sensible questions and straightforward answers would be met straight-forwardly. We spoke out of conviction not tactics. We heard afterwards, but I cannot vouch for its truth, that the staff member organising the uprising had said he would have brought them out indefinitely if 'Hoggart's group' hadn't shown them that some members of staff were taking their arguments seriously. The thing petered out a day or two later with less gain in open government than some members of staff wished. Apparently the Vice-Chancellor said I had 'stabbed him in the back'. Translated, that seemed to mean he expected all senate members to rally round him in defence of the entire current system.

Soon afterwards most universities, though not quite all, settled to the calm which still envelops them. There are occasional sit-ins even now, in the Nineties, but they have an unexpectant air; they are no longer going the way the world is going. The steam went out; there were minor rather than major changes in the style of British universities. It was true to the nature of the country that there should be such results, that the troubles should have nothing like the violent edge of continental or American uprisings. This place catches fire slowly, like damp timber; and there are many socio-psychological blankets to smother it, but gently. The English troubles had a very English complexion and died a very English death.

Movements like that have a natural span and then fade away. This fading was helped by the ending of the Vietnam war in 1975. The oil crisis, starting in 1973, put a firm end to expansion and to something of the sense of openness that that had induced. Jobs began to be more difficult to find. All in all, the landscape of the Seventies and Eighties was bleaker, less cheerful and inspiriting, than that of the Sixties; and universities' funds were squeezed more and more; no one was riding high.

Little had been gained. Student members joined a number of committees at many places, but most of them soon became bored. Most committees did not turn out to be sinister, conspiracy-ridden, shams and so were not the places for revolutionary rhet-oric. They were dull, hard-working, often wrong-headed for well meant reasons, and faced with increasingly intractable problems as money became more scarce. Since then, the universities' largely unquestioned involvement with and services to government, industry and commerce have become matters for which they gain good official marks. The change could hardly have been more total.

So far as I know, no study has been made of what happened to the British student leaders of the late Sixties. To know might modify the frequent snide remarks to the effect that they are all now in PR or market research or the mass media, especially broadcasting. Some are; I know one in market research and two in the mass media. Another is in the head office of a union, another in a university sociology department and another living on a pittance as a full-time worker for a far-left fringe party. As could have been expected, some found work in which the edge of their ideals and anger could be kept moderately sharp; and some slid comfortably into the system.

Still, the overall record for those years is not bad. Expansion proved that more need not mean worse, if people paid their dues to its implications and needs.

The student demonstrations brought at least a little more light into university government. Much more important, they reminded those willing to listen that it is possible – idealistic, heroic and, I would say, right – to see the university as, above all, a moral community.

The wrongly styled 'permissiveness', for all the tensions it involved, was more of a gain than a loss. In its time. Looked at over the gap of a quarter-century, that change in the climate seems to belong to quite another century, seems innocent, almost pre-lapsarian. It does not conceivably belong to a period in which a 'quality' Sunday newspaper, wooing university freshers with fashionable advice, encourages them to assume that the men will have condoms in the back pockets of their jeans and will expect to use them, soon, with all but the more nervous girls, with any who casually attract them or are attracted by them. All this under the malign shadow of Aids. A new world.

PART TWO

INTERNATIONAL LIFE AND BACK TO BRITAIN: THE 1970s AND 1980s

CHAPTER 6

A WORLD APART: UNESCO, 1970-5

After half of the three years' leave of absence from Birmingham had passed René Maheu, the D-G, invited me, one evening in Tunis where we were talking to the government about the restoration of Carthage, to meet him in the bar for a drink before dinner. Odd, because he rarely went into bars. The usual secretariat reaction to such a break in his routine whilst on a mission abroad would be: what have I done this time? Unwittingly insulted a very important person?

He asked me to stay for two years beyond my contract, to the time of his own retirement. It was a surprising and touching request and I muttered some hesitant, non-committal thank you. 'Well, you are the best AD-G I have,' he muttered in turn. Then, as though he could not bear to present such a bouquet, he half took it back again, discounted its value. 'Not that the others are any good.'

I

The British lack of much concern, amused dismissal or near contempt for some international organisations have been constant for almost half a century. We played a good part in the setting up of the UN, and intelligent and devoted Britons were drawn to its service. Some at UNESCO had been there, when I arrived, since not long after the 1945 founding conference in London.

Few academics, intellectuals or artists would nowadays allow themselves to refer to UNESCO as other than a small joke. The prevailing attitude was caught by a Vice-Chancellor not long after we had come back from our five years and a bit. 'I wouldn't call myself a Hoggart-watcher,' he said, protecting his higher vision from the start, 'but some of us did wonder what possessed you to go to that place.'

I agreed to go there in what a friend, urging me to accept, called a 'walking-the-plank spirit' – that which leads us to take on certain commitments not because we particularly want to, and even though we know that much in them will be boring or unpleasant, but because we have been asked to walk the plank in the service of a valuable idea.

I knew enough about the organisation to be amused by its rococo weaknesses. I knew little about its great cruelties, neuroses, unhappinesses and sudden kindnesses. I had some idea of the importance of its work, even at a time when many nations had shoved it to the edges of their interests. A quick visit to the debates on culture, at a late-Sixties General Conference, had allowed me to hear a remarkable intervention: a delegate from Mali pleading for funds to record the oral memories of old people, because Mali's history itself was still almost entirely oral and would almost entirely die with that generation of old people. 'When an old man dies in one of our villages,' he cried, in a spectacular Afro-French blend of passionate oratory, 'a shelf-ful of books is lost.'

My name had gone on to the list of possible candidates in that late summer of 1969, and we heard little for many weeks. Only odd hints filtered through: that Maheu didn't want me. No ill-will, but he wanted an Asian because the Asian states, rightly, felt under-represented on the top managerial board. All candidatures had to be put before the executive board (at the time, twenty-odd senior representatives from all the world's regions, who met for long sessions twice a year), even if with a polite lack of enthusiasm for some from the D-G. It was odd that Maheu put forward, with more warmth than he showed for me, not one but two Asians – a distinguished Japanese academic well known to the higher councils of UNESCO, and an Iranian Minister for Education, inevitably related to the Shah. Was Maheu after all splitting the Asian vote so that the European candidate could come in? I don't think so. He probably thought one of the Asians, perhaps the Iranian, would carry the vote easily, leaving the Japanese and me trailing far behind; or that the two Asians would share almost all the votes, which would allow him greater freedom to argue for his preferred one of the two.

The board gave two or three votes to the Iranian, about the same number to the Japanese and the rest to me. I doubt they were influenced by my professional record. The English member spoke strongly on my behalf but it seems unlikely that that would have swung so many votes in my direction. I suspect board members were reacting, as they did every so often, against a too obvious attempt by the Director-General to manipulate them. Given such a result, he had to appoint me and did so with reasonable grace.

He capped that some months later when we were on a difficult mission together. He growled in an interval: 'I didn't want you, as I'm sure you've been told. I had to bear other considerations in mind. But I'm glad now that the board had their way.' As did the Tunis invitation, that admission must have needed a considerable effort, from a man with his high charge of professional and personal pride.

A few weeks after I took up the job, the senior US career diplomat there stopped me on a corridor. 'You'll know we voted for the Japanese. State Department orders, to do with our relationships with them. But I'm glad you made it.' Academics are sheltered; that was my first direct experience of the amorality, in this instance a petty immorality, of much diplomacy in the pursuit of short-term national interests.

After the nightmare of leaving Birmingham, Mary, Paul and I (Simon was at work in Manchester and Nicola up at the university of York) arrived in a bitterly cold and, at first, apparently inhospitable Paris. That mood passed in about six months; it began to fade when in the second month we moved with our furniture into a large, empty and at first glance not at all smart apartment on the Boulevard Haussmann, a quarter of a mile from the Étoile. This fulfilled the first of three promises we had made to ourselves on agreeing to move: we would live centrally. The other promises were that Mary would so far as ever possible come with me on missions, and that we would pay for the children to come over as often as they wished.

I began immediately to work harder than ever before. My brief was enormous, complicated and complex. A typical day meant ten to twelve hours in the office and more when major conferences were running, more work at home in the evening and early morning, and in more than five years only two weekends without a loaded briefcase. We went away about one weekend in six, sometimes with one of the children, and grew to love the areas within a hundred miles of Paris, as well as Paris itself; but the briefcase went with us. That is the sort of load a high-level government official would have, but not part of a normal academic pattern. Like many academics I had always worked hard and long; the difference, and it is crucial, is that an academic largely chooses the things on which to spend the hours. Government ministers, senior managers in business and senior civil servants are attending to a continuous stream of material which contains many things that bore them, or should never have come along anyway. There can be, though, a sort of pleasure in learning how to cope, how – you hope – to do a respectable job without killing yourself or letting it get on top of you. So there was a tonic element. It was a new world, not chiefly because there was a lot of work but because you were no longer the master of your own time.

For me, the grind was relieved quite often because I had a madly mixed brief. Any week might bring news of an earthquake and so the need to arrange for urgent international aid to protect damaged national cultural monuments, or about the arrest of a writer for publishing a book of which his government disapproved, or a demand that the Hague Convention be invoked to protect holy shrines from the troops of a newly invading power.

Meeting all this in those first few months, I neglected to notice sufficiently how much support Mary, exceptionally, needed. Alone in a new city with no friends at hand, the two older children in England and Paul working at a charitable foundation in India, her mother newly dead. And there was I, almost entirely engrossed in the weight and detail of new work and also caught up with the sheer harshness of the new setting as it was at that time. After about six months Mary regained her resilience, a stream of visitors from England began to arrive in what was by then a very agreeable and homely apartment, and I began to see outside my own preoccupations; but it had been a failing on my part.

A provincial from outside the life of public power could learn a great deal from all UNESCO's doings; about governments and the ways they work, about national and international public personalities who threw shadows larger than any I had met before (such as the quintessentially French Maheu), and about the much more melodramatic world outside parochial Britain (a very long way from Hunslet, even in styles of melodrama). You learned about the world outside parochial Europe also, the vast and varied spaces of that outer world, its different ways of interpreting human experience, its complex and shifting physical and mental landscapes, its beauties of sorts we never knew as we walked in the Lake District or West Country. Above all, you learned about poverty and, entwined with it like bind-weed, the simple acceptance of corruption as an essential lubricant of daily life. An old hand – an Englishman – said, when encouraging me to go (he could not have been more accurate): 'Go. Your world and yourself will never be the same again after UNESCO.'

I came to dislike the shabbier sides of nationalism, the intense concern with face and so with protocol, which is all about national face. In this the British could be as tiresome as less secure countries; perhaps more so, since some of their representatives carried around a large, still Imperial sense of what was due to them. At a grand international conference the leader of the British delegation, a minister, called in the conference office to put his name down as a speaker at the opening plenary session. The official in charge of the list told him he would be the third speaker. 'Third. Who are the others?' 'Mexico and Senegal have already put their names down, your Excellency.' 'Do you mean the United Kingdom is expected to come after those two?' He turned to me: 'We can't have that, can we, Hoggart?' I supported the officer. Maheu was invoked by the British minister and was uneasy, since he felt some indebtedness to that particular politician. At the next morning's staff meeting he began to bully the officer concerned: 'I'll have you back in Paris by the next 'plane.' I interrupted and explained the circumstances. In the end he stood by his secretariat.

An English peer who attended a contentious session of a big conference sent a note congratulating me on 'putting our curly-haired coloured friend in his place' during a debate. That had been neither my intention nor what happened. In the face of such attitudes, most people decided there were two kinds of Briton, those who were straight, tolerant and hence excellent chairmen, and the arrogant or flatulent.

I made two or three trips to Britain as the D-G's representative at important occasions and noted, more sharply than ever because of being away, much the same habitual and hardly conscious rudenesses towards people who had been instantly assigned to a lower rank. And massively self-assured insularity. On one occasion I decided to use for the first time my red, diplomatic-status, UN passport. The immigration officer knew nothing of such things and was grumpily suspicious so, to save further delay, I produced my British passport. 'Why did you try to use that thing, then?' he said, as though anyone who preferred another passport to the blue one was a pervert.

After a few such incidents it was easy to begin to feel detached from the little snobby island. The aggression and straight rudeness common on the streets of Paris seemed preferable, and the aspirations of an international cultural agency more attractive.

Too many of the ambassadors attached to UNESCO soft-footed about, following their telephoned orders, seeking more financial aid than was their country's due, trying to bend the rules about the representation of their country's nationals in the secretariat, or about fees and expenses. One visiting Soviet dignitary, supported by his ambassador and a Soviet member of my staff, spent a week trying to have a large personal payment – which had to be in roubles – made in US dollars. He knew I was refusing to waive the rules and told Maheu at a luncheon that I had been 'unkind'. Maheu smiled and said he was sure I was doing all for the best. Whether he then released the dollars I do not know.

With some of the attached diplomatic staff one wondered whether there was any shifty order to which, with whatever regrets, they would demur. With others, one became able to distinguish by their manner when they thought their brief justified and when they knew, and knew you knew, that their orders were shabby and unjustifiable. It would be naïve to think of Foreign Ministries as moral agents before they are national instruments. But UNESCO is the one international agency founded on the assertion that free speech, objective speech, and its free circulation are inalienable rights. It is a relatively small and not very important organisation. One might have expected Foreign Ministries to be a bit more moral – well, fair-minded – there; but the old rule held most of the time: push your national interests.

UNESCO was hardly a prime posting for civil servants or career diplomats so, with one or two admirable exceptions, those given the rank of ambassador there were not among their countries' high-flyers. The Soviet Union sent, at the level of ambassador, clever and tough people; the Kremlin recognised the importance to itself of all international sounding-boards and especially of some major UNESCO themes (human rights, communications, the Arab–Israeli dispute, and one or two others).

Most US ambassadors were not career diplomats and were, professionally, jokes – people to whom the President owed a minor debt – say, for help in his presidential election campaign. There was a butterfly-spectacled Southern lady who had helped Nixon's campaign. There was a real estate agent from New York who had helped one of Nixon's successors. Robert Frost's death was announced during a sitting of the executive board; a poet, very much within UNESCO's sphere, so the Americans asked for time to read a brief tribute. The ambassador mangled 'Mending Wall' so badly that Maheu turned to me and said with pure Gallic contempt, 'They send us people who don't even know their own poetry.'

The dance of protocol was more important to such people than to, say, the Soviet ambassadors, who were usually younger, aware of UNESCO's likely place in their career pattern, and not inclined to give themselves airs on such a posting. The others greatly enjoyed being called 'Excellency'.

Most movements in the minuet of diplomatic niceties were comical and, where they were embarrassing to Mary and me, usually self-induced. Our decision that Mary would come on missions whenever possible meant we had always to travel tourist class, since we had to pay Mary's fare and UNESCO rightly saved by paying only a tourist fare for me; there could be no subsidising of one by the other. But an Assistant Director-General flew first-class; for him to do otherwise was so much against protocol that my first French secretary could not bear to ask for two tourist-class tickets at the in-house travel agency. She returned with one first and one tourist class.

At Lima, the welcoming party at the first-class steps in the middle of the night had to rush back to the tourist steps, gladioli held high. At that moment, smiling on the steps, I realised I still had on the blue-woollen-with-gold-trim travelling socks provided by Alitalia.

At Moscow in 1975, whither I had travelled alone because it was near Christmas and Mary preferred to prepare for that, the Soviet authorities knew I was travelling tourist class because they had just pushed a resolution through the executive board ruling that, within Europe, only the D-G could travel first. Yet they could not bear to place a Zim limousine at other than the first-class steps. I trudged to it through deep snow whilst the loudspeakers boomed in French for 'His Excellency, the Assistant Director-General Hoggart'.

On the return journey, I was trapped in the VIP lounge till very near the time to leave for Paris. A deputy Foreign Minister tried to give me a fat envelope of roubles, 'for incidental expenses'. That was one of the oldest tricks in the book. The packet went forwards and back until I asked my interpreter to buy champagne for everyone in the lounge. The minister and the interpreter thought that a nice move.

The Zim set off – to the first-class steps. I decided not to demur, knowing things would be sorted out at the top. The stewardess's smile froze when she read my ticket; she almost pushed me through to the tourist area. I expected to have the last remaining seat, near the loo. But status held; no tourist-class passengers were being allowed on until I had been seated.

The saddest diplomatic story I heard was from an Eastern European ambassador. He was a gentle man who would have much preferred being a musical scholar to being a diplomat. Perhaps they had sent him to UNESCO, the most cultured of postings, because of his years of service in one of the harder diplomatic jobs, as chief protocol officer.

As we became friendly he began to reminisce. His worst experience in the protocol post had been when a Middle Eastern potentate had paid a week's visit. His demands on hospitality preceded him: he wanted a different European woman in his bed each night. The request had shocked the protocol officer but he knew he would have to meet it. But how? His more knowing juniors told him elegant prostitutes practised, chiefly seeking Western businessmen, in the most expensive of the bars in each of the city's two international-class hotels. It would be easy to line up a different woman each night.

Greatly pained, he agreed. But a financial record had to be kept. Again, a junior solved the problem. On one day the VIP had apparently received the gift of a small refrigerator, on another a suit, on another jewellery, and so on.

I was not myself born to be a diplomat. Over the years I did come to respect those who seemed unusually honest diplomats but, as is by now plain, acquired little respect for the trade in general; too much mere spokesmanship. Perhaps attitudes were more impressive above the level of most I met. It was hard to take many of them seriously, and especially their interminable and often pompous speeches. In my first month the Deputy Director-General, an Indian and not short in a sense of his own importance, sent me a rebuke for teasing the executive board. Some members could be more relaxed. The Netherlands ambassador was a poet, not on the make and very happy in his placing. At the end of my first year he stopped me in the corridor on the way to an executive board meeting and said, 'My friend, we are glad you are here and like your style. But do restrain your jokes with the board. Some of them have little sense of humour and may tell the D-G you do not treat them with proper respect.'

I expect they did, but Maheu was too shrewd to take me up on that. He had other aims, especially in my early days. With all new senior colleagues he had to take the measure of their resistance to his generally autocratic manners. He was himself exceptionally clever and exceptionally pugnacious and soon despised those who proved to be neither clever nor bloody-minded if pushed. 'He will fight you quite early to see how soon you bleed,' said an African. 'If he draws blood he will eat you alive.' A Scandinavian, retiring after many years at my level, said UNESCO was a harsh place and even a provincial Englishman would soon find himself banging the table and shouting at his subordinates in the Maheu manner. The pity was that Maheu did not behave in that way because he was naturally bad-tempered. He did so because he cared intensely about the organisation, gave it all his time and effort, and so exploded when member states sent him, with glowing testimonials, people who were lazy and cowardly.

His early career had been largely with the French diplomatic service; he then joined UNESCO in its first years. Eventually, he became the first 'internal' D-G, drawn from UNESCO's own ranks. He was intensely proud of this and determined to justify his appointment. Hence the enormous energy he put into the job and the force of his anger if things went badly wrong. A British member of the executive board said that, when he was very angry indeed, she could feel the heat from his thighs a couple of feet away.

It was often an erotic energy. He was not conventionally handsome, but stocky and with a very solid face which suggested authority, a short fuse and decisiveness. Women whom he wanted to attract felt great sexual power radiating from him, and were often captivated. That he had been an early lover of Simone de Beauvoir surprised no one but impressed almost everybody. In his attitude to sex he could also be like the British caricature of a Frenchman, one in whom we do not quite believe until we meet him: Maurice Chevalier being wolfish, or as if delivering a line from a French boudoir comedy.

He liked that role too. One day I was asked to send down to him, sitting in a meeting of the executive board, a minute on some urgent matter. It fell to a good-looking American girl in my office to deliver it. She was wearing a very low-cut dress and smiled cheerfully when I raised my eyebrows at it. She came back slightly chastened. As she had bent towards Maheu to hand over the minute he had taken a bold look and said, 'Your boy-friend must have good sport with you.' Such stories passed around immediately, little sparks in the generally heavy atmosphere; he's a card, at any rate, was the reaction.

Day by day, he gave a magnificent example of how to work for what one believed in; and then threw all away by an act of irresistible self-indulgence – such as appointing a woman with whom he sought close relations to a post beyond her capacities. The supine and incompetent then took this as their excuse to ignore all his good work and justify their own fiddles.

His other great external interest was sport – from rugby to the Olympics to cycling. I bought a bicycle after a year or two, bored with driving the two miles from our flat over the river to the Place de Fontenoy each day. On advice, it was an Oscar Egg; one of those little folding affairs, in cream. I rode it one day to a lunch at Le Doyen in the Champs Élysées, given by a German minister. The doorman ordered me to the rear entrance. Told I was joining the German lunch party, he bowed and said, 'May I then take care of your bicycle, Sir.' Coming out with Maheu from the lunch I found the bike in the front foyer, ready to be ceremoniously handed over. Maheu was enchanted. 'An Oscar Egg! What a cyclist he was! Victor in the Tour de France! You have chosen well!'

Apart from current close personal relations, the most compelling of the few things which took his mind off UNESCO were the contacts which still remained of his life in the rue d'Ulm and round about with Sartre, de Beauvoir and their circle. He simply assumed that French intellectual life outclassed any other. We had Lévi-Strauss to give an important public lecture one evening and Maheu deviated from his habit so far as to go with me to meet his admired old acquaintance in the front foyer. He introduced me, and Lévi-Strauss said he admired my work. Half a dozen notches straight up Maheu's scale of values.

He could be unjust to members of staff, and ready even to cut corners of principle if he felt this might further some cause close to his organisational heart. For months I kept a resignation letter in my desk, one which told him in what I had convinced myself were carefully honed terms that I was resigning not on personal grounds but because I objected to his manner of running the place. I never sent it but, especially in the first years, fought him regularly. At one point, in a large meeting, he bullied one of the directors on my staff until the man was almost in tears. Maheu could not resist that, because the officer had been inefficient and, more, because he toadied towards him. Maheu enjoyed flattery for only so long, then would turn on the flatterer and try to destroy him with contempt. On this occasion I decided after fifteen minutes or so that Maheu had gone far enough and found myself banging the table and saying, 'This must stop. Take me on, not my officer.' The Scandinavian's prophecy had been fulfilled, but not in the way he had expected. Maheu was furious and told the Deputy D-G, 'If Hoggart won't work with me, I will not work with him,' as he stormed out. Once his anger had subsided he put the incident to my credit.

The early part of his last year brought the worst dispute. The post-Dubček government in Czechoslovakia had turned its attention, belatedly, to its nationals in UN service. It began to put pressure on some of them to return home, so that others could be appointed who were not tainted by Dubček's thinking.

Maheu decided he could not stand strictly on the letter of the official agreement which protects international civil servants, identified those among the Czechs who were most useful to him, and suggested a trade-off. One who was to be sent home was on my staff. He was a respectably efficient officer without being outstanding. He was, with good evidence, deeply distressed at what he guessed awaited him back home and asked for my support. I told Maheu that if this man were let go on the grounds of inefficiency one might as well let half the sector's staff go. The correspondence went back and forth, with Maheu becoming increasingly angry at my obstinacy and my becoming increasingly rigid. In the end he said that, if I persisted in deliberately misunderstanding him, he would without my agreement not renew the Czech's contract; and did not.

The Czech took his case to the UN Staff Appeals Tribunal at Geneva. He asked me to speak on his behalf. I told the Deputy Director-General, by that time an American, that I intended to do so. 'That must be your decision.' he said, rightly, 'but confine yourself to a description of his competence and do not criticise the D-G. You know, of course, that he will take his revenge on you anyway.' The Czech won his case, Maheu refused to reinstate him and so paid a sizeable amount in damages; the Czech stayed in Paris and took a job at the Beaubourg which was then being built. True to form, Maheu told the DD-G, 'Hoggart will pay for this.'

His opportunity came not much later, when I was myself beginning to look for a post back in Britain. Even though I knew what he might do, I felt I had to ask him for a reference; this was *a propos* the Secretary-Generalship of the Arts Council. Before he posted it, and with the old wolfish grin, he showed me what he had said. The letter was until the very end exceptionally complimentary. He had then inserted the dagger or poison. Knowing it would dissuade any chairman who might have to work with me, he added that my considerable analytic powers might make me inflexible when circumstances required considerable flexibility. He had had his revenge. Freed from its code, that sentence meant: 'In the matter of the Czech member of staff he stuck pig-headedly to the letter of the law on UN appointments and refused to recognise the larger political perspective and hence manoeuvres within which a D-G must work; and so refused to agree that his member of staff should be surrendered.' Or, in other words, Hoggart could be a stiff-necked puritan, which was true. I was told the warning had had its intended effect on one or perhaps two members of the interviewing committee.

In spite of such fights – and they were clearly fights not just between two individuals but between two different cultures – we ended as wary but respectful friends. I was one of the handful invited to his farewell party ('the few I respect') and went to see him a day or two before we left Paris, and six or seven months after he had retired. He was moving into the last rapid stages of leukaemia; it was as though his frenetic work up to the final day at UNESCO had fended off the disease, but now it was making up for the delay. He was staying at the apartment of Nadine, his companion for many years (his wife had been, also for many years, in a mental institution). Nadine was on my staff. After his death, she wrote:

> I know things were not always easy between the two of you. But you were true fighters and I think came to understand and appreciate each other at the end. I personally was very grateful to you for being so honest to me.
>
> Please share with Mary and all those you love my very fond wishes.
>
> Nadine.

The relationship with Maheu gave a most impressive example of how personal, social and professional values differ from society to society. He loved Britain for its hold on things concrete, its professional probity and its sense of the comic; he thought its intellectual life 'provincial', and in his intellectual glossary that was a very dismissive word. He had himself a Southern village boy's love of his native soil – when the village oak blew down he bought another – but that did not connect with his thinking mind;

the roots of that were in Paris. He knew my own love of France was as qualified as his for Britain, though for different reasons. We all tend to think we know much about cultural differences from our reading, especially in literature, and in some irreplaceable ways we do. Yet there is bound to be a difference in kind between that and the knowledge which comes from meeting those differences day by day, decision by decision. More than anyone, Maheu gave me that experience.

Differences in particular professional practices between cultures and countries are less important, more irritating and often more comical. In an international organisation, even more than in a national body, you cannot allow someone, from a society in which it is taken for granted that you fiddle the authorities so far as ever you can, to claim inflated expenses on a mission. You cannot let an officer cook the books so as to give privileges to a visitor from his country. If you do let such things happen the place will fall apart into a chaos of multiple bad practices, all justified on the most important cultural grounds.

Yet the most blatant instance of professional fiddling I met came from an Englishman. A BBC producer came over to talk about a programme they might wish me to take part in. I could only meet him at lunchtime and took him to a quite expensive bourgeois restaurant near UNESCO. Having paid the bill, I screwed it up and threw it into the ash-tray. 'Aren't you going to claim on that?' 'No, we can't claim for hospitality expenses. A reasonable amount for that is incorporated into our salaries.' 'Oh, in that case I'll claim it on the Beeb'; he smoothed out and pocketed the bill.

It is not a sign of European or Western arrogance that UN staff rules are, all in all, those of the technically and administratively highly developed societies – beginning with time-keeping. Those were the only widely agreed sets of rules which had been proved in large and complex organisations over time, and exported to colonies across the world. A director immediately below me, a most intelligent African of high birth, arrived in his office late most days, took long lunch hours, and disappeared clutching *Le Monde* in the not-so-late afternoon. His staff naturally grumbled, so I asked him to keep nearer to laid-down hours. He was angry and contemptuous and told me, in a letter of the greatest grandeur, one much more impressive than mine, that he had no intention of following the West's slavish and unimaginative commitment to clock-watching. His African sense of time and of a life of quality was quite different and, he left me in no doubt, better.

Very widespread was the assumption that nepotism, including bribery, was normal practice. This could express itself in unjust-ified and excessively large gifts, in letters and telephone calls hinting that it would be to your advantage to be aware that so-and-so, about to pay a visit from his government, wished this-or-that, or in near-bullying. Behind that in turn, like a rusty but still firm foundation, was sometimes a disregard for the rights of individuals – everything depended on rank, status, power or access to power, the army, the government, the party, the church. All the time, if there were demurrals about some forms of bad behaviour, the over-riding force of their own cultural values was invoked – to justify this or that sharp practice, privileges for a few, prison for a dissenter, or forced female circumcision.

Some of the above has turned out more sombrely than I had expected. Perhaps what I, in my provincial and academic ignor-ance, was shocked by in international agency life struck more deeply than I had known, and remained there even after five years in which to get used to and understand better why things should have been so. Standing back, I am freshly surprised and very pleased that nevertheless so much good work was done in the place; and that those who rose to the remarkable demands of principle made on international civil servants came not only from the developed and sometimes rather holier-than-thou democrac-ies, but from across the world; that those principles did move some people to detach themselves from the wombs of their cul-tures so that they could try to live up to the professional moral Esperanto of the international civil servant.

2

Only a lazy or determinedly armour-plated individual could have failed to learn a great deal about himself, his weaknesses and strengths – both little understood before, because not put under such pressure from outside. It was as if the personality was stretched tight across a frame so that the strong parts showed their strength as not before and the weaker parts frayed and cracked as not before. I do not mean to imply that, having learned about these things somewhere in the recesses of your personality, you could from then on control the weaker parts and consolidate the stronger. But it is useful to know these things; and bit by bit, if you will, you may slightly improve your practice; probably no more than that. But at least you are not so much taken by surprise or shocked when the weaknesses show again.

Above all, you could learn what questions, what issues, what values preoccupied you when matters reached an extreme, what principles held you so that – as you then for the first time realised – they proved to be more important to you than almost anything else, excepting always your close personal connections. Luckily, it scarcely ever came to the point, for people such as me, where one had to choose between those alternatives, between poverty for your family and sticking to final principle. Members of prosperous democracies are fortunate. We do not see the prison cell, exile or even the firing squad before us, except in nightmares. Many from other countries see these things immediately, as they contemplate any important decision of principle from within the fragile cocoon of the protective status at least formally given to an international civil servant.

So you learned also about the weaknesses of others and, in some, saw enormous courage under pressures and threats. Most lived in a condition of basic insecurity; some illustrated unforgettably the meaning of the phrase 'moral courage'. In particular, you learned that the cost of moral courage to individuals varies enormously, according to social and cultural backgrounds. For some the cost of even a slight stand can be frightening: 'Hold them cheap / May who ne'er hung there.' For others even a large stand on principle can be little more than a tremor, a nuisance, a loss of some money but no face, a hiccup in a career.

If the choice is between staying in Paris on a good salary even by Western standards – a Paris your wife and children now feel more settled in than they do 'at home' – and going back to a pittance in a remote back-water of the Third World, you need considerable courage to stand on principle. It is worse if you are going back to a government which has changed since you left and may expose you to poverty or prison or worse. Since, in my time, almost all members of the secretariat were on contracts of rarely more than three years, the triennial review was an agony; you would fight to the limit, invoking your ambassador and anyone or anything else within reach, to resist not being renewed, no matter how plain might be the evidence that your time should be up.

My hardest instance concerned a Soviet member of staff. He came a year after I did and at a high level, as a director. He proved to be a deeply self-protective, face-saving incompetent, a feeble *apparatchik*. That was plain to his subordinates within a few weeks and they made me aware of it. But he had to stay until his first contract had expired. Then I told the Director-General he should not be renewed; his division was suffering badly. The Director-General expected trouble from Moscow. The Soviet ambassador, a bright lawyer with whom I got on well, came to see me. The Kremlin wouldn't like it; they'd expect at least two more years. Surely the Kremlin wouldn't want to be represented by such an incompetent (the ambassador did not demur about the incompetence). Finally the D-G 'phoned and said, 'I've given him another year.' I see now he was right, though at the time I wished he hadn't done that. That man was succeeded by a hospitable Georgian. A year after he had arrived he came into my office, smiling broadly: 'Have you ever wondered why you have not been invited to the Soviet Union?' It was not difficult to guess. The man sent home had told the bosses at his research institute that he had been sacked because Hoggart was a senior agent of the British Foreign Office. That is how, a few months later, I did go to Moscow and, very much more enjoyably, to Tbilisi, my Georgian colleague's home-town.

Though not so melodramatically, people from rich and stable countries often fought against 'separation from the service', or from the denial of promotion for which they felt themselves due; especially promotion from top consular status – P4 – to diplomatic status – P5 – and the CD plates.

One officer from the United States had had several renewals of contract – it was rumoured Mrs Nixon was a friend and had influenced the decisions to renew. More likely, a mixture of inertia and the inability of his senior officers to understand the man's specialism (modern art) ruled. But I was told again and again by visiting experts that the officer was out-of-date and generally muddled. The muddle I soon saw, since a paper he wrote for a world conference was such a mess I had to pay an English expert to rewrite it entirely. But he outlasted me at UNESCO.

The out-of-datedness was an occupational hazard. When specialists are appointed to UNESCO's staff they are expected to be at the frontiers of their disciplines. As the years pass at their desks they become increasingly out of touch. A few become expert administrators as they also become more and more generalist, but useful generalists who have the respect of outside experts; they learn how to run a good programme. Others never learn how to manage a programme, refuse to recognise they are losing touch with their specialisms, and cling more and more desperately to their jobs, even though the three-year contract was designed regularly to inject fresh minds and up-to-date knowledge.

The entirely defensive phrase 'my programme' rings through UNESCO's halls whenever there is a sign of possible change; 'my programme' is the barque on which 'I' float on a sea smooth and comfortable most of the time but always likely to become hostile and tip me out. When the sea becomes very rough, when major changes are threatened, the boats large and small lock together into a flotilla which can ward off all but the most determined executive board or Director-General; so it always is with big institutions; self-preservation of the institution rules, even if that means destructive reinterpretation of its purposes.

Much of all that seems, and is, sad. Professional insecurity is almost always founded in or breeds personal insecurity, and life at UNESCO encourages that kind of fear to spread like spilt ink. That the institution is not rooted in one national culture but floats in a rootless professional space, makes the disease spread more quickly.

Inevitably, the worst cases stand out in the memory. Once again, one has to put the balance right by recalling that many people, from secretaries to directors, went on doing their jobs reasonably well, or even very well, without recourse to rage or tears. The only occasion on which I recall collective near-hysteria was when Maheu, who proposed to attend a conference organised by our sector in a member state's capital city, said we must provide his secretary for that two weeks. A group of secretaries wept together in the main corridor at the awful prospect. My own French secretary, she who had challenged me about a confidential reference for one of my former students, told them not to be silly and said she could look after both Maheu and me. She did and brilliantly; and in the course of the week told Maheu sharply she couldn't do several things at once for a man who kept changing his mind. So she too was invited to his small leaving party for the respected ones, those who had stood up to him. The old man's sense of the theatrical was creative and catholic.

Did I learn something about myself during those five years? If to 'learn' suggests the ability to profit from new knowledge then it suggests too much, and 'saw' would be better. 'Saw' much, but did not always learn how to absorb what was seen. There were pitfalls all over the road, some of them self-made, both with members of my staff and with diplomats. Early on, I wrote a comical piece about 'UNESCO-speak' but found that some colleagues reacted miserably, as though I had torn holes in their professional linguistic carapaces. Again, without identifying individuals, I tried to show how one bad practice led to more and more. But some people could not change their methods; they were designed specifically to prevent them from toppling into the outer world again.

The delegate from an African state, a French-trained professor of sociology, became a friendly acquaintance. Then one day, pushed by his francophone group, he tried to exploit that friendship by asking for quite unacceptable advantages to be given them at that afternoon's meeting of the general conference. I told him the claims could not be met and advised him not to raise the matter, since he would fail and have to fail and that would mean an unnecessary loss of face for him and his group.

He stood up in the meeting and made demands even more outrageous than he had made to me; and half-hinted I had not resisted them when visited that morning in my office. When my turn came to speak I began by saying, cheerfully, that the ambassador really was 'being a bit naughty' because . . . etc. He looked wounded and then he and his group walked out, went to the protocol officer and complained that I had treated them – the ambassadors of sovereign states – like children. It suddenly became clear that to them, whose command of English was more bookish than idiomatic, the word 'naughty' was used only to children who were misbehaving. I had applied a word to them which, they assumed, I would never use if I were replying to, say, another Englishman. But of course I would have done so; the phrase was part of idiomatic speech in England at that time; or at any rate of mine. But it was a gaffe.

There was a similar early clash with the Byelo-Russian ambassador. He wanted us to withdraw a new book on his country's poetry because the Oxford editor referred in her preface to a famous literary critic in their country who had, the ambassador said, been 'a collaborator in the Great Patriotic War' and so been expunged from the record. He threatened to expose my intransigence to the D-G and I, still fresh from what now began to seem the quixotic air of the English provinces, told him to try the Queen as well if he liked. After a moment of complete incomprehension, he broke into a smile. 'Ah; it is the famous British sense of humour.' He was friendly thereafter and even introduced me to one of his Deputy Foreign Ministers as the typically humorous Englishman.

I fared less well with the Chinese ambassador. When mainland China finally joined UNESCO, in the early Seventies, their officers combed all our publications for references unpalatable to themselves. The sleeve of one of our splendid recordings of types of music which were in danger of being lost referred to Tibet as 'a country with a long tradition in temple music'. He took 'country' to mean 'a sovereign state', accused us of questioning China's historic right to incorporate Tibet, and demanded the record be withdrawn. No explanations – which had to be largely semantic, such as, 'We might say Wales has a long musical tradition, but that does not imply it is a sovereign state' – satisfied him; he shrieked higher and higher for a few minutes and left, threatening to report me to the protocol office. The sophisticated Mexican in charge there soothed him by saying that, though a reasonable fellow, I was an English provincial academic and did not perhaps understand all the niceties of diplomatic life. He promised the offending reference would be removed in the next edition of the record. 'We've never sold out a first edition of any of them,' I said. 'I know,' he replied, 'but now you see why I'm a diplomat and you're not.'

Altogether more pleasant in the end was the encounter with a new ambassador for Poland. It was Poland's habit, at the several-days-long session of the committee on culture during the biennial general conference, to put down a resolution on the rights of cultural minorities. Everyone knew this was a disguised criticism of the Soviet Union, the Soviet delegates withdrew to a coffee bar whilst it was being debated, and it always went through. On this occasion the new Polish ambassador was in one of the coffee bars too, and missed his cue; so the resolution was not put. This was late on the final day of the culture committee's meetings.

The ambassador came up as we were gathering our papers and began to bully. He was not going to be popular in Warsaw. I referred him to the just-departing chairman of the culture committee but, their work now being done, he said he had no further powers. The ambassador became more hectoring. I stood with him until the hectoring stopped and then saw he was on the verge of sobbing. I made a quite irregular proposal. Sessions officially began on time but, because delegates straggled in, work always began half an hour late. I persuaded the chairman of the committee which followed that on culture – luckily, it was on the social sciences – to start work on time at his first meeting the following morning, and allow the Pole to put his resolution then. After all, the subject was as much sociological as cultural. The hall was nearly empty, those few who noticed smiled, and the resolution was passed before many participants had arrived. It was to the Polish ambassador's credit that he felt a handshake was enough acknowledgment and a case of vodka not needed.

In spite of clumsinesses and steppings out of line, a fair number of member states seemed to think things were not going too badly on my side. Some time in the autumn of 1971, I was informally asked by a representative of the 'Geneva group' – the Western powers plus a few others – if I might be willing to be groomed to run for Director-General on Maheu's departure in a few years' time. I suppose they knew it was the longest of long shots. It was time for a non-European, probably an African or Asian; they must have known that better than I. Nor did I want to end my working days as an international civil servant, fascinating though that was in many ways; I wanted to go back to England and academic life.

Even more, I wanted to be able to speak in my own voice once again, in lecturing and writing or just chattering. With few exceptions – such as giving the Reith Lectures, making a film in the *Omnibus* series for the BBC, and speaking at Allen Lane's memorial service – I had forgone external activities and expressions of opinion and, though speaking publicly about UNESCO's affairs could be interesting, the rules were inhibiting. I felt unable to push the boat out, to provoke, be a bit loose, to fly kites; this was intellectual life in a vacuum bottle. I had learned to recognise the value, and later the rarity in most member states, of being able to speak freely, not as the bosses wanted or diplomacy required.

This prompted me to think again about the nature of moral courage. I realised then that what sometimes seemed moral courage in myself, in what I said and wrote, could be a form of personal pride. Below that level, when the element of self-regard had been so far as possible discounted, there came into play a deep obstinate, stubbornness. I tried not to let that be the prime impulse, but most of the time it had to do for a purer form of moral courage. It came out most when I was defending not myself but people below and around me who were trying to do their jobs properly but being hounded by member states' delegates, usually from their own countries, or by the D-G. Maheu spotted it and sent me a letter in the marvellously convoluted Johnsonian/French style of English he adopted towards anglophones when waving a big stick: 'I must warn you against the tendency to set yourself up as the corrector of truth in systematic defence of the secretariat.' From his point of view it was a fair rebuke; other people, no matter how much they themselves may be self-deceiving, are often the best judges of self-deceit in us. We edit, we distort; we can't lift ourselves by our own psychological bootstraps. But to try to do so is a fair exercise.

So some lessons were taken from those years, even if not always properly learned. Some of them will be plain from what I have already written. They vary from the fairly precise and particular to the enormously wide. When I try to take stock, the items which come to mind always cover that sort of span, as though the mind now wants to hold both the very small and the very large in play at once and all the time.

For instance, it is not easy to forget the power and fragility of the oral cultures which still predominate in several parts of the world. They put the Gutenberg revolution in a fresh context, and show up much current talk about 'the post-Gutenberg revolution in perspective' – being brought about, it is said, by the new communications technologies – as the short-term response it is.

A sense of the great number and great anger of minorities remains too: in particular, their anger and contempt for whatever larger nationalism they feel themselves trapped within. The Polish resolution at each general conference was one example of that. The Yugoslav minorities were just as active and now, in the Nineties, there and in other parts of Eastern Europe, the resentment has exploded. In former colonies of Africa and Asia the belief that cultural differences ('integrities' is one of the favoured terms, but has become a weasel word) were being harshly wiped out was a prime force making for revolution. One of the most impressive speeches I heard at UNESCO came from a francophone African leader – on the difficulties of defining a culture after seven successive waves of colonisation over the centuries. Too often the political result of that urge has been a range and a rage of new nationalisms no less dominating than those of the Europe they were rejecting.

UNESCO, ordered by its governing bodies to promote 'cultural development', was as always trapped. Are all cultures equal, and if so in what senses? It fell back on that word 'integrity': all cultures were equal since each had its own 'integrity' and 'authenticity', and those must be respected. Within that warm mash, virtually any horrible principle or practice could be submerged.

Ten years after leaving UNESCO, I heard a Basque politician talking about the strength of his feeling that he belonged to Europe – very different from the kind of minority claim which practises the 'ring fence round my culture' style. 'I am', he said, 'a Basque before I am a European. But I am also a European because Europe is made up of many cultures and many languages which are in important ways one, in their history and traditions. What I am *not* is a member of that invented nation, the Spaniards.' A Slovene – this was in 1987 – talked about being part of the tapestry of Europe but not 'a Yugoslav'.

Above all, experience at UNESCO strengthened far more than I had expected the belief in the importance of human rights, and in particular of the right freely to speak and write and publish. That is worth repeating because, though it seems self-evident to most people in our part of the world, it is a scarcely attainable luxury in the majority of nations. That some of the upheavals of late 1989 in Eastern Europe were about more than material deprivation, were about also the importance of free speech to self-respect, is one of the more heartening facts of the century.

To all this the West's best contribution is not technology but the principle of individual rights. To hear tens of thousands of southern Javanese hailing Suharto as 'Papa Presidente, Papa Presidente' in a sustained child-like croon is to realise how far there is to go, and how important it is to help people get there. One of the few activities at UNESCO about which I feel unqualified pleasure was the successful struggle over several months and against several member states to issue a more than usually honest book about the nature of apartheid. Some African states hated its frankness as much as some double-crossing Europeans.

Much of my writing before UNESCO had been about aspects of Englishness, and in some ways that has continued. But neither Mary nor I feel English in the way we used to. To live for years in France, even though partly insulated within a large UN enclosure, is to have your Englishness challenged again and again, and often found unattractive; and sometimes attractive. Much more than that, the international life invites you to open yourself to the enormous, shabby pattern of human need and the range of – usually defeated – aspirations right round the globe; to open yourself also to the different ways in which, in spite of the corruption of so many governments and the recurrent brutality of some individuals and groups, many people show courage and fellow-feeling.

A sheaf of snapshot-memories remains; different ones come to the surface at different times in response to hidden triggers. As I write, two keep recurring, one bizarrely comic, the other depressing.

The first is of a call in the very early Paris days, invoking the 1952 Hague Convention for the protection of cultural property in the event of armed conflict. A high-ranking Muslim telexed from Alexandria to complain that the Israeli occupying soldiers were pillaging the treasures of the St Catherine monastery on Mount Sinai and had burned down part of the monastery itself. Our commissioner under the convention, an elderly Dutch admiral, came back to report that the Israeli troops were protecting the treasures extremely well but confirmed that a wing of the complex had burned down. One night Brother Ignatius, one of the handful of monks in residence, had drunk too much of the cactus-spirit they distilled, gone to bed, started smoking and fallen asleep. Months later, we saw a basket of bones drying in the sun in a small courtyard, before being put in the ossuary. 'Brother Ignatius,' our guide said with a half-smile.

The reappearance of the second particular memory is easy to explain, after the events of late 1989. During the main official cocktail party at a huge international conference on the environment in Bucharest, one of my officers, a Romanian, was very anxious I should have a word with his president. We had met formally on the receiving line, and the queue to talk to him at that later moment was very long, so I said it didn't really matter. The officer persisted so much I began to suspect he was afraid of a rebuke from Ceaușescu's entourage if he failed to bring before the president one of the two senior officials of UNESCO present. I went. When my turn came I said, which was true, that his officials were running a most complex conference very well indeed. He blinked, the lids of his cold pale eyes flickered at me, and he said, in a tone of utter gracelessness, 'They'd better.' That was all.

3

The last months at UNESCO veered between the touching, the hilarious and the sombre. I had been due out in early 1975, after Maheu's departure late the previous autumn. Two or three weeks before he was appointed, the new D-G, who knew I wanted to get back to England, asked me, as the most experienced AD-G, to stay at the least a further six months, until the end of July, to help him settle in; I agreed. From that moment professional things began to go awry.

That final general conference, for me, was marked by the first violent outbreak within UNESCO's halls of the Arab–Israeli dispute. The secretariat had been ordered to prepare a report on Arab accusations about Israeli cultural and educational misrule in the Occupied Territories, and the main burden of investigating the charges fell to my sector. We worked very hard to provide a thorough and fair report into each accusation; multiple visits by experts from untainted countries were dispatched. Their evidence showed that, though Arabs in the Occupied Territories obviously hated being occupied, the specific charges against Israel were virtually all baseless. In several of those areas – for instance, archaeological work – the Israelis had done better than the Arabs. This was in the report but not stressed in the oral presentation to the general conference. Other charges against Israel may have produced different results, but the Arab drafters had had to choose subjects for charges relevant to UNESCO's brief.

The report had to be presented to the general conference by a senior secretariat member and that, I suppose, might have been Maheu himself since the issue was so grave. He left it to me; perhaps, we thought, because he was tired, on his way out, fed up. Later we learned that he was ill and hadn't wished to say so; he seemed still to have a shred of hope that he might be offered another term. On that occasion at least I was, or aimed to be, as diplomatic as I had seen the best of others being. The effort was bound to be useless. In such a setting you shoot the messenger before anyone else. I was violently attacked in the meeting as a stooge of Israel, and the following day had three death-threats, which may be a record for one Englishman in one day. Balance was not quite maintained: an Arab group and then an Israeli group 'phoned during the morning, but in the early evening an even more confused terrorist group, of young Israelis, joined in. From my office window, I saw the CRS move over the Place de Fontenoy to start searching the basements. Nothing untoward happened and I went home. I did not feel particularly brave or defiant, since it was evident that one could do little – except from then on to feel under the car for *plastiques* before each journey – and life went on normally. Since then, I have had two other threats of assassination (early Eighties and 1989), with much the same reaction, and am told it is normal.

The threats meant little, the attitude of the new D-G a lot. He was politically in check. A black African and a Muslim, he owed his election to the support of those groups and the supineness of many other member states. It was extremely difficult for him to be even-handed about the Arab–Israeli dispute, even if he had wished to be.

It was my duty, after the conference debates, to write him a minute of advice on what best to do next. There is no consolation in the fact that, a year later, he step by step had followed that minute. At the time he felt unable to do other than let the Arab fury ride; he put the minute angrily aside with yet another of the kind of remark I had heard before – Hoggart was an agent of the British Foreign Office. Within a few weeks it was clear that all material on Arab and Israeli affairs, which should have been handled by my sector, was being dealt with in the D-G's office; a 'phone call to a friend there confirmed that. I do not remember feeling angry; miffed, perhaps. By then I had learned just enough about diplomatic/political life to know why a D-G often felt hemmed in. Even if one disregarded the nonsense about my sup-posed links with the Foreign Office, the new D-G was right to assume that my memos on the situation would propose actions likely to be no more palatable to the Arab states than the report on the subject which I had had to make to conference. Why should they react less intemperately a few weeks later?

Obviously, my usefulness was coming to an end. I had no job to go back to. Over the years I had had five or six good offers and refused all, chiefly because they would have involved breaking contract with UNESCO. I could have hung on in UNESCO for a few more months. But then whatever force my resignation might have had, as an act of principle, would have been lost. It would undoubtedly have been said that I had waited until I had found a UK billet before running up that flag. Within a week or two, Goldsmiths' College invited me for interview as a possible Warden (Principal). So I sent my resignation letter to the D-G an hour

before I set off for the airport and that interview. It was a polite
note, saying I didn't think I was doing much good there since a
major item in my duties was to be handled elsewhere, and so I
had best go. He replied equally politely and I left three months
before the agreed time. A pity in some ways though not in others,
and not really avoidable.

I spent much of the remaining time trying to push on a project
as close to my heart as any I had worked on in UNESCO. The
Katmandu Valley in Nepal, one of the most beautiful areas on
earth for its harmonious marriage of a striking but well cultivated
landscape and sympathetic urban clusters, was in danger of
destruction by development. Already the first slab-sided international-class hotel had gone up (with very high-level Nepalese
financial involvement, was the rumour). We began gradually to get
together a team of environmentalists, town-planners, architects,
experts on preservation (there were very many temples in wood),
public-health experts (various diseases were endemic) and the like,
so that a comprehensive plan for the area's survival in all its
beauty and as a healthy working community could be drawn up.
I went there, with Mary, to make the first moves. It was important
if at all possible to see the King, but that proved difficult.

At a grand reception in our honour, Mary threw out all their
plans because no woman had been at such a function before.
They brought their wives, all in elaborate long dresses, and left
them sitting in a frozen, unbroken line on the far side of the room.
Mary walked across the empty space and began to talk to them;
once their shyness was over they were obviously tickled, as at a
victory for women.

By contrast, I had a failure. Half-way through the party, I
was told the King's private secretary wanted to talk to me. A
breakthrough! He shook my hand warmly and said he understood
I had been at Leeds University. Did I know Douglas Jefferson?
Yes, he had been my tutor many years ago. And mine, he said,
for my MA. What a splendid man! That ended the contact. And
my contact with Katmandu. But a couple of months after we had
returned to England I had a call from Paris to say the team was
assembled; when did I wish, as its chairman, to leave? It had been
assumed that my interest in the project, in the final stages of my

time, had been inspired by the wish to set up a pleasant post-appointment perk. I said I was otherwise engaged.

So we left, with some people keeping their heads low in case the D-G accused them of an obscure complicity; and others writing letters we are glad to keep. It was early May 1975. I had been appointed to Goldsmiths' and their governing body had agreed I need not begin there until the following January. Meanwhile, a Leverhulme Fellowship at the University of Sussex, produced with apparent ease by Asa Briggs, would allow me to write the first draft of a book about UNESCO. I went up early to see friends at Birmingham and, walking into the Senior Common Room with them after almost five and a half years, met that familiar but always slightly surprising collapsing of time towards one who had been away by others who have stayed. 'Hello,' they said, 'haven't seen you for a while. All right?'

The re-entry into English life could not be easy for either of us; too many personal and cultural adjustments, of tempo and style, had to be made. A few months before we were due to leave, our landlord, the French ambassador to Eire, was recalled and gave the statutory three months' notice that he wished to reclaim his apartment. There was no point in moving all our furniture to another place in Paris, only to have to send it over to England not long after; better to find a small furnished flat in Paris. I had at that time no job to go back to but we had to start looking for a house in England at once. The children were by then all in the south. We drew a rough circle about fifty miles out from London and noted good railway services. Mary went over for a week, found three places well apart from each other, and called me over. By the usual mixture of choice and constraint we finally settled on a house in Farnham, in exurbanite Surrey. Not at all our natural habitat but pleasant in many ways; it has served us well. We were helped above all, in the search and much else, by the children, who rallied as a matter of course. Much basic work on the house was needed, from structural repairs through rewiring to total decorating. By the time all that was done we were almost back into English rhythms, had adjusted to the slowness of the working-pace and the endless talkativeness. 'What with those two habits and the tea-breaks,' a French sociologist said after a visit,

'I wonder when you English get anything done. You are easily the most lazy or the most relaxed nation in Western Europe.' And the most neighbourly, in practical ways, it is always worth saying; at all the levels I know.

After a few weeks I was almost ready to take up the fellowship. But not quite. I had only partly realised how hard it would be to settle again to the solitariness of academic writing. I was afraid of the blank paper and empty office waiting down in Sussex; only one telephone, and that internal and almost entirely silent; no busy office staff at my back, no urgent calls about cultural crises round the globe, no hourly sheaves of correspondence; no stream of visitors, most of them fascinatingly rarefied birds; instead, a condition of professional and intellectual agoraphobia.

I took out my first virgin pack of six-by-four cards and, for a start, put down some of the odd thoughts floating in my head. That neither lasted long nor, as can be one of the gains of such an early process when you are in trim, did it breed other thoughts. There was no flow; nothing 'on stream'. I had spent too long analysing other people's writing (especially so as to squeeze out the vague rhetoric of UNESCO-Franglais), or jotting down headings for others to follow or, where I wrote connected prose myself, doing so with an obligatory impersonality and inhibitedness. There was no link between head and heart, eyes and ears; it was one-dimensional prose.

Learning to read again was easier than learning to write, but still needed time. You may immerse but do not imaginatively submerge yourself in your masses of official reading; you are not offered the chance of getting in touch with another personality in the round. You stay poised above the page, reacting to it operationally, watching. At first, submerging in reading was not only difficult but seemed somehow wrong, as though this was not the relationship you should have with writers, too close and slightly embarrassing. Then it became engrossing again and going back to novels and poetry much more worthwhile and pleasant than the project itself, than trying to write a book about UNESCO.

The dislocation spread wider. In the first university coffee-bar conversations, I was badly out of touch with informal, English, academic talk – allusive, low-key, fragmentary, full of conniving or at least clubbish smiles, sometimes a little malicious; a rubbing against each other, a confidence in taking much for granted.

Academics found my first attempts at joining in too straight, too flat, toneless. I missed cues because by now I didn't know the acronyms or the people being most quoted or criticised. I had to learn who were the new members of the old stage army. But I had my own stage army. As I listened, a pageant of other figures passed across the internal eye: the tough and ever-watchful faces of military presidents in new states and old banana republics; the nervous eyes of cultural ministers in authoritarian societies; the quiet gravity of social rituals in the Sahel; the swish of soft walkers through the violet evenings of Java; the God-forsaken condition of the little Indians on the South American altiplano. I heard once more the voice of that Englishman: 'Go. But things will never be the same again, afterwards.' All in all but without a doubt, it had been a lucky break; perhaps a bit too long, but very well worthwhile.

The establishing of UNESCO, like that of the UN as a whole, is one of those rare instances in which the world of sovereign states has thought and acted better than it is usually inclined. The impulse inevitably faded as the close memories of the last world war faded. National interests again dominated and most member states did not try to keep the UN and its agencies more than barely alive, unless clear material or political gains could be made from them. In short, and it has been said often, no matter how hard and selflessly some members of the secretariat may work, the organisation is only as good as its member states let it be. The attempt at hope in this last paragraph may well be yet another example of singing against the wind.

CHAPTER 7

THE GREAT TRADITION REVISITED: GOLDSMITHS', 1976–84

In the late Seventies Britain seemed, to a returning migrant, like a punch-drunk boxer in a dingy fairground; unions and bosses more than normally at odds with each other, the government tattered and torn – all in all a much less attractive place than we had left at the beginning of the decade.

I said much of this in a television talk for Granada TV in the spring of 1976 – beginning with the by now accepted fact that, to a foreigner or a native who hadn't seen Britain for a long time, the overriding impression was of a country accustomed to being shabby and past caring. Continental Europe was becoming glossier and glossier, Britain more and more dull matt grey, like someone fed on bread, marge and too much tea. That wouldn't have mattered if Britain had had the air of a place confident that it had kept hold of better truths about the nature of the good life than the Continent. It hadn't. It was dog-in-the-manger.

Predictably, one tabloid paper put me on its front page: 'Come off it, Prof.' Another offered a chauffeur-driven car, with a photographer, to tour Central London's loos.

I

In the months after accepting the Goldsmiths' job and taking it up, I was 'very unofficially sounded out' about two vice-chancellorships, and two universities offered professorships. By then I had a new perspective on British university life, especially that of professors. Those last months at Birmingham, with their sixteen-hours-a-week succession of committees were a warning and a portent; I knew I could fall back into that routine. Most of the committees did not need specifically a professor's time and attention; nor were all professors effective members. Any reasonably conscientious member of staff could have shared the work and many now do; but in the Sixties most non-professiorial staff were not charged with that service; the sense of hierarchical duty held firm.

Whilst I was thinking about all this came an offer of what amounted to a research chair; a named professorship on the northeastern seaboard of the United States. No committee work, the lightest of loads (two seminars a week for one of the two semesters) and a salary large enough to have easily allowed regular visits to Britain; or even a permanent home in Britain with one sixteen- or seventeen-week spell in the States each year. Again, to refuse was not difficult, even if I had been willing to break my commitment to Goldsmiths'. During the years in Paris the children had each averaged a visit roughly every six weeks. That was not possible to the States, even on the most generous of salaries; and, grandchildren having started to appear, we wanted no more long separations, least of all long-distance separations.

So it had become plain, even before Goldsmiths' had advertised its vacancy, that it might be sensible to look for a job in charge of a congenial university institution, if possible one with interests near my own – say, one committed to recruiting more than the usual kind of eighteen-year-old undergraduates, or ready to cross traditional boundaries between disciplines, or both. Being in charge of such a place could hardly be heavier administratively than an Assistant Director-Generalship at UNESCO; and, with good support from senior colleagues, the committee work need be no heavier and might be lighter than that of a professor.

There was, it proved, excellent supporting staff. I could decide which committees I really did need to chair, and hand over the others. The average of my committee load was about ten hours a week, much of it taken up with the absorbing business of setting out to alter Goldsmiths' status within the University of London, and about a third on university business down at Senate House.

After the Sussex fellowship months we had moved, in January 1976, to a small terrace house opposite Goldsmiths' side-door, and there passed the working week for eight and a half years. There was hardly any room to entertain but the place was wonderfully convenient; and at weekends we went to Farnham. The children, and then their children, enjoyed being at both houses.

The 'Goldsmiths' Institute' had been set up in 1891 by the Goldsmiths' Company, one of the major and most respected of the mediaeval City Guilds. The company receives income from, most importantly, hallmarking silver and gold objects, and validating the currency of Britain and some other countries. It has long used much of its spare money not only for promoting education in its own crafts but more widely. It still does so, more and more imaginatively. South-east London, where many craftsmen then lived, was a most suitable place for a college, devoted not so much to the company's professional interests as to the higher education of adults in an educationally deprived area. It soon had, among much else, a flourishing school of art and an equally flourishing school for teacher training. It began to prepare students for the external degrees of the University of London; like an Ibadan or Kampala university college, in New Cross and Deptford. Some years later it was handed to the University of London, and there given a status which proved troublesome for many years.

From the beginning, it grew very quickly, run by a succession of exceptionally devoted 'Wardens'; the nomenclature given to senior members of the guild, though Goldsmiths' Wardens were not by that fact members of the company. The title was and is a pleasant reference to the college's origins. That it still causes the holder to receive unsolicited literature offering school equipment for delinquent children, or suggestions that his pupils might like to enter an essay competition on 'Why I would like a Career in the Armed Forces', is a harmless incidental; perhaps such things occasionally come the way of Wardens of Oxford colleges.

The comely John Shaw building has for decades been busy from eight-thirty in the morning to about ten at night every weekday; and on many weekends we ran or hosted one-day or two-day conferences, seminars and suchlike. The hours between 8.30 and 9 in the morning and 6 and 7 in the evening were the busiest; to get along the corridors then you had to squash against the walls of the main building by now a century and a half old (it had been originally the Royal Naval School). I calculated that about seven thousand people – students, academics and other staff – passed through its doors most days in term-time. Its 18–to-21-year-olds came from all over Britain as they do in most universities. It drew several thousand part-timers from a large area around – a few miles west into London until it met the magnetic pull of Birkbeck; more miles south to Croydon and beyond; not so far to the north because the river intervened and was not easy to cross; but then up to more than thirty miles east, into the heart of Kent where many commuter trains and buses ran. Two main Kent-bound roads went past the college's doors.

Congenitally shabby through such intensive use; and because – another anomaly – Goldsmiths' was funded by the Department of Education and Science, not by the better-endowed University Grants Committee. All these characteristics – the manifest value and success of the work being done, the way it broke some of the class barriers in British higher education, the esteem in which it was often held in Britain, abroad and within a wide radius of its buildings, and above all the intense vitality you felt the moment you crossed the threshold in the crowd, saw the tattered linoleum, smelled the cheap but largely unattractive food and heard the gabble – all this made Goldsmiths' a place people either loved or hated at once and then did not change that first impression. If they disliked it they tried to leave soon. If they loved it, if it felt immediately right, they stayed and worked far beyond the call of duty, led by the Wardens and the Registrars.

The Registrar from whom I first learned the mystique of the place, George Wood, was a perfect Goldsmiths' character: not what you'd call a tidy man; like a friendly bear, loving and lovable, happily married but childless, and preoccupied, seven days a week, with Goldsmiths' business. Among much else he made up sometimes for the tightness of our budget. Inevitably, he had 'friends at Elizabeth House', the home of the Department of Education and Science. No department of state likes to let money revert to the Treasury at the end of the financial year, so George would receive cryptic 'phone calls in late February. Could he quickly commit, say, half a million? He never failed. One year we renewed the central heating system in record time. Another year we ordered hundreds of thousands of pounds' worth of books and stacked them ceiling-high in rooms we somehow made available until we could catalogue them. Almost predictably, George Wood died of a heart attack, after attending a reception for the university's extra-mural summer school. His successor, Pip Leedam, was in his mould; and also had a heart attack but survived, to carry on the tradition.

Throughout my time the Deputy Warden, Tony Firth, made up the top trio. On the face of it he had seemed an unlikely applicant for the job; he had been for many years entrenched in University College, Oxford. I never once heard him hark back to Oxford, except to tell a few funny stories. Like the other two of us, he was picked up and absorbed by Goldsmiths'.

Goldsmiths' is like that, a remarkable inspirer of devotion; and that devotion runs right through to the long-serving academics and, perhaps surprisingly, since theirs is often the most repetitive part of the work, the administrative staff at all levels; it is more than a place where they earn their wages. It is part of their London and they are proud of working for it.

Goldsmiths' had to remain open, to be manifestly accessible, not to be like those university institutions which have so little contact with their districts that they could be transplanted without either the neighbourhood or the academic staff noticing. Cardinal Newman saw that characteristic over a century ago: 'A university does great things, but there is one thing it does not do; it does not intellectualise its neighbourhood.'

Goldsmiths' had been established to intellectualise its neighbourhood, to be open. In such a district openness has special dangers. One became used to young lads dashing in at one door and out at the other, picking up a briefcase or a jacket or simply a plate of food from the cafeteria. We always knew the fences' going rate for stolen credit cards on day one and day two; after that, they were valueless. During one long vacation we found a student's pigeon-hole for mail was being used by a local dealer as a 'drop' for drugs sent from America inside large, hollowed-out medical text-books.

The district has had a bad record for crime, petty or serious, from long before the immigrants arrived, from the murder of Christopher Marlowe in a Deptford tavern and before. 'The arse-hole of London' was a common nickname, though it would have been easy to find other places that title fitted at least as well. I rarely went into the pubs but even so soon learned which ones to avoid, especially in the late evenings: this one was a haunt of boxers and their gambling and not friendly to strangers; nor was this other, the headquarters of one of the 'heavy mobs'; or this, an IRA contact point. Down by the river one or two had become gentrified, so you didn't wish to go there either, or pay their prices.

But it was good, especially in the early evenings of summer, to walk through the streets of Deptford, looking at the remaining eighteenth-century merchants' houses and noticing how many of the small, late-nineteenth-century, terrace houses had been taken in and done for, whose owners meant to smarten the district.

Obviously, it was dangerous for unaccompanied girls to be out in the dark; we had one girl murdered down in Deptford, in a condemned block of flats. Muggings of old and young were frequent, especially at the bus stop just outside college, and so were burglaries (we had two at our house). Yet Goldsmiths' still kept itself accessible and felt it would have been against its nature to do otherwise. Insalubrious though the area was, some of us who could have afforded to move did not seriously think of doing so. To stay there was very convenient, of course; more important, we felt it right – almost like nonconformist ministers or C. of E. vicars and curates – to live over the shop. The college belonged to its district, was making offerings to its district and assertions about the elements of the good life – music, literature, art, history, philosophy – which it wanted to give its neighbours, which it believed they had the right of access to, and which they had over decades responded to.

In New Cross and Deptford and points around there were a great many black immigrants – 40 per cent was the estimated figure – many of them young men out of work and haunting the pin-table saloons all day. Most begged money from their mothers, many of them cleaners at Goldsmiths'. One of the cleaners, who looked after the administrative offices so that I knew her quite well, was fighting particularly hard to make sure her children climbed out of the district; she already had a daughter in secretarial work. She was usually going off duty at about half past eight in the morning, just as I was likely to be coming into the office from the grotty local swimming baths. One day she told me she had begun to write her autobiography and had already almost finished the account of her first fifteen years in a large family in a Jamaican village. She was a perceptive and comical writer. When I left she had enrolled in one of our evening classes for adults, so as to find out whether the typescript, prepared by her daughter, could be got into publishable shape. She was in New Cross but not of it. She refused to accept the valuation of herself and her family which the dreary surroundings offered her.

On those mornings I met another attractive character, the baths attendant who seemed to be known only as 'Perry'. Short, stocky, bald-headed, he looked like a retired bruiser but was a former swimming champion. His sweetness of character showed in his face and in his voice which was light and musical. A huge scar ran from front to rear in the middle of his scalp and one eye seemed to have a detached retina. In summer, at East Coast resorts' pleasure parks, he had dived from dizzying heights into shallow water. One day they forgot to run enough water and that career ended. He gathered the cockroaches off the surface of the Bath delicately, with a long broom, telling me all the while about the tasty sandwiches he had invented for his wife and himself, to sustain them if their journey from Gatwick to the Balearics was delayed. If the 'plane was on time, he gave the sandwiches to someone who was delayed. One day he asked if I had ever looked up and noticed the beauty of the Victorian wrought ironwork.

In a way which these universities on large, landscaped campuses could not often know, Goldsmiths' setting could remind staff and students every time they came up from the station to college or stood in the litter-strewn road waiting for a bus, that to be able to have full-time higher education was a huge privilege and one denied to most people. We had some 18–21-year-olds who could ignore everything around them not part of their college group-life; we even had a few rugger hearties who broke windows and furniture and puked out of the windows of their halls of residence. But if I had to choose one kind of student – whether full-time or part-time – to suggest Goldsmiths' peculiar strengths it would be a girl of about thirty who had struggled out of a succession of dead-end jobs, been given a Local Education Authority grant for full-time study, and enrolled for a degree in English. After a seminar in my room during her first term I asked how she was coping. She lived on the other side of London and was finding the travel difficult; and she had had to learn the routines of study. 'But,' she added, 'it's wonderful. I can't get over the fact that I'm being *paid* to read good books all day.'

Small wonder that the college's general atmosphere and its attitudes towards its students were good-hearted, indeed often soft-hearted. Many had had to fight to get there; even the 18-year-olds who had come along on the annual examination-train, clutching their grants, had to learn to live in one of the dirtiest parts of a shabby and expensive capital city, so the college felt particularly protective towards them. Those who had come to take the one-year postgraduate diploma in education had often come because they had heard of the college's humane ideas about teaching. Our Nicola had done her diploma in primary teaching there five years before we arrived.

As a result of this kindly disposition, little stink-bombs detonated around the place every six months or so. There was the occasion when one department, full of sympathy for a bank robber who protested his innocence of a particular raid – no one is more morally outraged than a villain nobbled for a crime he didn't commit – and was finally released by the Home Office, offered him a place on a course which would have prepared him for social work. Before he took up the course he was caught red-handed – robbing a bank.

There was a student on a course preparing youth workers who, in spite of agonised efforts to help by his tutors each of whom saw such a decision as a personal failure, clearly should leave after the first year. He fought hard and invoked in his defence every possible rule allowed. He did have excellent references from the heads of the institutions in which he had been placed for periods of direct practice. In the end the staff were driven to say what should have been said at the beginning: that the references were forged.

The greatest test of Goldsmiths' good-heartedness and hospitality came about the time I arrived. Colleges of education were being closed all over the country and the Department of Education and Science had to work out plans which would be as fair as possible to their staffs and find the best use for their buildings. Two colleges near Goldsmiths', one owned by the Inner London Education Authority, the other a Church of England foundation, were offered to us. Negotiations with the second were mild, those with the first eyeball to eyeball. I merely sat in on that tough encounter – the first occasion I had seen direct DES–LEA negotiations which involved a substantial amount of money. The ILEA representative, no doubt as he had been instructed, fought hard for the highest possible price for the buildings. All was formal but very courteous – coffee and biscuits at the start – until the DES Under-Secretary decided the time had come to end the discussion. 'Now look here, X,' he said, using the man's surname for the first time, very curtly and as if slapping a glove at his face, 'That cock won't fight. You have our offer and it's final.' 'X' accepted. I had never before heard that 'cock' image used in the course of a discussion, during a verbal cock-fight, a tough argument. How long is it since cock-fighting was outlawed in Britain? How long will some people still find it an available metaphor? It has a brusqueness, a brutality as of a bit of a m'lord brushing off an attempt to trick him, which the ILEA official clearly found not to his taste – this in the DES, in the late Seventies.

We were handed both sets of buildings, one fairly recently built in deepest Deptford, the other a handsome Edwardian pile in Camberwell. We were given the student numbers released by the closure of the two colleges, but not for the training of teachers. That suited us well; our university degree candidates in a number of subjects greatly increased.

There remained the matter of the staffs. As a result of finely humane planning by my predecessor, all academic staff, including those already at Goldsmiths', were assessed by a committee with an outside chairman and expert external advisers. I am still surprised and glad that we were able to solve the problem with so little hurt. Some – most of them happily – took early retirement, some found work in other colleges of education, some could be placed in Goldsmiths', in departments other than those preparing for University of London degrees, some were already equipped to teach for those degrees, and the remaining few set out to bring themselves to that level. It was a small triumph by all sides; I suppose other places did much the same.

ILEA had its money for its buildings. So had the Church of England foundation; they decided to set up a trust which would use the interest for relevant good works, and asked me to serve on it. A slight enough commitment but well worthwhile. We sat, quarter after quarter, considering worthy applications. After a year or a little more I had a letter from Leslie Paul, he who had written the first draft of the Albemarle Report with me twenty years before. We had kept in touch. He was now old and retired, had a minute pension, was diabetic and lonely. His housekeeper of many years, a retired headmistress, had died: he needed support.

The trust was delighted to help. Here was one who had done the church good service – in writing a report on the pay and conditions of the clergy – who had a Lambeth (Church of England) MA and had fallen on hard times. A string was pulled which brought him the trust-subsidised post of Creative Writer in Residence at a large and successful Church of England college of education; the trust bought his library, gave him the proceeds but let him keep the books until he died, after which they were to go to Goldsmiths'. He could now not only manage but feel wanted. He loved being a Writer in Residence, could regularly discuss the poetry he had been writing for some years, and could afford a comfortable small flat; he bloomed for his last year or two. I saw him in the flat a few months before he died; the tetchiness at not being appreciated which had developed in recent years had virtually gone. Few trusts can have acted so quickly and to such good effect.

Goldsmiths' hospitality, often as casual as that of a large household where one extra mouth never makes much difference, was suspected by some and admired by others. When I arrived the college was providing lodging and services – rather on what could be called a self-catering basis – to what also might be called the international mother-centre for the Laban School of Movement and Dance. Another curious tie from the past: I had met Laban in Middlesbrough in 1947, when he was still having to proselytise all round Britain. By 1976 he was dead but his method was being used around the world.

Soon another candidate appeared. One evening in early summer I had a 'phone-call from John Vaizey. He had just finished a report for the Gulbenkian Foundation on the condition of orchestral training in Britain. The report was timely since not only was training of that kind patchy but the BBC had decided to close its training orchestra in Bristol. Vaizey was going to recommend that a post-graduate training orchestra be established; he already had promises of funds totalling £500,000 over the first five years, from the BBC, the Musicians' Union, IBA and others. For various reasons he thought the centre might best be established at Gold-smiths' – which did have an exceptionally good music department – rather than at one of the more obvious establishments. Would we accept, if he managed to make his recommendation succeed with his committee and the likely sponsors?

A small story but worth telling. When you are in charge of a large institution the weight of day-to-day business and constant accountability work heavily against chance-taking. There is always much else waiting to be decided in your statutory work; risks which may be costly; people watching and ready to charge you and your institution with fiscal carelessness, band-wagoning and anything else they can pin on. On the other hand it's silly, if someone comes along with a very good idea and needs an early answer, not to do your best to push it as soon and as far as you can.

I had been lucky enough to be given this lesson at UNESCO, that institution hedged in with more restrictions on financial movement than even the most bureaucratic national civil service. There, one morning, Peter Brook had telephoned from his Paris base in the unfashionable part of the Left Bank. He was almost ready to set off with his troupe on their now celebrated and fruitful tour across the Sahel. For some reason I now forget – perhaps someone had let him down – he was about $10,000 short and the deal had to be completed that day. I knew I could just about release that amount if two 'phone-calls proved successful, one to a member state, the other to the Deputy Director-General (the D-G being away on a mission). Both calls succeeded. The American DD-G said mildly, 'We have to be willing to take chances, whatever the regulatory jungle, and I'm taking a chance; on your judgment.' The money was released within two hours.

The decision on the music proposal was similar. That what became known as the National Centre for Orchestral Studies should be based at Goldsmiths' was decided within a couple of days, after the Deputy Warden and I had talked and made two 'phone-calls, the first to the chairman of our governing body. It worked well in spite of two obstacles. A very few people in the main music colleges, naturally put out that the centre had not been offered to them, whispered that the best new executants would not go there. They did, and the campaign died away.

More serious was the increasing squeeze on local education authorities' spending. Since almost all our entrants had done their full executants' training courses, they were not eligible for further mandatory grants and had to apply for discretionary awards. By the late Seventies most education authorities were forced to reduce discretionary awards so as to fulfil their mandatory duties. The director of NCOS, Nick Tschaikov, and I wrote dozens of letters year after year pointing out the value of this, the only post-graduate orchestral training centre in Britain. Some of those who saw the point squeezed one or two grants a year out of their budgets. One or two didn't answer letters. The Scottish Office was best of all; it gave us six grants a year and let us choose the holders without referring back to them.

Nick Tschaikov's brightest idea, among many, was to decide not to have a full-time resident conductor. Instead, we would have a father figure, a regular guest conductor, distinguished and hence very busy, but also prepared to give some regular times each term to NCOS. For the rest, Tschaikov exploited the fact that most well known conductors pass through London. He knew almost all of them and saw to it that a succession of internationally known conductors and executants came each year to prepare NCOS for a concert under their batons. The most exotic was Herr or Monsieur Schwalbe (he was Alsatian), first violin in the Berlin Philharmonic. Plump, elegant, he carried a Strad wherever he went. At the end of our first meeting he kissed me and declared: 'My friend, you 'ave 'eart.'

Goldsmiths' governing body, the Delegacy, was even odder than such bodies usually are. Because of the college's peculiar status – it was integrally a part of London University, but did not have its own charter as 'a school', and so had limited freedom – its governing body had to be a committee of senate. Delegacy was too big, too disparate and met too infrequently to be able to cohere; so most power lay with the chairman (also selected by Senate House and usually well chosen) and the Warden. Not that either of them wanted so much influence; they had to exercise it so as to get the business done.

There were some excellent lay members who wished the college very well and gave it all the time and thought it asked. There were local education authority and borough nominees, some helpful and useful, some ignorant and opinionated: 'Chair, I move this item lie on the table'; 'Chair, I move we move to other business'; 'Chair, I move this item is *ultra vires*'; 'Chair, I move we move to the vote'. It was like a ballet in a second-hand linguistic furniture store where all the chairs came to life. Whether of the left or right, some of the councillors had a permanent love-affair with the more esoteric and rebarbative of committee jargon.

There were elected staff members, most of them valuable. There were student union members, but several of them attended only when they were 'mandated' to speak on some issue directly concerning specific and usually parochial union interests: refectory prices, changes in grants, hall of residence rules on damages for drunkenness.

There were nominees of senate, predominantly from other colleges of the university. They usually arrived knowing little of Goldsmiths' but thinking it was a sort of foster-child which Senate House in a fit of charity had taken under its wing in more relaxed days. To their credit, almost all of them came to realise that the college was academically equal to most full schools and in some respects more interesting; they became strong supporters in the councils of the university. Those and the enthusiastic lay members and a few of the others gave the Delegacy, all in all, a good central core.

That most student union presidents had little stature was a disappointment, even though not a surprise. In my student days, union presidents were social bigwigs; this was exemplified by the custom which required the president, in black tie and tails, to lead the Vice-Chancellor's wife on to the floor for the opening dance at the union's annual and expensive ball (to which most of us would not have dreamt of going, even if we could have afforded to).

When I had left British university life at the turn into the

Seventies, student officers were still political heroes, their views on nuclear disarmament jostling with those on university government and support for sexual liberation.

Few student officers of the late Seventies had either of those foundations for assurance, neither the socialite nor the political. Nor was the atmosphere easily ignitable. They were uncertain and constantly on the look-out for causes with which to foment what were sure to prove to be small demonstrations. They picked up the predictable bag of current causes – they were by turns Green, Feminist, Anti-Racist, Gay. But they didn't do enough homework on these issues, so their attachment to them had the air of expediency. Or they picked up an internal college issue and inflated it.

On one occasion they presented a 'demand' that we provide all-night lighting on the public road, for three or four hundred yards to the back gate of the college. A girl had been chased by a prowler. She had been seen on to the train by her boy-friend at Charing Cross, near midnight, for the fifteen-minute journey in a dangerous because corridorless carriage to New Cross, and the almost half-a-mile walk from the station. The suggestion that her boy-friend might have seen her to college, given the risks late at night in our area, was dismissed as male chauvinism.

Most officers of the teaching staff union were in a somewhat similar dilemma. They belonged to the Association of Teachers in Further Education and that was, understandably, more like an industrial trade union than the Association of University Teachers. It bargained much more than it discussed academic matters. Here again, Goldsmiths' members were afflicted with uncertainty because of the college's uncertain position within the university. Staff union officers tended, on issues in which parochial interests and matters of academic principle were mixed, to go for the parochial position. This may be true sometimes in some full universities; in a mixed body such as Goldsmiths', at the time part proper university institution, part a place which did not feel itself of proper university status, the union stood almost always for the second end.

Early in my days there, a temporary member of staff, noting an omission in his contract of service, argued that because of the error he had the right to a permanent post. His college union branch and its national office supported the outrageous claim. In the end, shamefully, the union said the man would settle for £200; it was as though a would-be bank-robber had settled for a packet of crisps.

I gradually became wary of my own tendency to over-react when principle was sacrificed to short-term and short-sighted interests. I was angry by nature at that kind of behaviour; I was angry because it demeaned the idea of a university; I was angry because in other countries I had seen real struggles of principle within the universities, and seen the bravery of a few who fought for freedom of enquiry and publication – and often paid heavily for their stand.

I tried to be more relaxed on such issues and to some extent, though not entirely, managed that. One side of me would have preferred to be like those wise old, grand old, academic-administrative owls who smile and roll with the blows and then settle the business, probably over a sherry; or don't settle, but don't make a public statement of principle.

I was furious when, after a house fire at a party on the main road nearby in which several young blacks died, some members of staff and students – the day after – placarded the college with Socialist Worker demands for campaign contributions based on the assertions, even now unproved and quite unlikely, that the fire had been started by racists and that the police were dragging their heels, being racists all. We launched a college fund, on straight humanitarian grounds.

When the college's more aggressive feminists stuck powerfully adhesive labels on a sequence of fine drawings of a woman's large and beautiful backside, on show in the senior common room – both the woman and her husband, the artist, were proud of the drawings – I weighed in with a piece in the College Bulletin.

It will be plain that the head of Goldsmiths' had a closer engagement with the people living nearby and with Goldsmiths' members of all kinds than is usual in large university institutions. You could range in a day from trying to think big thoughts about the future of higher education nationally to meeting a local deputation which was sure that, since we had such a large building and were the local college, we should find room for a crèche or an old people's club or a multi-ethnic food and dance festival. It was surprising that so many odd deals were made and initiatives kept going, until the DES accountants caught up. That style had been Goldsmiths' for decades; each Warden was expected to be not only a bit of an academic statesman but also a skilled New Cross counsellor or barrow-boy.

The atmosphere, the feel, of Goldsmiths' was decent and gentle above all. Goodwill breathed from the bricks of the building; it combined with excessive modesty, bred from a feeling that the inhabitants, out on a London limb, were slightly looked down upon by those university institutions to the west. Once they decided that you, their Warden (they very much liked the title), were fighting that corner for them their goodwill surged.

An incident towards the end of my time there threw into relief the best side as well as the weaker. The department of mass communications was promising but in a mess. The head of department left, so there was a chance to make a new start and a move forward. The field of applicants from outside was very good and we made a splendid appointment. But one or two of the staff had had their own internal favourite and set out, persuading a few students to join them, to make the new man's life and mine difficult. It was a nasty operation, and involved some staff giving false information to the press, and students spraying obscenities on the department's walls.

Then the great majority of staff showed they rejected the whole operation. Even more, both the staff and student unions rose to the height of this issue of academic principles, in support of the new man and me. The business stopped. Within a few months the new head of department had shown his considerable qualities and the whole department was behind him. For me, it was a good final curtain.

Goldsmiths' weaknesses grew directly from its goodwill. It hated to close its doors to anyone; it agonised even more than is usual about possible examination failures; it rallied to any member in difficulties; it often made judgments more with the heart than the head, bent over backward to be fair to even the most obstreperous. It was a sort of family, and most visitors felt this the moment they stepped over the threshold.

2

Just after the turn of the century, the Goldsmiths' Company had decided it was not really its business to run a sort of university college. In 1904, they offered the whole outfit to the University of London, with the hope that it would eventually become the University College of South-East London. The university accepted Goldsmiths' in what subsequently looked like a fit of absence of mind and promptly put it, like a pot white elephant, in a mental and institutional attic.

What really to do with it? It had some professional and academic departments of university standard. But didn't all that teacher training suggest it was really a teacher training college? And it had a school of art. Art history or aesthetics might be university subjects, but this place actually trained artists and this was not a recognised field of study in London or in most universities. The word 'recognised' runs through University of London literature like a mantra – 'recognised' teachers, 'recognised' subjects and the like; all sacred incantations.

Then there was Goldsmiths' work in the community around. How did one judge that? Few seemed to know that that work was a major example of the long-standing Great Tradition in extra-mural education by the universities (work which had first drawn some of us to its service immediately after the last war). What a mongrel! But there it was now, inside the house and obviously full of life.

They decided to incorporate it into the university's central structure; it would have no legal independence. Academically, they did not see their way to making it a 'school'. They made it an Institution having Recognised Teachers of the University of London. For decades thereafter, there were a number of those. But when the colleges of advanced technology left, for university status or CNAA accreditation, Goldsmiths' became, particularly after 1972, more than ever an anomaly.

The University of London is, or was still when I arrived, a massive and historically fortuitous growth, a great academic wen within the great metropolitan wen, a casual and accidental hotch-potch.

Senate House in Bloomsbury brooded over about fifty different institutions, from colleges as big as many independent universities and with international reputations in several main areas, to places with fewer than two thousand students and some departments so small they had no more than four or five staff members. The heads of a good number of the schools, large and small, were cushily housed and serviced; some almost to the level set by Scottish vice-chancellors. In an outer ring were important post-graduate schools and a few assorted sports such as Heythrop College and the British Institute in Paris. It had all grown, all happened, without much planning. Each part sheltered under the great Senate House wings or shadow, the larger places more and more restively; each part had a large sense of its historic consequence, its ikons, its household gods, its 'plate', its traditions, its style.

In an ordered world growth would not have happened in that way. The university became big enough to house some of the finest departments of any university in the world, and some of little account. It trained many who became its own best scholars and their loyalty to the institution was often unshakeable; they were not listening for a call to Oxbridge. What post could there be more exalted than their present one? Some of the most loyal gave their works for publication to the university's Athlone Press, which therefore over the years built up an unusually good backlist; but it was not by the late Seventies a particularly effective house and was precipitately sold off soon after.

The impeccable English nose for consonance between class, educational opportunity and civic geography had ensured that from the beginning the university's schools and institutes would be overwhelmingly canted from Bloomsbury towards the west, with a branch line up to the intellectual north, Hampstead. From Russell Square up to tiny Westfield, from Regent's Park out to Royal Holloway in Egham, round Gower Street, the Strand, Aldwych, out to Kensington and so on. One exception, to the east and north of the river, was Queen Mary College which had been formerly the People's College in the Mile End Road. But it was now a 'full school' and, unlike Goldsmiths', had forgotten its origins in education for workers and part-time students. It thought of itself, with some justice, as one of the more powerful scientific and technological colleges.

So, before the Sixties expansion, you looked westward past Royal Holloway, itself very conscious of being out on a limb, and found no university institution until Reading, with its exurbanite feel. South, nothing until, well to the south-west, Southampton; north, after Westfield, nothing for ninety miles until Leicester and then the small Midlands group; north-east, nothing until Hull. South of the river and east right through to the Channel, nothing after Goldsmiths', nine miles east of Senate House.

There was among academic staff much loyalty to particular colleges, there was loyalty to particular departments across the university, there was intense loyalty to its major self-governing academic parts – preeminently to the Academic Council, to which some people gave unstinting service year after year. When, in the late Seventies, the Vice-Chancellorship became a full-time executive post not a one-year honorific, there were always people willing to give up their scholarly work so as to take on one of the hardest jobs in the British higher education system; in an exceptionally dreary office in an exceptionally graceless building, where even the refectory food still reminds you of *1984*. But there is no point in labouring yet again the architectural damage the federal University of London has done to Bloomsbury over decades; it is a lesson in the shortcomings of one kind of federalism: that in major imaginative decisions few are truly caught up, or qualified, or both.

No doubt these factors – size, spread and diversity – explain why at a level below the legal, the formal and the representational, the University of London does not cohere humanly. Partly this is because hardly anybody can live near the shop; the centre and west of London are too expensive. Some older and some better-off academics can manage Hampstead; some have settled for the slighter but still comfortable charms of Muswell Hill, Putney, Clapham; but the more typical University of London lecturer may be seen each day, battered briefcase bulging, scurrying at about five p. m. for Liverpool Street, King's Cross, Euston, St Pancras, Waterloo; for Essex, Herts., Middlesex, inner and outer Surrey.

It needed the Thatcher government to convince the university that it should 'rationalise' itself, that those small departments –

often with inadequate plant – on those expensive pieces of land could no longer be afforded. So, slowly and painfully, with anguished cries about the death of great traditions, marriages were arranged. Bedford went to Royal Holloway's site, and a joint college was created. There were other such marriages so that by now, though the university cannot be called, in the current jargon, lean, it does look, structurally, less like a doodle with Lego.

For all its great academic distinction, London has long suffered from the main ill of all over-large, over-centralised, over-bureaucratic and over-committee'd institutions, and especially of academic versions of such elephants; it is inherently resistant to change. When Chelsea College was incorporated in the late Seventies it brought with it an interesting post-graduate diploma course in contemporary cultural studies, much influenced by Birmingham. That had now to go before a sub-committee of Academic Council. The sub-committee paid a 'visitation' – another favoured term of art in higher education's procedures – and the Principal of Chelsea asked me to join him and his colleagues in making the case for this subject not yet recognised in London. We did our best and it wasn't a bad presentation; but the application was rejected. The course is small, the report said, poorly resourced, and there is not enough back-up from related departments. Maybe; but all of that could have been changed in a short time, especially given Chelsea's new status. I was more impressed by the insistent question from one member of the visiting body: How can new graduates, usually graduates in a single discipline, go on to truly post-graduate work in more than one discipline? As long as such attitudes prevailed there could be no post-graduate work in London which crossed disciplines, except by students who had graduated several times over, in different subjects.

There are too many gears and they grind too slowly, especially when they attend to bodies or people who seem slightly outside the federal pale. Before coming to London I had never met the concept of 'a Recognised Teacher of the University'. Members of academic staff of full schools, after the usual two years of probation, are 'recognised teachers' by virtue of their office. In slightly different places such as Goldsmiths', no matter how much the institution is incorporated, or how long it has been preparing students for degrees of the university and with what success, the

academic staff have after a due period to apply to be registered
as 'recognised teachers', and a committee considers each dossier
of application. From one angle this may be a proper device to
protect London's standards; from another it is an arthritic mech-
anism which should in respect of any place with a record such as
Goldsmiths' have long ago been done away with. Within a few
months I grew impatient with checking on such applications and,
like a Mother Superior to the Cardinal, certifying the scholarly
virtue and health of each applicant. I decided to make the issue
prominent by applying to become a recognised teacher myself;
the petit Péguy of London University's world.

The results were elaborate comedy, the most enjoyable foray
of all. A very senior administrator nobbled me on the stairs of
Senate House one day and said my application had 'put them in
some embarrassment'. Very sorry, but why? 'Well – heads of
schools do not usually ask to become recognised teachers' (the
first time I had been called a head of school). Why not? 'Because
they don't teach.' But I do, several times a week; for the modern
literature paper. Do other heads of colleges do that? 'Perhaps
not.' Well, I dislike the recognised teacher system as it is applied
to Goldsmiths' but so long as it exists would like to go through
the same hoops as my colleagues. 'I see, but still it is rather
embarrassing and I'd be glad if you would accommodate us by
withdrawing the application.' I didn't want to be awkward and
was pondering whether to agree when he went on, as one of
Austin Reed's senior staff might offer a nice dinner jacket to
someone who'd come in for a pair of flannels, 'Why don't you
apply for a higher doctorate, a D.Litt? With your publications
you'd surely get one.' 'Real', as distinct from honorary, D.Litts
are awarded after scrutiny of many years of academic productivity
at a suitably high level. I didn't quite see the connection, but
agreed to drop the recognised teacher application.

I had not thought of applying for a D.Litt at any time and any
place. Back in college I looked casually at the University of
London regulations for applicants for such a degree. Catch 22.
You had to be either a graduate of London or – one of its
recognised teachers. I expect the very senior administrator had
simply forgotten. Spurred yet again, I looked at the regulations
at my own *alma mater*, Leeds. I qualified to apply, so bundled up

my publications, and a year later was told the degree would be awarded. We named it after the very senior administrator.

The overwhelmingly most important of the inhibiting procedures in Goldsmiths' relations with the University of London was the college's status; after three-quarters of a century still only an institution with recognised teachers, with few rights and privileges; an external driving school but with instructors who had been approved by Senate House. Whatever the rights and wrongs of this as it concerned other IRTs, it was outrageously irrelevant to Goldsmiths', to its position *within* the university and to the length and quality of its academic record. Most members of the academic board did not understand the situation and the few who did believed they had more important matters to concern themselves with. They may have had; we hadn't anything more important to settle. When I arrived in January 1976, the college was still suffering deeply from the impact of the Murray Report of 1972 on the university – a grey, unimaginative document. It had recommended firmly against school status for Goldsmiths'. The college felt even more uncared-for by the institution which owned it, and didn't see exactly where it should aim to go. Unless we simply gave in, there was much ground to be made up, starting at once.

It was the old, old English story all over again: the invisible but steel-clad assumption, or at least the sitting-at-ease with the notion, that there must be classes in everything, higher orders and so lower orders. Birkbeck, a school since 1920 but for part-time students, was often assumed to be less important than the fulltime schools (though the accusation would be denied, even by some within Birkbeck, whose pride would be hurt); Goldsmiths' was even lower in that invisible but rigid ordering. Those angry denials are entirely predictable. As I keep saying, few academics have thought much about the unjust social conditions that decide which students they will receive.

So where should Goldsmiths' aim to go? Its academic record was very good over a number of important traditional subjects, and in some subjects thin on the ground in London University, especially in the arts. It treasured its work for part-time students not only from nearby but from up to thirty miles away, and would not easily give that up so as to become a full school. It was establishing authority in some subjects not yet recognised by London, such as communications studies. It was the only university institution in the whole of south-east London, and the whole wide district valued it not only as a centre for part-time education but specifically as a genuinely university institution in their area. What should it do? Pull out; or stay there and seek to become a school though without losing its special identity?

The decision was not easy. Some people, including some local MPs, thought we should have done with the university and become a polytechnic. The Inner London Education Authority more than once indicated they would welcome us in that form and treat us well; I believe they would have. Easier to put aside was the off-hand remark of a senior DES official, ex-Winchester and Cambridge: 'Oh, whatever Hoggart says, it's the public sector for Goldsmiths',' he threw off casually to a colleague, on a railway journey, with all the arrogance of a man not quite at the top but sure he could convince his minister, who was just then beginning to learn about the question. That got back to us within a couple of days. If anything made us dig our heels in when the going became rough it was that remark; its style as much as its substance.

On the other side was the fact that Goldsmiths' had been an integral though largely ignored part of the university for all those decades; it was time for this clumsy non-regarding, this ineptitude of style, to stop, time for the unacknowledged child to be acknowledged. Its academic staff had long laboured at the university's undergraduate and post-graduate courses. They wanted to be confirmed in that role, not cast adrift. The – to me – more thoughtful local MPs and councillors and clergy and professionals, and those who respected and used Goldsmiths' facilities, felt as my colleagues and I did: that it was more than time for the full flag of the university to be raised in south-east London. All those soundings, rightly, ran in that direction. We decided, from mid-1977, to head that way and, after much statistical and historical analysis, made formal application in 1979. We were encouraged by a movement within the university's councils to pass some powers down to the schools from Senate House; well, not so much encouraged as given a further push since, if Senate House became less and the schools more powerful, we would be more than ever in a limbo, down a crack in the middle.

There then began the most extraordinarily repetitive pattern of events. We knew that academics are past-masters at invoking the Principle of Unripe Time but many of these were Grand Masters. We never lost heart but did wonder whether and when it would all stop. Each hopeful move, whether a successful 'visitation' or report, was quickly followed by a further cut in government funds for higher education. No matter how good the case for Goldsmiths', no school was then going to agree to admit another claimant on the funds allotted to the university (with few exceptions, funds are allotted centrally, and then disbursed by Senate House). The Department of Education and Science might say it would transfer our funds in the first few years to the University Grants Committee, so the cake would be bigger. No one believed them; after a year or two the cake would not have increased overall but there would be another mouth to feed from UGC funds. So, though the university never said, 'Go away,' it could not bring itself to say, 'Come in.' Even if the Vice-Chancellor of the day was as well disposed as he could possibly be, and some were, he and so we foundered on this reef for years.

Inventive procrastination became the outstanding characteristic of those years. It had taken years also for one of my predecessors to gain permission for professors to exist at Goldsmiths'; that was finally permitted by the device of letting one of the schools appoint a professor with our money and then detach him or her to us. That was an imaginative and generous stop-gap. But as the cuts bit deeper, and on the grounds that our 1979 application was being reviewed, the willingness even to make that accommodation fell away. As is the way of things, the professor of education left for a more famous chair; no replacement was permitted. Suppose something went wrong and they were left with another professor to pay for, one who worked entirely separately from them, except legally? We'll indemnify you, we said. They demurred: hang on, it can't be long before you become a school. The Goldsmiths' Company had offered money for a chair in English literature. That too lay dormant, a blocked promise, for years, and was finally regarded as lapsed. But in the late Eighties the Company re-funded a chair in education as a celebration of the achievement of school status, and so of the power to propose Goldsmiths' own professors.

Without warning, we received a formal letter proposing to withdraw our right to prepare students for degrees in psychology, because the control of that degree was being passed to schools. It was easier to send us that letter than to amend the rules so that Goldsmiths' retained its right; that was typical of the old attitude which was taking so long to alter. We objected, strongly, and the new rules were changed in our favour.

Still, more and more people in the university and in relevant places outside began to see that we had and were a problem; we were the thorn in the flesh, the clamant one on the wrong side of the blanket. We had a long succession of lunches with MPs, ministers, vice-chancellors and other educational eminences. We issued careful and, we believed, persuasive papers; we wrote letters to everyone who might conceivably take an interest in Goldsmiths'; and Delegacy members, as always, rallied very well. I doubt if matters could have been speeded up in those interim years. Too much ran against a favourable decision. Things had to have their course until, though financial circumstances had not improved, it became shameful to muck about any longer; and financial assurances from DES were at last made more convincing. That was in the mid-Eighties, not long after I had gone. It was and had to be a psychologically elephantine birth; then at a certain moment the waters had to break.

Meanwhile, at the turn into the Eighties, we pressed the Vice-Chancellor with powerful evidence and arguments until he announced that yet another report would be made on Goldsmiths' situation and future. A few weeks after the enquiry was under way and the immediate pressure was off, Mary and I went to stay with the Humphreys's on the north-west coast of Arran, for a short sabbatical. On the second night there, I was called to the 'phone in a neighbour's cottage. A bizarre-seeming call since, at the door in the cold and blustery dark, there seemed to stand Harold Macmillan in drag. It was one of his elderly distant relatives, settled in the next cottage on that remote coast. The report had arrived unexpectedly soon. It was also unexpectedly brief. Sketchy, in fact. The gist was that Goldsmiths' should not become a school and might as well have its painter cut. I gave up my leave and we went back.

I asked the Deputy Warden and Registrar – and, as usual, they could not have been more helpful – to let me closet myself for a couple of weeks to analyse the report. I have rarely seen so ill prepared and ill presented a document.

Once primed, we asked to see the Vice-Chancellor; and one morning in Senate House four or five of us from college faced him, the Chairman of the Academic Board and the officer responsible for presenting the report across a committee room table. We had twenty-odd pages of errors, omissions, elisions and biases, individual and cumulative, to point out. They all came together to work against Goldsmiths' claims.

After a couple of hours or so of that meeting the Vice-Chancellor – Randolph Quirk, who had taken office after the report was commissioned and proved particularly sympathetic to our claims – turned to the report's presenter and said, 'We consider this report withdrawn; yes?' It was withdrawn, but we had lost time and were back at the starting-line. More cuts in university funding were coming along and would delay us yet again and again. Still, the air was now clear as it had not been before and no honest observer with the slightest knowledge of Goldsmiths' history, formal situation and achievements could from then on deny the justice of those claims – the inopportuneness in view of financial constraints, perhaps, but not the justice. The university's part, in having such a report prepared and in failing to reject it before it left Senate House, speaks for itself; but at least the authorities recovered their balance and did when challenged discard it. A much more positive version was issued in 1982. As for Goldsmiths': there had not been, and has not been since, a more crucial moment – a more fateful morning – in the college's history since it was first given to the University of London; nor a more bracing.

The succession of 'visitations' (we half-expected their members to drop from the air on the back lawn) continued, said respectable things; and their views were forgotten as the cash screw tightened. With very rare exceptions, there was no ill-will. In happier times . . . they said; but you see how it is. How could we take on another member with claims on the rations? By now the Vice-Chancellor was proposing that some schools merge. Most fought hard; the V-C knocked heads together and mergers began to take place. In these circumstances, and it was now 1982, there was no hope that a complete new school could be added. The Vice-Chancellor then suggested, wisely and helpfully, that we associate ourselves with – later, 'merge with' – Queen Mary College opposite us, over the Thames, straight through the Rotherhithe Tunnel. At his instigation, QMC was already in discussions about a merger with Westfield College. All this would create a very large single school with, among much else, two particular sets of strengths: QMC's sciences, and Westfield's and Goldsmith's arts.

So began yet another round of long discussions. Again, the atmosphere was generally fair-minded. Some of our members feared that some of QMC's members were only interested in the asset-stripping of Goldsmiths' best departments, leaving little more than a rump on the south-east bank, doing largely evening work below degree level. They may have been right, but I think most people over there realised 'that cock wouldn't fight' – that this would have to be a proper marriage; we left them in no doubt. The talks were still going on as I retired in 1984, but foundered soon after. Later, there was talk of an association with Birkbeck College.

In the mid-Eighties, and here I am working partly from report, the latest Vice-Chancellor (the fourth since I had arrived and another helpful one) decided enough was enough with this matter of Goldsmiths'. My successor worked very hard to support him and others in this view. In 1987 a joint court/senate committee was set up, this time with a non-academic chairman, William McCall, a member of court. For the first time, the university had the good sense, the common sense, the grace, to put representatives of Goldsmiths' (three) on the committee. It reported quite soon that in its view enough was certainly enough, that Goldsmiths' had much to contribute to the university as a school and should have that status. This would have been an inconceivable recommendation in 1976, when we had set out on that road. Many things then began to slot into place which could, in principle, have been granted a decade before.

The University Grants Committee, which had played a one-step-forward-one-step-backward dance over the years (even though its chairman had once declared at a public dinner, at the turn into the Eighties, that Goldsmiths' was a uniquely valuable part of the university) agreed, and the DES at last said: well, if that's what you want we will go along with it. Finally, the charter was granted, as it should have been long, long before. It had been a dragged-out, muddy war and there had been better things to do. But it turned out correctly in the end so none of us could entirely regret trailing a pike for so long. It had also been, all in all, an enjoyable campaign; and, as so often, very English – very English-university-like – in its style.

In agreeing to the change, the university stressed that it wished Goldsmiths' to retain its distinctive strengths. The overwhelming hope must be that as the college moves through the Nineties it does just that, does not succumb to a version of academic drift, does not become just another school anxious chiefly to keep its nose academically clean with the more traditionally minded spirits within the university, that it remains psychologically as it is physically – slightly off-centre, ready to take unusual chances, a bit of a mongrel, a very good school in the usual senses but also part of its local community in a way the others, except for Birkbeck, are not.

3

To meet commitments outside Goldsmiths', and for most of the time there, I took to stretching the day at both ends, much as at UNESCO. The most peculiar invitation was to give the first 6 p.m. lecture in or near the hardly finished foyer of the newly opened National Theatre. Five attended, so we moved to a small empty room and sat on the floor. Two were former Workers' Educational Association students from the north, on holiday.

There were four or five university committees down at Senate House and the usual incidental lectures, seminars and conferences at universities and polytechnics here and abroad; all such things are common in the lives of fairly senior academics. I accepted these things chiefly on two fairly simple grounds, one more internal than the other. First, I had convinced myself they had some value and that I 'owed', to those who had over all the years helped me get out of the rut, a readiness to give something back. Second, I was glad to be wanted. I did not wish to be known as a person who was chosen, to be at the centre of any picture publicly; I preferred being at the back. The wanting to be wanted was private, an effort to make up for something lacking in my early background, not a seeking of celebrity or the grand. Perhaps this is at bottom no more creditable than the straight enjoyment of limelight; but it is different.

Why were so many things offered? Presumably word had got round that I was a useful – hard-working, at least – member of committees; and later perhaps that I was a respectable chairman. At some point a snowball had started to roll: because he has been asked on so many committees and then to be vice-chairman or chairman of some of them, perhaps he is good at such things; he must be a good, then he must be a very good, chairman; and so it went on. I knew by that time that the assumptions were largely matters of habit. I did work hard but so did many others; I was a conscientious chairman but never a very skilled one, always clumsy at compromise and awkward in many of the talents the best chairmen need. Occasionally that clumsiness would be taken as an instance of subtlety in chairmanly manipulation, as at UNESCO the effort at plain dealing was sometimes taken as an example of Albion's higher perfidy.

More than any other appointment I suppose that to UNESCO, which was after all a shot in the dark by those who proposed me and a bit fortuitous in the way it then came off, put me into the ranks of those of whom it could be said, 'He seems rather effective . . . look at the job he got.'

Of what became a substantial overload, one which was most evidently a paying-off of dues was activity to do with the UN and UNESCO: the presidency for four or five years of the British association of former United Nations civil servants (and, much later, membership of the executive committee of the Friends of UNESCO – formed after Britain pulled out), and a small stream of articles and speeches on UNESCO affairs, each trying to be both frank about and favourable to the organisation. The most robust activity was inspired by the Heritage Foundation, in the USA, which set itself to keep the USA and Britain convinced that UNESCO was an irredeemably corrupted body. Two or three of us on the other side were invited to grand dinners. It took me some time to realise what they were in aid of. When the penny dropped, I asked another marked man why we had been invited. 'Oh, they said they'd "decided to have a couple of *bien pensants* at each of our dinners".' UNESCO is, actually and potentially, too valuable to be treated like that, by people like that. That transatlantic foray ended with a very frank public debate in London, at which the Heritage Foundation could, if it wished, have learned something about the strength of feeling against their efforts.

The most mistaken agreement was to become chairman of the *New Statesman* board, in the late Seventies. There were actually two committees, one for the trust which owns the paper and its financial interests, the other a board which overlooks the progress of the paper itself. My predecessor had been chairman of both, and for a year or two after I arrived kept the senior post; I was asked to be chairman of the second, and that met more frequently than the first – in that evocative little alley, Great Turnstile, near Holborn tube station. It was, because of the frequency of its meetings and for other reasons, more onerous.

For people of my generation, and especially for those from bookless homes, the *New Statesman*, as has been said again and again, was one of the main promoters of emerging intellectual and political interests – all the more because under Kingsley Martin it was odd; quirky, impulsive, warm-hearted, irreverent, full of humane good intent and principles worn on the sleeve, and often wrong-headed – especially in relation to the Soviet Union. Before and through the war no other journal meant more, intellectually and emotionally, to young people somewhere on the Left. So when someone on the paper 'phoned to say two or three of them had been asked to talk to me about whether I might chair the second board, I was touched again. They were serious, warm and persuasive, and I found myself agreeing. I went very soon to see the former chairman, he who was giving up that second board. He said he hoped I would accept but he had better say it was the most difficult committee he had ever chaired.

It was also the most difficult I have ever chaired. The board had some very clever members, naturally. But there was more unpleasantness around that table than I have seen at any other committee. The discussions about political policy were rarely illuminating. There were one or two equable people who tried to help push the business along usefully. The member representing the editorial staff was decent, and anxious to promote the paper's best future in every way possible. But he was constantly moithered by insistent briefings from colleagues, some of whom wanted to see the paper as a sort of self-governing commune – which, since it was owned by a trust, it could hardly be. Luckily, as is not uncommon in such circumstances, the paper had some members, especially on the administrative side, who worked steadily, loyally and well, whatever the temperature in the board room.

Much in these disagreements stemmed from the fact that the paper was struggling. It had long lost the large readership which the immediate post-war period had seen, the period also of the birth of the Third Programme and of the boom in most weeklies of opinion. Circulation had seemed to level out but then began slowly to sink. We should know now why that had happened: television and its substantial treatment of current affairs and of 'opinion' generally; the growth of 'in-depth' reporting by the quality newspapers, especially the Sundays; and, more subtle and important, the growing unfashionableness of the very idea of wide provision for the intelligent lay reader, and the rise of more specialist journals, most of which had at least a few pages nodding at matters of unspecialist opinion, usually with a specialist slant.

These, at least, were the most obvious difficulties. At a more deep-seated level, the paper was being eaten away by the decline in confidence in progressive socialism. The prevailing intellectual mood, where it was not depressed by the nuclear threat and the behaviour of both the Great Powers in the face of it, was cynical about 'post-capitalism' and the rise of consumerism. Books praising the achievements of the USSR dried up; that future didn't work. Crosland's democratic socialism didn't fire the blood, was not inspiriting. The age of the Fabians, the Webbs and Shaw was well over; this was the age of Solzhenitsyn and Marcuse – and *Private Eye*. Left-wingers were either dispirited, with little sense of direction; or they each gripped more tightly their often scholastic factional recipe as the one true panacea – for the *New Statesman* as for much else.

All these elements brought about a climatic change, so that even Kingsley Martin would have been hard pressed to reverse a decline. But some on the board thought a change in editorial policy towards their way of thinking could transform the situation, and some thought a change of editor might – as is unavoidable at such times.

In all this the editor, Tony Howard, bore himself well; but his contract was due to expire. I had just taken over. The board, after much deliberating, rightly, asked me to offer him a renewal. His answer was dignified and an illustration of the difference between the academic and the journalistic worlds. He asked me to thank the board but refused the extension. Do what he would, the paper was steadily losing sales, he said, and he simply did not know how to arrest that decline whilst keeping its essential character. He was now in his middle forties. If he took an extension he would, at the end of the new period, be approaching fifty. He could not say confidently he would by then have arrested the decline; he would also be less employable than he was now. His instinct and judgment were subsequently proved right. The most impressive element in that short and cheerful interview was the self-reliance and decisiveness, of a kind rarely called on in academic jobs.

How do you find a new editor for an important weekly, especially one owned by a trust, not by an individual who can simply put out his hand and make an offer to someone who impresses him? It was decided we would have an appointing sub-committee and advertise for applicants. That caused some irritation. Journalists at that level of seniority do not like to be weighed publicly, and know that if they fail and their application becomes known, as it will, there will be mirth for some in their world.

Where there were difficulties with the procedure, the board asked me to 'have a private talk' with more promising candidates and report back. That too was not a procedure journalists relished. I remember having such a talk – not an 'interview', of course – with an MP in a House of Commons bar; neither of us enjoyed it or thought it a realistic practice.

The time drew near for the chairman of the top board to relinquish that also, and the word went around that the two chairmanships could and should be made one again. My own first spell as chairman of the second board was ending too; I was not interested in the renewed double job. I do not know whether, if I had been willing to take an extension and look after both boards, that would have been acceptable; but I rather think not. I had not been a total failure as a chairman, but neither had I been much of a success; it was the wrong world. We parted amicably and quietly, as was right.

My connections with the Arts Council and the Broadcasting Research Unit, both of them institutional continuations of personal interests spanning many years (and each, in the Eighties, undergoing major and largely deleterious changes), I had best look at in a separate chapter. There were also the European Museum of the Year Award Scheme, and the national Advisory Council for Adult and Continuing Education.

The museum scheme (EMYA) is little known here though quite well known on the Continent. It brings together two things of which Britain has been traditionally suspicious: the arts (and particularly museums which, though Britain has some of the best museums in the world, long-established and new, many public commentators assume are still dusty, over-earnest places), and the Continent itself – that home, to many British, of artistic pretensions and historical humbug. Yet the scheme, which has a European-wide committee, was founded by two Englishmen, Kenneth Hudson and John Letts. In each of the past dozen or so years it has given a prize to the new European museum which in one way or another has done most to further the idea of museums and especially of museums-and-society. I became involved because I knew Kenneth Hudson; he had been the producer of the second broadcast I ever made, an analysis of a short poem by Auden, and we had remained occasionally in touch. Over the years he had become one of the founding fathers of British industrial archaeology and one of the most knowledgeable of the world's museum experts. Museums, and their meanings, their relationships with cultural and social change, their politics, had become a passion, even an obsession. By the Eighties he was spending about half of each year moving – his abundant grey locks all awry, his ungainly pockets stuffed with nuts, raisins and a notebook, an instantly recognisable English scholarly eccentric – between northern Finland and Sicily, Greece and County Cork.

Hudson and Letts appeared at Goldsmiths' in the late Seventies to ask me to be chairman of the judging committee for this new scheme. They knew I was neither a museologist nor a museographer; but I had looked after the division within UNESCO which was concerned with museums, so I had something more important in a chairman for their committee than practice in running a museum – experience of the international politics which might erupt from time to time in their scheme. I thought it a rather far-fetched piece of persuasion, but liked both them and their scheme and agreed.

Within three or four years their argument proved not at all far-fetched. We give the prize in a different capital or major city each year and the rather grand ceremony was on this occasion in Brussels, with the Queen of the Belgians handing over the main prize, a bronze by Henry Moore. For the first time we had an Israeli candidate, the Museum of the Diaspora. Here my international experience came in useful. Could/should Israel be considered a part of Europe? There were arguments both ways. In the end the committee accepted that the nearest parallel in grouping of membership was UNESCO, and there Israel was regarded as within the European group. Those committee members who had seen the museum – at least two of the ten members see each entry – said it was without doubt a worthy recipient of one of our 'Highly Commended' plaques, of which we give a few each year; so it was decided.

On the morning of the ceremony I was at my desk in Goldsmiths' and due to leave on the mid-afternoon 'plane for a 6 p.m. ceremony. There came a 'phone call from our people already over there. An Arab terrorist group had telephoned to say that if we did not withdraw the prize to the Israeli museum the Queen and I would be assassinated – presumably as I handed her the Henry Moore for the main winner. With those at UNESCO that made the fourth death threat; the fifth, in 1989 and apparently apropos Salman Rushdie, was probably a hoax.

Such threats are very curious phenomena for the recipient. I do not think of myself as brave, and would certainly cave in under torture or claustrophobic imprisonment or ingeniously induced vertigo. Death threats seem different, less directly personal, more removed, more like being bombed from the air than being mugged in the street by an enemy. They can induce an 'if it's got your name on it', almost fatalistic, acceptance. They also induce a more civilian feeling, a bloody-minded resistance to being blackmailed, bullied, threatened because you don't fit someone else's ideology. So you know from the start, however uneasy or even scared you may be, that you cannot yield; if you did then the grounds for rational conduct, for sticking to principle, or for reasonable compromise, would all have been undermined; there is no alternative to sweating it out, unheroically but unshiftingly.

We decided that the Palace should be told and given our view, but also told that if the Queen was advised to withdraw we would understand why. She proposed to go ahead. At the moment of handing over the Moore bronze, I was too preoccupied in making sure the Queen got it safely into her hands – it is very weighty – to remember to think that this might be our last moment. Nothing happened. Perhaps it was a hoax. Or perhaps not; we do not know. I do recall that the Israeli museum director, who received his runners-up plaque from me, whispered as we shook hands: 'We know everything, my friend. Thank you.'

There have been slight murmurs from time to time that the committee's members should be nominated representatives of their countries rather than individuals chosen for their personal qualities. Now and again someone hints we should strive to make sure that over several years every country has a winner. So long as the present principles and present kind of committee last all those will be resisted. They would spoil the spirit of individual, disinterested, non-nationalistic enthusiasm and pursuit of good judgment. The visits are made cheaply and without fuss; we are, of course, unpaid; no one is buyable or wooable; nor are we often approached in those ways. Our only grand occasions are the annual prize-giving ceremonies and the grandeur at those is provided by the host city. We, in those gilded halls, look what we are – a dozen friends who give as much time as we can to something we think worthwhile and find fascinating.

EMYA's achievement has been to help illustrate year after year how museums have transformed themselves in the last few decades. It is rare to find an unreformed museum, odd objects in dusty cases, little intelligent effort at information and education and enlightenment for lay visitors, not a particularly warm welcome for other than scholars, and often overall a grinding, old-style-local-authority sense that you are there on sufferance and the museum itself there only because it seems to be obligatory to provide one, like the scruffy park and the shabby library. That's a caricature, but not untrue to the old spirit in some places. It has virtually gone, in favour of museums which open the life of a community to its inhabitants; and in this Britain is one of the leaders.

It is a hasty over-simplification to claim that the crowds who now visit museums of this kind are simply being nostalgic. If you listen to what they say as they go round, you hear much more than that; you hear people, above all older people, talking soberly to their grandchildren, trying to make sense of the gap revealed between the world they first knew – rooted in certainties, 'real' – and the world they now live in.

There is a charmingly old-fashioned style of address, in manner and language, which the British bring out on formal occasions, even when only two or three are present. I met it one afternoon in Goldsmiths', again in the late-Seventies. A letter on the top-quality blue notepaper which seems to indicate secretary of state or ministerial involvement said a visit to me to discuss a new quango would be appreciated. The responsible under-secretary duly arrived. After the statutory chit-chat until the tea appeared, he switched into formal mode and announced gravely and courteously that the Secretary of State (Shirley Williams) would be greatly obliged if I would be the chairman of a proposed Advisory Council on Adult and Continuing Education. I duly followed with an almost equally formal thank-you-for-the-offer.

I had no doubt I should accept and somehow find the time. Such a survey was overdue; I had spent my first thirteen years of working life in that field and, after UNESCO, had joined one of the only two university institutions in Britain which had a major commitment to part-time students, working for first and higher degrees.

Then down to practicalities; above all, looking carefully at the terms of reference and the provisional list of members. As a democratic gesture, they had advertised in the press for suggestions for members; many were proposed; many proposed themselves.

Within a few months of the council's first meeting the Conservatives came to power and we knew our time was limited. That government from the start made plain its distrust of quangos, those instruments of consensual not confrontational government. I do not suppose it helped our reputation that this particular chairman was on the Left. A guide-line of the new government was the firm smack of decisiveness, not the willingness to listen to on-the-one-hand, on-the-other, arguments. We wondered whether we would exist past our first three-year term.

Towards the end of our second year the new Secretary of State, Keith Joseph, sent us the expected letter, though its terms were not exactly as expected. He said the government thought quangos best used when, after the shortest period needed to fulfil their particular briefs, they were wound up. He would therefore renew us for one more period but that would be the end. We could have done with a year or two more since the field was so huge. But it could have been worse.

We had met Shirley Williams at our first meeting but never saw Sir Keith. Each year, at the front of our annual report, I put a letter to him, usually provocative, about the state of affairs in adult education, further education and part-time vocational education, but there was no response. We were, in that government's eyes, an odd engine created by their predecessors and now shunted into a terminal siding. The only ministerial recognition we had in that almost six years was a visit from the relevant junior minister – who reacted with alarm because we were, among very much else, planning to enquire into the need for more adult education in the nature of politics. Obviously, Red propaganda, not democratic political literacy.

I did once see Sir Keith in action, on other than Advisory Council matters. He seemed quintessentially a once-born man, without guile, cunning, a belly-laugh, irony or cynicism; clearly fascinated by ideas but in an abstract way, disconnected from the weight, the muddiness, the chiaroscuro of quotidian thisness . . . like a whirling planet, round and straight past whom all the debris of daily life whizzed without ever making any contact, ever impinging. I have not met anyone whose mode of being seemed so different from my own; or from those of most others I had known. Curious, fascinating – and much more attractive than the smooth or aggressive 'I know a hawk from a handsaw . . . no flies on Charlie' people who were more common in that administration.

Like all responsible quangos, the council was as educative for its members as it hoped to be for its audience. We did not slide towards the mushy middle; our debates had a good edge. But those on the Left gradually saw more in the Right's points of view than they had long grown used to allowing themselves to see; and those on the Right went through much the same change. Each remained basically of Left or Right – since such differences go deep into the personality – but each had modified that progressively simplified stance which too much conversation with one's own committed kind breeds. We all like to hear confirming and corroborative noises.

We were not at all a bad quango: we produced a surprisingly large number of publications, on all the most pressing questions, and they have had their effect on some people and institutions; we hammered hard at a definition of the field which was both catholic and intelligent; we marked a path between what was foolishly called 'the choice between flower-arranging and computer training'; we organised some seminars which at least slightly shifted opinion; we did all this without striking postures, and efficiently (we had excellent administrative help). We did it in a climate which was, after our first few months, mildly hostile or rather suspicious or dismissive. These were not the Sixties, when the great proconsuls steered their quangos over a balmy sea with a fair wind, nipping into the ministry from time to time for a friendly word over coffee with a senior official or a minister. Still, though the air was cold, sharp, unfriendly, you did know where you were, that some of the less attractive aspects of the British character were now the dominant style. Those council members on the Left knew this from the start, those on the Right soon learned it; I remember no one complaining.

Our last months were particularly productive. Among much else, we had a national seminar at Goldsmiths' on part-time entry to higher education and out of that came a useful booklet. Best of all was our last full-length book: *Continuing Education: From*

Policies to Practice(1982). That was a survey on the size and nature of the demand for part-time adult education and a set of planned and costed proposals for the decade ahead. It was a blueprint, based on sound evidence, for the medium term; and it proposed that when we expired a national development agency be set up to see this need met. It was backed by our last annual report, with the usual frank letter to the Secretary of State; and the usual lack of an answer. (Later and elsewhere, he did react to our proposals.)

There was not, as we knew there would not be, a development agency; but the national Institute of Adult and Continuing Education at Leicester was given more money; and the Literacy Unit, also there, was set on a firmer footing. There had to be nods towards vocationalism. It was all a good deal less than we thought was needed and very much less, in the funds provided, than the misbegotten Assisted Places Scheme for schools received. But perhaps the government went a little further in funding adult education than they would have done if we had not pitched our case so high and hard. In that sense, it echoed Pilkington and its effects.

For me, the most surprising and encouraging result of the surveys made for the *From Policies to Practice* book was the evidence it gave of *why* people wanted more provision of adult education. We had guessed the unmet demand would be large but not as large as it turned out to be. We had assumed, especially because of the hard-headed mood of the new government, that much of the demand would be for vocational training and retraining (evidence from 1991 suggests that vocationalism is now dominant). We had hoped there would still be some demand for adult education for the old high purposes. What we did not expect, back in '82, was the weight of people giving that last sort of reason. They used old-fashioned, value-laden, beautiful phrases, usually rather tentatively. They wanted more education so as to be more 'whole', so as to 'understand better' the world or society or themselves, so as to 'broaden' their minds, so as to have 'fuller' lives, more 'enriching' experiences. You wanted to throw your hat in the air. They were not at all talking like the images thrust on them by the persuaders of modern life, did not see themselves – they positively refused to see themselves – as 'consumers', 'clients', self-seeking atoms, 'targets' for politicians or advertisers, 'audiences to be delivered'. They recalled a wonderful phrase of Coleridge which I quote often: 'Men, I think, are to be weighed not counted.' That rings down almost two centuries and makes today's fashionable phrases about the nature of society, of the individuals within it and of our judgments on its purposes, show as the tinsel they are.

We went out with a modest farewell party. Just a middle of the day buffet in a hotel belonging to a chain which specialised in modest buffets. Nothing lavish; all incorrigibly English. One of the group on *From Policies to Practice* went back for modest seconds and tried to pick up another breaded scampi (no doubt thrown in the fryer from a large freezer bag). The supervising waitress, a large lady with vividly henna'd hair, bore down upon her and said loudly, in pure Cockney: 'Eh, you, you can't 'ave another of those. It's one each. That's the allowance.' Surprising that she didn't say 'the ration'. Very English. Very 'if we let you 'ave another, they'll all want one' – the language of the petty bosses who enjoy propping up the system from below. A rationing, just like the allowance of education provided for those who can't afford any sort of unmeasured largesse. 'The spirit that denies', Euston Road style. Not likely to be said in more prosperous places; they don't count the scampi there. That would be a good title for a book on the contradictions and divisions of Britain in the Eighties: *Don't Count the Scampi*. But outside, we now knew beyond any doubt, were hundreds of thousands who could not afford more but did seek more, who wanted a very important kind of liberation.

This was the Eighties way; not the nineteenth-century or pre-1979 way which saw the birth of those bright ideas I have kept celebrating: university adult education, free public libraries, museums and art galleries, the Workers' Educational Association, public service broadcasting, the Army Bureau of Current Affairs and the Open University. This was the old pinchbeck and pinch-spirited style come back, the style thought adequate for those who can't pay extra. It recalls another remark to go alongside that of Coleridge quoted above, one by Gotthold Lessing: 'We must not accept the wantlessness of the poor.' We must never say: 'Of course I don't read or watch them myself but if they want the popular press as we have it, or the trashier programmes on television, who am I to regret or judge their tastes? That's democracy.' As is, presumably, the increasing seediness of cities, the inadequacy of educational provision at most levels, the moral squalor of so many lives; for all of which we no longer have a language of judgment or of charity; in which for someone to say 'I want to know more so as to be a more whole [or even a "better"] person' sounds simple-minded.

CHAPTER 8

CULTURE, COMMUNICATIONS, CENSORSHIP REVISITED 1976–91

I was a member of the Arts Council for about five years, from 1976 to 1981, but it seemed longer. The extra work the council asked for contributed to that impression, and of these jobs the most symptomatic was the chairman's commission, in my first few weeks, to report on the Greater London Arts Association (GLAA), which received a large grant but about whose operation the council was uneasy. The member of staff deputed to talk to me was an American woman, one of a small number who had come to Britain in the Sixties and Seventies and started to work in arts groups. She was in charge of grants for one kind of art. She introduced me to some of the attitudes which, during our absence in France, had particularly begun to present themselves to arts funders.

I asked her approximately how many applications for grants she had each year. So many, it seemed, that if they had been allotted equal amounts, each applicant would have been given far less than was needed. How did she decide between them? She looked at me as though I represented some bureaucratic and unimaginative element in society which she had thought to have seen the last of on leaving a middle-class family. 'Decide *between*,' she said, 'we don't use that language here. We respond to demand from the grass roots.' She did not believe in making judgments between people and their work, their arts and their abilities.

I did know the arguments about not-making-distinctions-between but had not, before leaving England, heard them carried to this length. How *did* she parcel out the money? She refused to be led into discussion with this man on his élitist, bourgeois, paternalistic terms. I wondered whether to lighten the discussion by trying a joke: say – that method sounds a little like that of a harassed mother with a large and quarrelsome family, who puts the bowl of custard in the middle of the table and hits it with a spoon, so that they all got some. I didn't try the joke and she saw me out stiffly.

I

I had agreed to join the Arts Council because, after years of resisting the idea, I had decided that public funding for the arts was essential, not usually well argued – but right. From the Sixties much more public money had been made available, but usually on peculiar grounds – a mixture of afflatus and cheer-leading. Confused alarms of struggle and fight; Arnold would have enjoyed breaking apart this verbal plastic.

For me, the debate had run through thirteen years of taking classes of adults; six years writing *The Uses of Literacy*; reading many long essays in *Universities and Left Review* and *New Left Review* (I didn't agree with all of them, but they gave a sharp edge to the argument); and through UNESCO, which agonised constantly about the meanings of 'culture' and 'member states'' responsibilities towards it.

No society need give a penny to the arts unless it chooses to do so. No one can prove it should, as one may prove pure water and effective sanitation are necessary to healthy physical life for a community. To give public money to the arts has to be based on a particular value-judgment, on beliefs, not on determinable facts.

The basic unprovable case is so simple to state that it may seem, but isn't, banal. The arts are to be kept up because they are the most profound expression of our nature and experience. Without the constant and free practice of the arts, without people aware of the arts and free to come to them, however awkward they often are, a society is the poorer. For many people, no matter what their own level of education, this is a harder tablet to swallow than the case for universal, let alone free, education. Free and universal education can be smuggled in on the ground that it allows a society to be industrially and commercially effective. You can't do that with the arts – unless you begin to talk about the arts' contribution to the economy through payments for tourists' bums on seats; but that is a fourth-order argument and should be used wryly, even with governments which understand no other.

A society's traditions in the arts and the connection of those traditions with life and art today are not only to be kept up; their audiences should be broadened as much as possible, and certainly much more than is evident in twentieth-century Britain. Access to the arts has to be encouraged because they are, and once again Auden found the right phrase, 'a game of knowledge', a form of play but one which can inform our understanding. Yet, though pity and terror and love and the sense of possible redemption may be found in the arts, response to them does not necessarily make us act better. If there were that simple connection we would have lost the freedom to go to Hell or Heaven in our own ways. The arts stand available, offering insights we can take or leave.

If these claims are true, they are true for all members of society, even though most of us may entirely ignore the arts. I quoted Lessing earlier, on our duty not to accept 'the wantlessness of the poor'. Bishop Wilson, in the eighteenth century, made a similar point: 'The number of those who need to be awakened is far greater than that of those who need comfort.' The Advisory Council on Adult Education's last study found, we saw, that the number of those who are 'awakened' to the need for something in their lives beyond what they have been encouraged to accept is very much greater than we have assumed. That is a start, but no more than that. The 'wantless' are far more numerous.

The argument that people should pay for what they want and like falls, as to the arts, because most of us do not know what we like or what we are missing. How do I know what I like till I see what it's possible to have, outside my immediate tastes; and beyond the constant reiterations by the popular persuaders that those tastes cover a full and sufficient range for any normal person?

So one of the most important arguments for public financing of the arts is social, or cultural in the anthropologist's sense. It is based on the fact that the appreciation of the arts in Britain is exceptionally closely correlated with social class of birth or adoption, and with educational opportunities. The only way to shake off this unpalatable truth would be to argue that our social and educational system is so effective at winnowing out the imaginative that by and large these correlations do fairly represent the spread of ability, of the capacity to appreciate the arts. If you believe that, you will believe this is an open society, that the Ritz, or Eton, or the Carlton Club, are open to all and hence natural and unexceptionable elements of a democracy; or that British sports or British marriages or British eating habits or British housing are classless. Many, perhaps most, people in the middleclass and above are not artistically inclined – so the correlation between class, education and artistic interests is not a smooth fit. Still, this correlation exists and is a major limitation. If the arts are of value then the opportunities for revealing that value are cramped and biassed.

Obviously, most people who now patronise the more expensive arts – orchestral performances, ballet, opera, big theatre – are still, as always, well-to-do. Against that, the cheaper seats are filled by young and not well-to-do people. Even if the organisers adjust prices so that the seats occupied by those young people carry the highest subsidy, the most expensive and usually 'corporate' front seats and boxes (paid for by commercial organisations, as a combination of sponsorship and perk) are also to some extent subsidised.

The Arts Council has spent over the decades a great deal of money on ensuring that hardly anyone in Britain is more than forty miles from a theatre, each with a professional company far better than the sparse and irregular pre-war Reps. Cheaper seats for well upholstered bottoms again?

The major performing arts are now so expensive to mount that if public subsidies were withdrawn they would become inaccessible to all but an even smaller minority, the very rich and the commercially subsidised. The audiences would be even more skewed than they are now. But can this prosperous nation of fifty-odd million people refuse to help maintain at least an opera house, a Shakespeare Company and a National Theatre, each of international standing? If it does not support them adequately, or if the wealthy do not pay enough to maintain them, they will at best collapse into 'chamber' operations. To that large rhetorical threat anyone is, of course, free to answer, 'Let them collapse.'

Here is where yet again arguments are not often followed through to the points where they might hurt. The directors of, say, Covent Garden, faced with inadequate government funding, seek more and more commercial sponsorship, and more and more 'corporate' seats let at a very high charge. They salve their unquiet consciences by reducing so far as possible, whilst still balancing the books, the seats in the amphitheatre and points even further away or harder to see from.

The 'corporate' seat system is manifestly undemocratic, ugly, and should be scrapped. If a government wants this country to have international-class opera, as it should, then enough should be given to the Royal Opera House to allow it to be accessible, throughout all the seating, to many more people. All seats need not cost the same, but the range should be much narrower than it is today, and there should be no preempted places.

The hope that commercial sponsorship or patronage can be persuaded to give more to the arts so that governments can give less, is both forlorn and misguided. After a decade of this argument from government itself, it is plain that British business — here again we have to recognise the nature of the society we are in; if German business acts differently, so be it — it is plain that British business will not give more than a very small percentage of the arts' needs.

There is always a price to pay. Some more hopeful people like to make a distinction between patronage and sponsorship. Patronage has no strings, is done for love of the arts and because of their value to the community. Very roughly and optimistically speaking, it can be seen as the modern equivalent of aristocratic patronage. Sponsorship has a price-tag in terms of what plain gain the sponsor may have calculated will be received from the money given — perhaps in sales, certainly in accrued prestige and probably in fending off external criticism. The distinction is paper-thin. Most 'corporate affairs' directors in large companies, even if they wished, could no more resist sliding from patronage to sponsorship than a burglar resists an open window; they will drive the hardest bargain they can. In Britain, most arts bodies will help them over the window-sill. George Weissman, Chairman of Philip Morris in the USA, was smoothly, oleaginously frank: 'Our major products give people pleasure – cigarettes, beer and soft drinks – and to many people that makes us the bad guys. In our art support activities we're viewed as good guys and that's nice.'

Most commercial sponsorship is unsatisfactory because it is fickle, impermanent; long-term plans cannot be made on such a base; there is no long breath. Commercial sponsorship tends to play safe, putting its money on the known and fashionable rather than on the new and experimental. It leaves that to public funding much as commercial television, left alone, would have happily let the BBC have the risky or worthy-if-boring bits – thus pushing the BBC further into the minority cold. Commercial sponsorship wants a visible return on its money and, in pursuit of this, can be egregious. One drinks firm which had given money to a Covent Garden *La Traviata* – a minute amount compared with the public subsidy towards the production – slung a banner across the entrance, 'The "X" Drinks *Traviata*'. A spokesman for the Opera House, challenged about this louche appropriation, said, 'They've a right to claim a lot. After all, the Arts Council *has* to give us money. The drinks people don't.' Wrong on both counts. The Arts Council decides whether or not to give taxpayers' money according to quality of performance, spread of audiences and much else. The drinks people were not giving money; they were putting money out for presumed advantages. One should only deal with such people with a very long spoon; or, preferably, not deal at all; it's demeaning.

Does all this positive argument for public subsidies apply to literature? Suggest it doesn't entirely apply and you bring out literary people in angry defence of their assumed rights. But, drama excepted, literature is a hedge-industry, a solitary occupation by writer and reader. It needs publishing but not mounting.

Tens of thousands of books are published in Britain each year; but most are not, and do not aim to be, works of the creative imagination. Some books of that kind have always had difficulties. Times are harder now and will continue to worsen as publishing

becomes more and more a matter of marketing, of quick pro-
motions and as quick remaindering.

Biographers, to take one example, who may need several years
on a book and probably money for travel, are especially pinched.
Desk-top publishing will help some, but at the cost of narrowing
their audiences to professionals. If you sit on a committee of, say,
the Society of Authors, to give grants, you will be harrowed to
learn how many – dedicated to writing books which could never
sell widely but will be of great value – are managing on less than
the average manual worker's wage.

I have no cause to grumble about my own treatment over forty-
odd years of writing. Still, one incident shows the present trend.
A week after the first volume of this sequence appeared I was in
Leeds. The book was very well received. I looked at the display
of new books in the large branch of W. H. Smith's in the city
centre. No luck; the usual, predictable, fast-selling titles. I asked
at the enquiry desk. Never heard of it; what's it about? It's a sort
of autobiography, all set in Leeds. 'Oh, then you should try Local
History, over there, love.' 'I don't think it's likely to be there.'
Very helpful, she turned to the VDU. 'Oh, it's been published.
But he's not buying any. I could order it for you.' I went down
the road to Austicks, still a real bookshop. They had a score of
copies.

So there are certainly some grounds for helping some authors
along with the writing of some books. But on the whole it is
better for authors not to become bursary-holders, pensioners, or
on the look-out for prizes. Money given in several ways towards
widening readership should have precedence.

I still wish we could do without state support for the arts, and
not only for literature. And not because it encourages playing
safe, the practice of that kind of art which does not disturb the
authorities. Work with the Arts Council shows that the most
vocal claimants for subsidy are also the most ready to bite the
hand that is feeding them, almost as a matter of self-respect. They
are in no danger of succumbing, can well protect themselves.
You could argue that the lusher literary prizes may tempt to
accommodations more than state subventions, that large-scale
commercial sponsorship is more dangerous to the unfettered
imagination than an Arts Council or Regional Arts Association

hand-out. Yet one would like to see the end of state subsidies but only if the need disappeared, if there were a very great increase in interest in the arts across a much wider area of society than at present. The state could then wither away.

In all this I have deliberately avoided some common but confused assertions. It is said we should be able to spend much more because the total public subsidy for the arts amounts to no more, let us say, than a couple of Trident submarines. Defence is indeed horribly expensive, but if it is accepted as necessary those costs cannot be avoided. No simple transfer applies here; to imply it can is to appeal to unthinking sentimentality. Unless you are a pacifist, one kind of expenditure is inescapable, huge though it has to be; the other has to be justified.

Another unacceptable practice is the drawing of foreign comparisons, usually entirely unembarrassed by the consideration of historic cultural differences. We know the French and Germans and almost all other Western European countries spend more on the arts than the British. That is part of their traditions, perhaps to be admired but not easily or automatically transferable. Some of them also spend money on water cannon to quell rioters, or more than we do on the secret services; those too are part of their traditions. Some spend less than the British on public libraries, parks, allotments; and their range of voluntary activities within the community is often much less than Britain's. You cannot legitimately yank out one bit of a culture which suits you, as a stick to beat Britain with whilst conveniently ignoring others. Best to make the case for this place, this society, this culture, here, now. There are good enough internal reasons for spending more on the arts without the benefit of dubious comparisons.

After such arguments, it is almost a relief to meet two related and outright objections to public support for the arts, both from the Left. The first claims that public support goes overwhelmingly to 'the high bourgeois arts', is therefore a reflection of bourgeois tastes and tends to reinforce and disseminate those tastes to people for whom they are irrelevant; the high arts are determined by their social origins.

Most of the recognised, traditional arts in Europe have been created for middle-class audiences, for people who were literate enough and prosperous enough to pay for them and appreciate them. Those arts were conditioned by their social backgrounds. But not wholly explained by them. It should not be necessary to say once again that art can break out of the ideology of its time; that the novel, for example, can be both a mirror and a critique of the societies it describes. And can do more, can explore with insights most of us cannot match, for the greater pleasure of whoever reads it, experiences common to or apprehensible by all times, places and people. To discourage access on anti-bourgeois grounds is like refusing a child the opportunity to discover the most nourishing foods on the ground that that sort of thing is a bourgeois trick; that, in the absence of any folk-art in developed societies and to avoid bourgeois adulteration, let people in today's cities eat fast food and read the *Sun*. Here the far Left meets the slick entrepreneurs. People have chosen what they want; who are we to judge them?

In any event, the claim that public support for the arts today goes almost entirely to the traditional high arts is mistaken. The Arts Council, always nervous, is constantly looking for community arts, folk-art, popular art, alternative arts to support; in my day it had a special panel with that brief. Nor are those from the 'grass roots' transmuted into tame recipients, 'embourgeoisified' by these attentions. They hold all the firmer to their belief that such subventions are at least as much, if not more, their due than are subventions for readings of classical poetry, with harp accompaniment. One 'radical' playwright even claimed: 'I should get a regular weekly wage from public funds just as the carpenters at the theatre do.' Reducing art and the artist in the name of democracy.

The more subtle argument, especially against the Great Tradition in literature, is that its representative works glorify individualism and weaken the claims and the understanding of the community spirit. The argument that the novel in particular is rooted, from at least *Robinson Crusoe* onwards, in a sense of the power and importance of the individual will, needs no rehearsing. It is not an overwhelming argument; the novel has also illustrated and enhanced the sense that we belong to communities. Even if the novel were almost exclusively a celebration of personal will, its achievements in that sense have been wonderful; it is illiberal to discourage people from meeting those insights out of a hidden and dangerous feeling that they can't cope with them, have to be shielded. *Agit prop* lies that way; and, in the end, censorship. And nonsense, as when one proponent of community art said, 'The frescoes in the Scrovegni Chapel at Padua are not to be regarded as the product of a particular genius, Giotto's, but were team work in which all concerned, including those who held the ladders, were communally contributing.'

All in all, it is difficult to know why, over the last twenty years or so, British governments have progressively given more money to the arts. Some people, among those who already know and enjoy the arts and can make their voices heard, have gladly done so; they want their pleasures to be more widely shared. Some of our governors have crept towards thinking that the arts might well have a quietening, a 'civilising' effect (a late-twentieth-century version of 'we must educate our masters' – our new, ignorant but powerful masters). But all in all the confused mixture of purposes about the justification for spending public money remains, even as the money made available grows, if prudently.

2

Members of the Arts Council are chosen by the usual mixed and circuitous routes. In the middle-Fifties the Independent Television Authority, anxious to show that it was of the people, was reputed to have made up an advisory board from as strict a population cross-section as possible. It could not work, that bundle of people few of whom had had committee experience. The mixed route which draws on experienced people, plus some who seem likely to learn the trade quickly and well, has more to be said for it than its critics allow. Those critics call for a more 'democratic' selection and usually mean two artists, two provincial councillors, two actors, two writers, all chosen by the relevant unions; a formalistic dog's breakfast of interested parties, and a recipe for imaginative croup.

Governments have not habitually loaded the council with their own nominees, though they have usually taken an early oppor-tunity to redress any political imbalance or fancied imbalance.

Harold Wilson was thought to be rather too active in that way. As with other committees, I did not certainly know the politics of most members of the council in my time; I could have guessed at most, as they could have guessed mine. But conscious political inclinations were by almost all members left in the cloakroom with their overcoats – except for a little falling over backwards by most members to be fair to applications from people whose politics were not theirs. There was, though, one member appointed by the Conservative government and a very active figure in the higher Tory echelons. I do not remember him opening his mouth except when asked, or to replace his cigar. His cigars were very large; from behind them he looked round the table with a very small smile. Was he wired for sound? A bit like UNESCO once again, playing the 'spot the KGB man' game.

I suppose my own invitation, from the Labour Minister for the Arts, was inspired by his knowledge of some things I had written. That I am a socialist would not work against me, but nor would such a fact have worked against someone thought to be knowledgeable in the council's work, even if known to be on the Right. I guess also that Roy Shaw, at that time still new to being Secretary-General and a close friend, pointed out that I had just come back to England after being involved internationally for five years with Arts Council-like matters. I was appointed in 1976, reappointed for a further term, made Vice-Chairman in 1980, and precipitately dropped in 1981.

It may be just as well to say here that members were not paid (though that practice has latterly grown in some public committees). The only Arts Council perk – and it was well worth having – was the right to a couple of free tickets to any performance subsidised by the council. Without them, you could only have informed yourself at considerable personal expense on how well grants were being used.

A few Council members do – are asked to do – little more than attend the monthly meetings; others do a lot extra, especially the chairmen and vice-chairmen of the Scottish and Welsh councils and the chairmen of the 'panels' which overlook the council's attention to the different art forms. Some time after I had produced the report on the Greater London Arts Association, I was asked to chair the Drama Panel – by a call from the council chairman at a quarter to eight one morning; perhaps a time when resistance is low. The formulation was a little like that *apropos* the *New Statesman*: 'most difficult committee we have; hope you'll take it on'. Perhaps it was; but Marghanita Laski, who chaired the Literature Panel, complained about 'the literary pressure group's total lack of philanthropy'.

Presumably you are meant to be slightly flattered at being given the role of bronco-rider. It was certainly a tricky committee, for two main reasons: it was made up of groups of specific interests, some conflicting; and some of its more talkative members did not want to accept the constraints of their brief. Of the different groups, the managers were the most quarrelsome, the critics the quietest, and the actors and actresses the most helpful. A committee on funding for opera and dance showed similar short-sightedness and one-sidedness, especially among staff officers.

Sticking to the promotion of your own causes, failing to declare an interest where you should, fighting people in the next box openly or covertly, are common in all branches of the council's activities, among members of staff as much as in the panels.

The council's monthly meetings were duller than I had hoped. I had not expected high-thinking debates on why and how to make the arts more accessible. I did expect a general sense that this was a major issue for the council. Except for some members from the provinces, and they tended to have a narrow geographical focus, most council members had one art in which they were knowledgeable and fascinated, or had a wider range and were amiable kinds of culture-vultures – successful men in the city, high bourgeois or aristocratic ladies, some dons and some trade-union officials. There was a little log-rolling for personal interest and, when matters went wider, an always polite disinclination to discuss questions of principle – social and cultural principles – with which to guide the business of disbursing those millions of pounds. Large 'abstract' debates would have been difficult to bear, especially in that hot, gilded, anachronistic salon looking across Piccadilly at Green Park; but so was the relentless, casual, well mannered pragmatism and practicality. I doubt if more than one or two members at any one time, of all those people who had either read deeply in their chosen art forms or widely in the accepted and usual arts, had ever read one essay on why the arts reach so narrow a group in society – and that is only one issue which, whether council members know it or not, lies behind all their actions.

In most respects, staff members reflected council members' attitudes, though often with a nervous edge. For almost twenty years the power of their day-by-day executive leader, the Secretary-General, had progressively yielded to that of the Chairman. Allen Lane's adviser, W. E. Williams, was the last dominant Sec.-Gen. He saw himself as a public servant but not a civil servant; with his Royal Charter, he could distance himself from parliamentary control. He looked to his chairman for support outside, especially in the corridors of power. He knew his chairman would see himself as a guide and friend, and would not hesitate to take him for a talk over a drink if things seemed to be going wrong; or, at the limit, might advise him not to seek an extension of his contract. It was Williams who said, to a chairman he thought too interventionist and too often around: 'You are the admiral; I am the captain. Now please get off my bridge.' Those days had gone.

Most council officers were extremely hard-working, too hard-working to be able to think other than on the run. They were under constant pressure from warring or near-warring claimants and clamants, from a few members of council and panels, and sometimes from Very Important People outside (one chairman of an applicant company did not scruple to emphasise that their Patron was a member of the royal family, and unusually keen that a particular application should succeed). Under all these pressures and aware that most of the press, if it ever refers to them, does so with amusement or scorn, council officers have grown insecure, learned to speak fair rather than frankly, to play both sides against the middle, to create a protective shield of people who know they will as reward be well looked after, to smile and smile and be fed-up. Echoes of many UNESCO officers. All the new profession of cultural intermediaries, the controllers of the cultural taps and the money which can come from them – the Arts Council, the British Council, the BBC, UNESCO – all learn these protective styles. They are also reasonably well paid;

and they enjoy being minor Maecenases and being courted as that.

Their condition will not greatly change. They are British, and in Britain the few journalists who like the arts and may even think the Arts Council doesn't do a bad job in its difficult circumstances will not readily say so publicly. It is easier to side automatically with the unofficial bodies, the more clamorous claimants against the 'arts bureaucracy'. That attests to your own unstuffiness.

So staff members are not greatly able to help members of the council think better about what exactly they are trying to do in giving away all that money. Keynes would have wondered what world he had wandered into. His high bourgeois justifications, assumptions, have been thoroughly discarded, even though the main institutions which embody those assumptions still get large slices of the cake; and some staff members – like vicars gone pop – slide into an ill-digested, reactive populism. One senior officer with many years of selfless service to the council, uneasy at saying the arts should be supported because they have special value, said: 'Look. One man likes driving fast cars, another likes gourmet cooking or gardening or hot-air ballooning – and another likes Mahler. There's no more to it than that.' No wonder many staff members are pushovers for the more aggressive applicants, anti-highbrow or highbrow.

Conversely, some staff members all the time, and all at some time, protect the specialist purity of their particular arts against any attempt at what they see as vulgarisation. This is not an opposition to crass populism; populism and their kind of élitism can sit together within attitudes like these. It is a simpler and more old-fashioned English prejudice, similar to the prejudice against adult education ('earnestly dissecting T. S. Eliot or analysing Rembrandt's or Beethoven's art, in chilly schoolrooms during the evening'). In these things members of the English intelligentsia can be thoughtless once they move out of their specialist areas, about which they do usually know a great deal. Their education has often given them a well developed artistic head but a weedy cultural trunk.

Roy Shaw wanted one monument above all others to his time as Secretary-General: that the council should have an education department whose main purpose would be to work against that lack of interest in the arts among the great majority of the population, those who have had limited education. He knew from years of work in the Potteries, at the University of Keele, that, given the right opportunities, many more people than is usually assumed could respond to the arts. It was typical that fashionable journalists used to refer to Shaw – a university professor, an exceptionally good teacher of philosophy and a cogent writer – as 'a provincial educator'. Obviously, the council had slipped up in that appointment.

The response of many in the council and many of its officers to the education proposal was disdainful. They talked as though it was proposed to brush the bloom off the butterfly's wings; they made the usual jokes about solemn adult classes; they edged away as if some shabby, earnest old man with wire spectacles had sidled up in the foyer of the Hayward Gallery and implored them to explain Picasso's work.

Shaw had his way. I doubt if most members were convinced, but after a certain time custom suggests that you no longer resist a deeply felt proposal by the chief executive. The department was an immediate success.

I worked with the council at a difficult time; but, then, all times are in different ways difficult. The move into the Eighties brought the decline in the influence of quangos of which a good deal has been said earlier; it also brought increased governmental intervention in the work of bodies with the Royal Charter; the hedge that charter has habitually provided was brushed aside. The defences of the Arts Council against the process were weak.

The manner of my own abrupt and unexpected departure from the council is a good illustration of the change in climate. The vice-chairmanship of the council is an internal appointment, by custom but not by regulation. It has no term; some vice-chairmen have held the post for many years. In 1980 the Chairman asked me, with the approval of members he had consulted, to be his Vice-Chairman. In 1981, at a routine meeting between the Chairman, the Secretary-General and the Arts Minister, about which members of council had reached the end of their term and who might succeed them, the minister suddenly said that my time was up too. They pointed out that by custom and precedent the vice-chairmanship overrode normal council terms of service. He insisted; they resisted. Finally, the minister said something to this effect: 'I have no room for manoeuvre. Number Ten doesn't like him.'

So I went. I wonder now, for the first time since it happened all those years ago, why the two didn't refuse. I doubt if the minister would then have pursued his shabby little instruction. But they were difficult times, so. . . .

The point of the story is obvious: it confirmed that governmental intervention in the work of such bodies started very early in the Eighties. Fiats from Number Ten and compliance from some of her ministers. Or, worse, a disposition in some ministers to be more royal than the Queen, to guess in advance what she might like.

3

In 1960 Dennis Enright gave his inaugural lecture as Professor of English at the University of Singapore. His subject – *Robert Graves and the Decline of Modernism* – seemed innocuously academic; but one sentence, on the Singapore governments's error in trying to impose a Malay culture on a predominantly Chinese population, caused a tremendous political uproar.

Some time later the Enrights took a break further north, in Malaysia. Painted on the retaining wall of a large dam up there they read: 'Balls to Enright.' 'It would need a revolution to make you or anyone else so melodramatic a figure in English cultural life,' Enright said.

In 1981, I almost reached that level of theatrical notoriety. The Arts Council had to make some cuts in funding to its clients. Because the Chairman was ill I, as Vice-Chairman, had to take the press conference announcing the cuts.

At the council's monthly meeting some weeks later, police guarded the door of 105 Piccadilly. During the meeting a very large procession of protestors marched past the building, banners high, singing songs of hate, especially about Roy Shaw and me. Some banners called me 'Hangman Hoggart'; others demanded 'Hang Hoggart High'. Not as dramatic as Dennis Enright's retaining wall, but remarkable for England. Heartening too; people were getting mad about the arts, and taking to the streets.

From the beginning of the Sixties, the Arts Council had been given more or less continuous increases in grant, some of them very high. W. E. Williams's motto 'few, but roses' as a guide to the choice of clients could be forgotten, and was against the 'let's not make distinctions between . . .' mood of the time. Judgments on quality could be fudged: 'You never know how they may turn out. Let's give them a chance.' There were continuous increases in the number of organisations aided, and in their range of activities. A catholic, generous but insecure procedure, and one which came to haunt the council.

By the mid-Seventies, the increases in grant to the council began to slow down. It began to spread the butter thinner, but managed to avoid actually cutting off some grants altogether. Complaints from clients increased; increases were not now keeping pace with inflation and many, perhaps most, of them were suffering. Fund us adequately or cut us off, was said more than once, though obviously as a rhetorical debating point.

In late 1980, the council decided at last that some hard judgments, on both policy and quality grounds, had to be made, and in early 1981 proposed to stop grants to some of its clients (3 per cent).

The response was unhappy but, for the first few weeks, not violent. The National Youth Orchestra protested but without rancour. Michael Croft, who ran the National Youth Theatre and the Shaw Theatre on the Euston Road, soon revealed that he would fight viciously.

There were several reasons why it had been decided that grants to Mr Croft's enterprises should be stopped. The rules against the council funding amateur organisations had been bent in the prosperous times so that the National Youth Theatre and National Youth Orchestra could have grants; that could hardly be continued when professionals were going to the wall. NYT was the kind of body which could attract patronage or sponsorship – not easily, but more easily than most others (so it proved). Third, but few people at the council and few critics in the press would say this openly: the Shaw Theatre company was not in very good shape; and the National Youth Theatre 'has seen better days, become coarse'. It was Croft who had organised the procession with banners. It was Croft who wrote letter after letter to the press and appeared again and again on radio and television. He had a right to defend his children hard. But he ignored facts, and explanations; he distorted wherever and whenever it suited him.

Some months later I gave a public lecture at Birkbeck College on the Arts Council cuts and their reception, chiefly as an example of inadequate treatment of arts issues by the mass media. Michael Croft was in the audience. From then on he pursued Birkbeck with threats of legal action if they printed the lecture. We amended it more than once and finally Birkbeck's lawyers said it could be printed. Croft's lawyers sent a final letter, and Birkbeck caved in. I have the page proofs, but the lecture has never been published.

More important than Croft's behaviour is the light the incident threw on press attitudes. Virtually all journalists provided willing ears for Croft rather than for the Arts Council. They took almost all he said at face value. Literally hundreds of pieces were written on the issue. I checked on a hundred, taken at random: ninety-three simply assumed the Arts Council was in the dock. In the jargon of communications studies, rarely has reality been more cavalierly constructed. Most journalists extended an unweeded generosity to Croft and an equally unweeded cruelty to those who had had to make the cuts.

The language used by virtually all journalists in this extended incident were Orwellian in their 'four legs good, two legs bad' insistencies. Any 'free, small, radical, unofficial, experimental' body must be in the right. This is the Gallant Little Belgium syndrome, and its favoured nouns, epithets, verbs and metaphors are of 'victims' who are 'stunned', 'bewildered but struggling, hitting back', thus showing they are 'youthful, brave, crusading, gallant, adventurous, plucky, pioneering, undaunted, militant, campaigning'; in short, 'true Cavaliers'. Vicarious machismo.

By contrast any official, semi-governmental, national, quango-like public body must be congenitally in the wrong and its members old stuffed shirts. They are by definition 'undemocratic' and composed of the sort of people who compile 'hit lists'. The Arts Council is a group not merely of 'bureaucrats' but of 'bloodless bureaucrats' and 'faceless bureaucrats, bourbons, mandarins, élitists' who have 'set themselves up as arbiters of taste' (i.e. they have had to make choices). They are, and again I am choosing only the more recurrent epithets: 'brutal, indecently zealous, swingeing, underhand, despicable, disgraceful, patronising, arrogant, dictatorial, inept, callous, impetuous, arbitrary, Draconian, miserly, and secretive'. If at any point they reply to this barrage they are 'petulant and jittery'.

Their 'victims' suffer a 'shock, purge, bombshell, massacre, outrage and assassination'. They have been 'thrown on the scrapheap after the rug has been pulled from under their feet.' They have been 'abandoned, stripped and chopped at a stroke' by (the favourite anti-Arts Council image) 'the axe-happy hatchet men of 105 Piccadilly'. What a litany! 'It's the waste, the waste that I resent,' said Granville Barker. It's the dull predictability I resent.

Still, there were better lights. The *Financial Times* recognised that in such situations 'the Arts Council is always the villain', and the *Times Higher Educational Supplement* took a full and balanced look. Melvyn Bragg, who had not long before left the council because of the pressure of other work, said a lot of hard, plain and unfashionable things in more than one publication and was savaged for his pains by some of those cut.

The most striking form of this role-playing as the People's Tribune is trial by television. Shaw and I were asked to appear in a television discussion about the cuts. We had seen the previous programme in the series: it was ill conceived, ill prepared and ill conducted. They were planning a Roman circus; representatives of those cut packing a theatre, Shaw and I facing them on the platform. We would have been willing to appear and be questioned toughly if the arrangements had been sensible. We were not willing to feed the Sergeant Buzfuz pretensions of an interviewer who played to the audience. No one capable of concocting such a mess can claim to be presenting an even moderately 'responsible public forum' (as the aim was described to us). 'The right to know' is not a synonym for intrusive demagoguery. We refused. The director said he had hardly expected the Vice-Chairman and Secretary-General of the Arts Council to take such an 'undemocratic' position.

Why do so many journalists, so many arts journalists in this instance, behave in the way I have described? Not only because they congenitally like to be on the outside shooting in, though that is so. Much more importantly, because little in their training, in so far as they have any training, prepares them for taking part in a responsible discussion about the arts themselves, about the justification and nature of public funding for the arts, about the inevitable making of choices (whether as to those who shall serve on a quango, or those who shall be given grants by that quango).

They would have to learn about many more, interesting and particular, questions which any acquaintance with the Arts Council prompts: about the pressure groups – not always nice in their manners – of creators, performers and boards of directors behind each art form; about the enclosed society, mythology and language within each art form; about how, and if possible why, almost all fringe activity is of the Left whilst the Right, though noisy in assertion, is creatively hardly visible; and about the effects of this on, especially, the development of drama in the last two decades; and about how far the claims of people promoting community and alternative arts should be balanced with provision for the historic or classical forms of art. As we have seen, the Arts Council itself is too busy coping with immediate problems to give all such questions adequate thought; and I have not met an Arts Minister who was greatly aware of such an agenda.

Journalists writing on these issues today suffer also from not having a sure sense of any serious audience out there which will listen to them; I believe them mistaken. People do not change so quickly and easily; but if we are constantly fed monkey-nuts we will gradually come to act like monkeys, and want no other diet.

Even the non-tabloid press feels itself under pressure to soup up all issues, to personalise, to sensationalise to the degree and in the manner their special kind of readers are thought to like, never to be solemn or arty or – God help us – educational. So there appears a nervous catholicity, a hectic brightness, a premium on being smart and knowing. Never mind the subject; look at the style. In such a world Huw Wheldon's editions of *Monitor*, in the early Sixties, which we used to say were made by artistically inclined bank managers for artistically inclined bank managers, seem sure, serious, well informed. In today's pursuit of the smart and striking, injustice to people and to ideas can easily be committed, as we have seen. 'It is well to be frank. It is even better to be fair.' This entire incident would make a model analytic exercise for trainee arts journalists.

4

The institution whose duty it is to make British culture better known abroad, the British Council, has been, even more than the Arts Council and for forty years, in the centre of the arguments about purposes. For years Beaverbrook's newspapers campaigned against the council and its works – arty-crafty, suede-shoed Oxbridge types using public money to promote abroad their airy-fairy picture of British artistic life . . . everything silly, short of nose-flutes. In the late Seventies the Berrill Report on the Diplomatic Services short-sightedly saw the council as a not very useful appendage of the Foreign and Commonwealth Office. Council headquarters in London and council officers working all over the globe were again badly shaken. Then the Conservative governments arrived and put the emphasis on the practical, the vocational, the quickly cashable. The Overseas Development Agency began to give the council more and more contracts for work which was marked more by hard-headedness rather than a sense of a more imaginative role for it in the Third World. The stage was well set. More and more roughage had to be found in the council's programmes, to make it look more thrusting, masculine.

It all recalls the early days of English departments in the universities. Was the study of literature a proper, scholarly discipline? Wasn't it rather a pleasant leisure-time occupation for gentlemen? Roughage was introduced in the form of linguistic studies, from Anglo-Saxon to Middle English to Old High German. They were compulsory in the English degree course at Leeds in my day and I do not regret them; but in academic politics they were a face-saver.

Similarly, the British Council began to neglect literature and the arts generally in favour of linguistics and, later still, informatics. Linguistics led to the teaching of English and for that there was a vast demand abroad and from people willing to pay. Linguistics and the teaching of English thrived. English – more strictly, American – was the new dominant world language. Yet people wanted English English, English taught by the English; so it burgeoned.

In 1985 the council asked me to chair a committee of staff members which would report on the way they promoted British arts across the world. I imagine they had been prompted to make the offer because I had not long before written a report on a small but useful body, the Visiting Arts Unit, which with funds from the British Council, FCO and the Arts Council, gives money to help foreign artists of all kinds perform in Britain. Being concerned only with the arts, with no roughage to give it more body, VAU was particularly ill funded.

The British Council invitation was followed by a typically Eighties'ish encounter. I told the senior officials I was interested, but perhaps not the best person. I had in mind Mrs Thatcher's reputed suspicion of me as 'that man who criticises me and my government', in its policies on education, the arts and especially communications. I didn't need to say that explicitly. The council people said at once: we know what Mrs Thatcher is said to think of you; but we would like you to take on this report; and anyway she won't be here for ever. I agreed.

It was plain that the council is greatly admired across the world, as a model for artistic offerings which don't smell of government propaganda. The Germans had used much in the council's methods and style as models when they set up the Goethe Foundation. But now many countries were wondering what had happened to the council and its hold on its own purposes. One Indian intellectual said, 'We can get computer skills from many countries; only you can offer us Shakespeare.' Increasingly, the council didn't. A representative in Africa, offered a good Shakespearean touring group, telexed back that he hadn't time for such 'marginal' work nowadays. In the Council Centre of a European capital city I found the librarian taking the English classics off the shelves. He said he needed more space for informatics, cassettes, tapes. No nonsense about literature as the gateway to an inner understanding of other cultures there.

A senior official in London said they hadn't room nowadays for the literary eccentrics they sometimes used to appoint; 'short-haired mad executives' were more in favour, it seemed. A very senior Foreign Office official, in reply to my asking why relatively less and less was being spent on the arts, said, 'You've got to realise that the arts simply aren't sexy these days.' Odd to hear that unpleasant current image in one of the innermost sanctums of Whitehall. At least he gave a direct answer; a man slightly below that level had, on being asked the same question, taken it as a criticism of FCO policy and told me three times that we would be going outside our brief if we did that. We were to assume they gave funds to the council according to their judgment; we were to advise council how to use those funds better, not to suggest that the Foreign Office should increase them. That is exactly what the report did.

There always has to be a tag and the tag for this period became 'Cultural Diplomacy'; the council was the cultural arm of FCO and its business was Cultural Diplomacy. It was also, as the FCO had itself increasingly become, an arm of British commercial and industrial promotion – Rolls-Royces carrying sprigs of royalty to the opening of British Trade Fairs in the great cities of the world. An ex-ambassador delivered a much-admired lecture on the role of culture in promoting our commercial interests, with the aim of making the FCO less penny-pinching in its decisions on the size of the council's grant. I could almost swear I saw, in the foyer of a foreign theatre playing *Macbeth*, stalls promoting Scotch whisky, tartans and shortbread.

The Director-General of the council delivered a formidable lecture, analysing the inadequacy of the concept of 'cultural diplomacy' and proposing instead 'cultural relations' – disinterested offerings to and from countries, in the pursuit of greater understanding; bread on deep and distant waters. I do not know how many paid attention to it.

When the report was in draft, in the summer of 1986, I asked a senior civil servant if he would comment on it. We met at lunchtime in the cafeteria of the Royal Festival Hall – feeling slightly conspiratorial and ready to slip behind the potted plants if anyone showed interest in us. Handing back the report, he said, 'I've only one piece of advice. Don't sign it.' Why? 'Well, you know what's said to be your reputation with No. 10.' I have heard this kind of thing more than once but do not know if it was true and have never met Mrs Thatcher.

I replied to the warning not to sign that the Prime Minister would not be likely to read it. 'No. But her backbenchers know she is said to dislike your work and many will react as they think she would wish. It will be ignored.' I said this seemed greatly exaggerated. 'You do not seem to realise,' he said, his historical comparisons wobbling, 'that to today's backbenchers you are the equivalent, as a left-wing bogeyman, of Harold Laski in the Thirties.'

I told the council officers of this advice; they laughed and said, 'Sign.' One result of the report, at least, was that the Literature Department was given more funds.

5

It is plain that behind almost any discussion today about the arts, and indeed about any of those areas of British culture with which I have been involved, lies the evaded question of value-judgments. The more striking examples given earlier – the GLAA woman with the custard spoon; the devoted senior officer of the Arts Council equating fast cars with Mahler – are entirely typical across large parts of society.

It is true, and most people in our kind of society would say so today, that it is better to be free to find our own rules than to have them imposed by church or state. But it is precisely in these kinds of democracies that this openness is comprehensively abused by people with their own ulterior purposes, does not lead to our being left alone, let alone aided, to find our own beliefs. We are besieged by a mass of apparently conflicting but actually consonant voices, each peddling its own patterns of overt or more likely hidden beliefs. All of them – politicians, advertisers, tabloid newspaper hacks and many another – are interested parties; the ways of life they offer have overwhelmingly at their centres the notion that it's all a matter of taste, and of changing taste, since that's what keeps the wheels of this kind of society turning. Openness becomes emotional promiscuity, choice becomes whim; but underneath is a passivity, the acceptance of things as they are and are offered. Above all, you mustn't resist, like a stone in the water, snagging the inchoate flow. Or make distinctions. We are soon at the Beatles as good as Beethoven loony terminus; or at this, from an Oxbridge academic: 'Lavatorial graffiti are not to be distinguished in any qualitative way from the drawings of Rembrandt.' Or this, from a similar source: 'Great literature is a meaningless expression. I believe every great writer would rather be Raymond Chandler than James Joyce.'

In this perspective, pop music is as good as classical, or perhaps even better since more widely enjoyed. Or: though pop music may not be quite of the order of classical, such a distinction is mistaken: each is *good of its kind*; we should not set one against the other. The difficulty is that the argument is circular. At the popular level judgments of value almost immediately slide into measures of effectiveness; it must be 'good of its kind' because so many people bought the record. It is possible intelligently to go further; but by then you are after all making judgments which aim to be intellectually persuasive, not echoes back of the audience ratings.

Arising from the same group of attitudes is the 'stay as sweet as you are' syndrome, favoured by intellectuals who wish to appear neither highbrow nor populist. In linguistic thinking they were given a big boost by, in particular, Labov's studies in the USA, as they were transmuted and sometimes misapplied when they reached here. Labov illustrated the subtlety of speech and linguistic interaction between members of street gangs and so damaged, it was believed by some, the argument that unless such people employed publicly received speech they were unable to cope with their experience. Those who led off from Labov and some others here were so anxious to show the subtlety of communication among disregarded sub-groups, and especially their capacity to make critical judgments on, say, their favoured forms of music, that they ran the risk of appearing to say that there was no need for everyone to have access to public forms of discourse. The fact that they can make judgments about 'their kinds of music' takes away any need to suggest that taste might be broadened and – if the word may be used – enhanced; and removes the need to admit that after all their world is very limited.

I remember always at this point a further education lecturer in London who had a class of young men apparently highly sophisticated about and certainly very well supplied with elaborate audio-visual equipment. The lecturer introduced them to a Consumer Association report on video recorders. They had not seen before an analytic survey on anything in their world and were at first puzzled, then amazed. They had bought on the recommendation of the advertisers, the exciting packaging, and peer-group talks. Now they saw a sober record of comparative quality. The climax came when one of them called out, 'Bloody hell. I've been conned.' That was a step up in critical literacy.

At every level of artistic talk, at every place where the arts are discussed, the fog swirls. To sit on the planning committee of a local arts festival is to have a succession of lessons in bad language – misapplied ideas in fashionable jargon, good intentions and undernourished thinking. It is good for such a festival to try to appeal to as many people as possible; but choices have to be made throughout. You find instead resentment and suspicion of the 'highbrow', and unqualified support for the presumedly popular.

The evidence is everywhere, of the almost palpable fear of being thought to put on airs. A senior arts executive in the BBC, speaking on Radio 3 and with total assurance, said recently: 'There is no longer art. There is only culture – of all kinds.' Some of our arguments come back to haunt us.

Especially in public libraries, and not only in their attention to information technology – the machinery not the message. There is also their defence, on democratic principles, of the practice of buying multiple copies of the most popular fiction at the expense of any copies of what might be thought 'serious', let alone 'better'.

Our own town library offers the usual shelves of records and cassettes. Far from feeling it has any role as an aid to the development of musical knowledge and judgment, it has one whole shelf labelled 'Easy Listening'. That's a come-down from the impulses which founded the public libraries. They would have done better to label a shelf: 'Hard Listening, but worth it.' Are they trying to compete with Our Price record shops? Can they see no difference between their role and that of a commercial operation? What are the schools of librarianship doing – concentrating on training in information-processing-with-marketing?

UNESCO met the same dilemmas on a world scale. 'Culture' had to play a sizeable role in its thinking. But it was plain that no distinctions could possibly be made, in those halls, between cultures. So they slid into asserting that all cultures are of equal value. As a start that might discourage, let us say, Western chauvinism. But by what criteria are all cultures of equal value, by what definition of the word 'value'? Are tolerant cultures no better nor worse than cultures which practise enforced female circumcision? The question is worth examining. That was just what UNESCO dare not do. It learned to slide at difficult moments between the two meanings of culture – culture as the way of life of a whole society, and culture as its body of imaginative and intellectual 'artefacts'. We can all admire Benin art.

6

My continuing interests are by now very plain. Those in broadcasting – its peculiar nature, its relations to individuals and to society (especially the public service idea) and the constant urge in governments to censor it – have run from the middle Fifties to the Broadcasting Research Unit of the Eighties.

What turned out to be the founding conference of the Broadcasting Research Unit, in 1980, was a very British affair, in its Establishment style – the venue was Leeds Castle in Kent, the lushest of all British conference centres – and in its free-ranging, non-conforming mixture of scholarship and practicality.

The chairman was Edward Boyle. I had not seen him for two years and did not at first recognise him as we gathered in the library for pre-dinner drinks. His suit hung loose; his neck was scrawny; he had obviously lost three or four stone. Walking round the grounds later he insisted that everything was under control, Leeds Infirmary had been marvellous and his colleagues wonderful. He was dying of cancer but entirely in his usual manner, with unobtrusive and unself-pitying dignity.

He chaired the meeting in his usual manner too, fair and well informed. In turn, we all behaved in what we tell ourselves is the British way; undemonstrative, respecting his wish to carry on normally. He died in 1981.

BRU was, in its decade of life, the most consistent contributor to the British debate on public and political aspects of broadcasting; there are, so far, no signs of a successor. Its founding father was Kenneth Lamb, at the start in charge of BBC Research Policy, after having been in charge earlier of much else within the Corporation. He had for a long time wished to see a body which would study broadcasting policy and practice without being part of any broadcasting organisation, and hence open to the charge that it was not objective. Some universities and polytechnics ran research on broadcasting but not with the focus on the future which Lamb had in mind. He pushed hard at his idea for years, and finally received powerful support from the then chairman of the BBC governors, the late Michael Swann. He persuaded the Hosa Bunka Foundation in Japan to pay in large part for the Leeds Castle conference.

Few people have read and even fewer bought *The Future of Broadcasting*, the conference report. A pity, since it was readably edited and full of good ideas. But the climate for that kind of study had already begun to change. Still, the Broadcasting Research Unit idea was given the essential push forward by the meeting, and quite soon the Markle Foundation of New York, the British Film Institute and, a little later, the Independent Broadcasting Authority had joined the BBC as core funders; there was enough to go ahead.

I was then invited to another of those 'let's check on what he thinks and make an offer of the chairmanship if he seems right' lunches. For my part I wanted to be sure of two things: if the exact brief of the new unit seemed right, and if it was to be completely independent. I came away satisfied, and presumably my interlocutors felt much the same since they made the offer.

The focus of the brief was clear: it was to carry out studies, leading to publications, seminars and the like, on questions about broadcasting which were emerging because of new communications technologies or of changes in social attitudes, each of which, and this was the crux, might call for changes in national policy. In the current jargon, we were to work at the interface – the frontier, the line – where new technical possibilities raised the question of whether the existing ground-rules were adequate.

We were interested in satellites and their likely effects, and in cable. Those were pre-eminent forms of the new technologies.

We were even more interested in the future of public service broadcasting since both the advent of the multiple technologies and of market-oriented governments were being used to call in question the basic principles of the public service. We had no institutional axes to grind; but since the concept of public service broadcasting had been uniquely British or, at the least, had reached its fullest expression in Britain, we had to enquire into its future. It was a precise and useful brief.

Members of BRU's board were neither nominees nor representatives; they were there in their own rights, as producers, directors, executives in broadcasting, writers of various kinds with a special interest in broadcasting, research workers and executives in allied institutions. The core funders each sent an observer and behaved with propriety towards this latest and perhaps last of the free broadcasting quangos. The director for most of the unit's life was Michael Tracy, among much else the biographer of Hugh Greene and one of the many bright products of the Leicester mass communications post-graduate outfit (which had been set up after Pilkington, with initial ITA funding). It was a lovely committee – very well informed, good at arguing within itself but not destructively.

Like the Advisory Council on Adult and Continuing Education, BRU sailed straight into increasingly unpleasant waters. In this one area of Britain's internal life in which we had done better than any other country, a government – especially one which, whilst encouraging initiative and the free play of market forces, insisted on its understanding of and determination to support the best in our traditions and initiatives – such a government was setting about putting public service practice in broadcasting increasingly under pressure. It is all too easy to point to the limitations of the early BBC; that is itself a limited judgment and plays into the hands of those who see broadcasting as only another arm of their money-making operations. The fact is, though, that the principles of public service broadcasting are a superb example of democratic thinking. Whatever the better achievements of the governments of the Eighties may have been, whatever their other faults, the damaging of the public service principle was one of their blindest and most illiterate acts. Their definition of 'public service' was typified by the Tory MPs who bayed at the BBC's

Chairman and Director-General for reporting the Falklands conflict disinterestedly; for people like them, the public service equals national propaganda.

The proconsuls (but they had almost disappeared; Michael Swann was one of the last), the gatekeepers of opinion, the intellectuals and the artists did virtually nothing to protest against the demolition. They had for years been given time and attention within British broadcasting far beyond what they would receive in an open market, one which recognised no social imperatives, only those of profit. They had accepted these privileges as their and their arts' right, and not noticed when the structure which allowed them was being dismantled.

There was the Hunt Report on cable of 1983, commissioned by the government and written by a retired senior civil servant; like a minute written to a government's brief or at least within its frame of reference, without wider historic or social vision. There was the Peacock Report, meant to be mainly about money but honest enough to stray more widely and in the end something of a disappointment to the government but, again, lacking in perspective or depth in its sense of the role of broadcasting. So we moved along to the 1989 Bill which became, after some modification, the 1990 Act, the final confirmation of the sentence of death on the public service ideal and a disgrace to the nation of Milton and Blake and Coleridge and Mill and Arnold and Orwell. It went through in that half-twilight which, on matters of public importance, envelops what intellectual community we still have.

Meanwhile, BRU continued to publish its findings; and some people listened, nodded but were unable to do much to stem that tide. We issued thorough studies showing, for example, that in spite of what the putative new commercial broadcasters and some politicians of all parties say about what they love to call 'a regressive poll tax', most people do not resent the licence fee; they think it very good value (compared with the costs of satellite reception, it's the bargain of the century). We proved that, as against what the new censors and the demagogues assert, Channel 4 is not generally believed to be the home of disreputables, of homosexuals, lesbians and the like; an odd channel, certainly, but one which people have a right to watch if they wish; more general tolerance there than is shown by those who claim to speak for the silent majority. We proved that newspapers with major interests in the new forms of commercial broadcasting, especially satellites, were consistently producing biased reporting against the public systems. We proved that, in spite of the government's insistence on the need to open the radio networks to audiences it claimed were starved of a wide and nourishing diet, most people thought the radio channels satisfyingly broad and nourishing. We found, though this was not new, that people made a distinction between glossy international programmes such as *Dallas* – which most of them watched – and programmes with more content closer to their own lives. They watched the first kind regularly but 'got much more' from the second. Myth after myth, cliché after cliché, went down; but few paid much attention. It all proved once again that anyone who claims to speak disinterestedly for the public in a commercial democracy should say to himself every day, in opposition to what the profit-seeking persuaders say: 'People aren't as shallow as we're led to think they are.' To which a Leicester survey of people who take the *Sun* added its coda. 'So you get your political information from the *Sun*?' they were asked. 'Of course not. From the BBC.'

I was most directly involved with preparing two of BRU's shorter publications and these, perhaps because they were short and demotic were, as we had hoped, more widely read than the larger studies. In preparation for giving evidence to the Peacock Committee, we decided to try to define the fundamental principles of the public-service idea in a bolder way than had been done before. We wrote to about a score of people either in broadcasting or very knowledgeable about it and asked if they would set down in about two thousand words their understanding of the central principles of the public service. I read the essays again and again over two weekends until there emerged those principles which had most caught the writers' minds. They fell into place with exceptional ease, with no ragged ends or minority riders. Nine principles overrode all others. These were then laid out in the tightest fashion, one or two lines each; and under each principle were three or four of the most striking and cogent statements of it given by our contributors. By agreement, none of the statements were attributed; we wanted the purest statement of agreement on principles, free of the prior influence of known reputations, or the lack of them. That booklet, on the main principles of public service broadcasting, went into two impressions. We heard of one senior broadcasting executive who kept it in his briefcase – as a reminder of what, at bottom, he was still trying to fight for; there were other such sightings.

The second booklet of that sort, *Quality in Television*, appeared in the later Eighties, a much harder time even than the Peacock era to talk about such things. It was harder, also, to try to define what constitutes quality in television even than to winnow out the main principles of the public service idea. We used the same procedure and drew out statements of intellectual and imaginative conviction and force. No one went to either of the disabling poles: quality as being traditionally highbrow, or quality as whatever turns on the biggest audience. It is worth half-breaking the rule of anonymity to say that no other statement on quality in the medium has included an archbishop quoting Alastair MacIntyre on the philosophical meaning of 'professionalism'.

The divisions into which we finally disposed the material were deliberately non-ideological; they were generic and professional. But each section came to life with powerful expressions of faith from people who knew the business intimately. Like *Main Principles of Public Service Broadcasting*, this second lay (that is, not research-based) publication had hardly any public notice, nor did we expect any. In the profession it received less attention than *Main Principles*, for by then those who cared about broadcasting had their backs pressed even more tightly against the wall. The definitions of quality were therefore painful, like echoes of a more Adamic past, statements of an integrity broadcasters could no longer afford to try to uphold, ghosts of a passion they were no longer allowed to exercise. For scholars of no more than twenty years on they will bring to life, as at the very moment it ended, an era of uniquely single-minded professional probity; by some at least. That people could think of broadcasting in that way! That they had the time to do so! That the system within which they worked allowed, even encouraged, them to develop so powerful a sense of the possibilities of the medium and its value for the individual and for society! No one could practise it now, in 2010, they'll say. They may be surprised that, as early as 1990, we had had to write of it as of an era fast fading.

Towards the end of BRU's decade of life, the hardest decade in British broadcasting's history, we swam even more against the tide and drafted a *Charter for Democratic Broadcasting*. As I write it has not been published, since it only reached final shape as BRU gave up its independent status. The change was not due to any failing on BRU's part; it had carried out its brief well and even those who had now to withdraw funding did not stint in recognising this. But the Markle Foundation had already extended our grant well past the point at which they usually stop founding-funding; the BBC decided it could no longer afford to fund such outside activities, given the tying of its finances to inflation-proof rises only (though the cost of new communications technologies has long outstripped inflation, so the BBC is now impeded by a built-in deficit). ITC, the successor body to the Independent Broadcasting Authority, does not have the power to fund outside research, and the British Film Institute, though helpful to the last minute, has ideas of its own for television research, ideas not particularly close to BRU's special brief. Still, it had been a worth-while ten years.

The spirit in broadcasting at the beginning of the Nineties is easily indicated. A friend sent a pilot script to a television company long respected for its willingness to spend time and money on good programmes which might attract a sizeable and intelligent but not mass audience. The script came back quickly, with a note which ran near enough like this: 'It is an admirable and moving treat-ment of an important issue; but I am afraid the market is not right for that kind of product just now.' Even more striking than the quick dismissal of something which would, a few years before, have been considered at length is the new language, the language of the market, the product and the consumer. Against such lan-guage, talk of public service principles would sound like a sermon competing hopelessly against a huckster's patter. The man who replied like that had been a good broadcaster and in some ways still is; but he has had to pick up the attitudes, and so the lingo, of the new era. Those who write about radio are in much the same case. One professional commentator refers to his medium as:

'Radio, which is the most dated medium in the country, inclined to take an unfashionably puritan view of events.' 'Dated' and 'puritan' are the face-saving evasions there.

Or read the statements made at any convention today of broadcasters preparing themselves for the kind of competition which the new Act will encourage, discarding anything which might interfere with the search for secure large audiences, consigning sixty years of wide-ranging and varied provision to the dustbin of broadcasting's dodos. Such as this, from a senior executive of a large commercial broadcasting company: 'Who wants to listen to waffle about some minority play when you can turn the dial and listen to pop, jazz or rock?' We always get the operators for whom we provide comfortable living-space.

It really should not need saying that the new multiplicity of channels will narrow not widen choice; there will be a greater number of outlets, a smaller number of different types of programmes. Profit will decide how much – how little – provision should be made for those on the fringes, geographically, intellectually or in their tastes. There will be immensely more concentration on the dead centre of existing tastes; and that concentration will reinforce those tastes, never challenge them or suggest there is a wider world outside.

One does not expect those in or about to enter broadcasting for the money to recognise or admit this. That it escaped the minds of even the more thoughtful in the governments of the Eighties is one of the mild surprises of these days. How can intelligent, well read and cultivated people swallow this mass of special pleading, these falsely 'democratic' arguments, be willing to accept this low fate for people out there? The answer is not difficult and points once again to the educational and class divisions in Britain. The great bulk of the population are indeed, to these fortunate few, 'out there'. Their tastes may seem limited if not deplorable, but then, 'Who are we to judge?' They have not noticed that one of the best achievements of public-service broadcasting has been the proof that some elements of the British imagination – think of the surrealist humour of situation and of language in the best TV comedy shows – are not class-defined but shared by all parts of society; that is a remarkable revelation. As is the proof that many people can appreciate programmes more demanding and wider in range than would have been suspected if chances had not been taken: 'How do I know what I like until I see what I can have?' A class-bound and rigid definition of taste is one of the costs of a half-way democracy, but not for that reason to be accepted as in any way worthy of a democracy. Yet, held by the more cultured few in a cabinet, such an attitude assists the destroyers of good broadcasting no less than do the arguments in outright support of commercialism by the intellectual spivs of the same cabinet.

The invention of the idea of public-service broadcasting is likely to seem, to later social historians, an admirable idea the British stumbled on almost by accident, a form of late paternalism which, in action, became better than itself, better than its originators could have foreseen. Even at its best its importance was not recognised by most of those in broadcasting or given to talking about broadcasting. Fear of not being associated with the routine dismissals of the BBC inhibited them from recognising its achievements. So they said with relief and repetitively that we had 'perhaps the least worst broadcasting system in the world', a nervous selling-short, a denial of what is on any fair count a remarkable domestic achievement, and one which is not likely to return or be repeated in another form. It would be useless to try to call it back in its old form, and there is no point in merely lamenting past times. But almost no one in a position of responsibility – Lord Whitelaw was an honourable exception – thought hard about how to keep the best in the old system as the floodgates were being opened; the unsustainable claim that the market could ensure that the best would remain also went unchallenged. The popular press pursued its BBC-bashing; the top-drawer press, afraid of seeming stodgy, let the case go largely by default; the BBC did not put its case well, being also afraid of sounding holier than the rest. Palliness did duty for principle.

Democratically elected governments can destroy in the name of democracy just as easily as create. Commercial democracies are habitually disposed to that sort of destruction in all areas, whether physical, or internal to the culture as people live within it. In the last decade we have had a particularly virulent sequence of that kind of government. We have not fought them because we have not recognised the value of what they were destroying.

Broadcasting was given legislation at the start not chiefly because of the shortage of channels but because of the recognition that it was an important new medium and should be used well in all our interests – not to issue the government's line, nor to make the advertisers wealthy. So legislation led to windows being opened, not knuckles censoriously rapped.

7

Government censorship, especially of broadcasting, increased substantially in the Eighties. The roll-call is sizeable: programmes such as *Real Lives, Secret Society* and *Death on the Rock* all met trouble; and there was the ban on interviews with members of the IRA. The Broadcasting Standards Council was created, and the Act regulating video tapes. No wonder Britain has such a long record of being called to appear before the Court of Human Rights at Strasbourg.

The Falklands campaign produced one of the most exact, small and ludicrous examples of the way things tend to work, and also of how they can sometimes be brushed off. It can be found in the Broadcasting Research Unit's large study of the news media during that campaign. A Harrier pilot, just back from his first mission, was asked how he had felt when he realised that this time the siren was for real action not another exercise. 'For a few seconds,' he said, 'I was scared shitless. Then it was all right.' Honest and brave and compact. But the Ministry of Defence told the TV networks it couldn't be broadcast. Why on earth not? Because a British pilot is not to feel, or to admit that he feels, fear even for a few seconds? He'd be a thick pilot if he didn't. Or perhaps he's to use only heroic not everyday scatological language? The networks had the sense to ignore the injunction, and broadcast the reply. The Ministry of Defence in turn had the belated good sense to let the matter drop. There can be gains: in the massive coverage of the Gulf War, perhaps because of lessons learned in the Falklands, perhaps because the Americans were there and transmit much more openly, servicemen and women of all kinds spoke to camera of their fears and how they proposed to overcome them when full-scale fighting began.

The above examples, except for the new Council and the new Video Act, are largely political. The council and the act more accurately illustrate the British style, which is obsessed with sex. It is easy — and just — to attack the exploiters. But some things in these attitudes reflect strains deep in the English character; puritanism sitting at ease with voyeurism. Governments come to power not by going against the grain but by finding a grain to run with, and at the right time. The attitudes of good democratic governments are in a few things, such as capital punishment and racism, slightly ahead of those of many, perhaps most, of their citizens. As has been remarked more than once: without legislation, the most popular programmes on television would be public executions.

In less dramatic or less manifestly illiberal matters than capital punishment or racism, governments can sail closer to conventional opinion — sexual puritanism is easier to go along with, for an intelligent minister, than a call for the return of the death penalty; and he can ignore its consequences much of the time whilst himself reading, seeing and doing much as he likes.

Middle England is still a sexually puritanical society in the narrowest of senses — small-minded, fearful, 'let's not mistake liberty for licence' intoners — whatever the changes the last thirty years have brought in the habits of some groups. The Eighties saw the illiberal side riding higher than for a quarter of a century. The New Puritans rode again, the suburban foot-soldiers of sex-obsessed, low-level, conventional morality. And the government met them half-way.

The paradox was that those Eighties governments were aggressively in favour of the free market; and in entertainment matters that encourage sex, violence and whatever else sells well. So they introduced new checks. They had freed the poachers but then had to enlist more gamekeepers: the new Council and the new Act. To the exploiter the message was: feel free to make all the money you can up to the limits laid down by, say, the Video Act. No sight of penetration, but simulate as much as you want, with all the grunts and groans you want. The classic pattern of the hypocritical mind; sexual humbug sitting at ease with commercial greed.

Because, in addition, we have no Bill of Rights, many gateways seem open but — we learn later — are invisibly marked 'No Entry'. The air seems clear and fresh but suddenly swirls with fog when an unwritten rule has been broken — the perfect climate for encouraging fearful anticipatory evasive action in bodies which are in one way or another dependent on government.

Hence much in the BBC's difficulties. It reacted bravely in 1957, over the Suez threats; it kept its nerve during the Sixties; latterly, its record has been less doughty.

It is more than usually important to be clear here. Broadcasters have sometimes to decide not to show programmes, programmes with political implications as well as others, not because they have been leaned on by government but because other factors are in play — for instance, about accuracy or about likely effects on some viewers. An important case here was the initial decision not to broadcast Peter Watkins's *The War Game*, about a nuclear attack on Britain. This was in Hugh Greene's days as DG, and he was not easily bullied. It was nevertheless to be expected that the Corporation would be accused of yielding to government pressure. It was said, and it may be true, that heavily 'advisory' 'phone calls were made from Whitehall. I heard from both Greene and Huw Wheldon another account.

They said they had expected to transmit the programme though they knew it would be harrowing and so objected to. It proved to be far more harrowing than they had expected. So much so that they were advised by a psychiatrist that a very few viewers, in a state of chronic depression, might be tipped over the brink into suicide; a late showing could not guarantee that some such people would not be watching. Both said, in a way I found convincing, that they were willing to release the programme for public showing in cinemas; audiences there are self-selected, choose to pay to watch; but that they could not risk having on their consciences a decision which might cause even no more than two or three people who saw the programme by chance to be brought to despair.

But in the Eighties the Broadcasting Standards Council and the Video Act of 1984 indicate the dominant interventionist style of government. Don't trust the BBC governors or the members of the Independent Television Authority; or, for that matter, the

Broadcasting Complaints Commission. So: enrol more game-keepers. What this means is not that the governors and the authority have not fulfilled their briefs; it means they have not accepted the government's own narrow sexual standards.

On the other hand, the established authorities have sometimes been pusillanimous, as though hesitant to deny the air to even the silliest and most untalented Fat Boy – 'I'm going to make your flesh creep' – among writers or producers. Some programmes which went out and still go out should have been thrown away, not because of the wish to censor but because they were valueless hitch-hikers on the attraction of immature vulgarity, submissions to fashionable triviality.

A council such as the BSC can hardly help falling into the classic British trap: 'standards' are defined as the 'standards of sex and violence' exhibited. 'Sex and violence' links a couple of nouns as indissolubly as 'bacon and eggs' and 'fish and chips' or, odd contrast, 'sweetness and light'. The first Director of the council announced early on that he intended 'standards' to mean more than sex and violence, to mean quality in all kinds of programme; and some of us cheered. Whether he will be able to escape from the trap is, as I write, unclear. Meanwhile, we will have to go on thinking that the BSC is a sop to the Moral Majority.

That other characteristic invention of the New Puritans, the Video Act, handed over to the British Board of Film Classification (formerly the British Board of Film Censors) the task of classifying all videos, whether for sale or loan, or for showing in cinemas or on television (again, riding over the duties of the responsible broadcasting bodies). The rules for classification would be hilarious if they were not also a melancholy reflection of the main British obsessions. The central considerations are sex and violence, of course. But being British we have to be fair and make what seem like reasonable rules: hence the wilting willy at the unopened door and so on. Such formalities reduce the force of more important injunctions. All societies have to protect certain groups of their citizens: children who may be abused actually or through images, women who may be violated. If there is serious and responsible doubt about effects, about the power of certain films to encourage these abuses, it is right to be safe rather than sorry. But the British approach reduces the area of responsible doubt.

So it is both an unnecessarily wide (as to the institutions it covers) and at the same time an unnecessarily narrow – though characteristically narrow – Act. But, and here we go again since we are in Britain, the Act makes provision for an appeals body to which those video-makers and -sellers who feel the BBFC has treated them unfairly can appeal; and the result of that appeal is final. I was invited to be a member of the appeals committee and had a small crisis of conscience. I disapproved of the Act. I also wondered: if not me, then perhaps someone worse; perhaps I've been invited as one of the more liberal side. A tempting chalice – but a proper one? I have now sat on the committee for three or four years and found no one there who represents the spirit which informed the creation of the Act. If anything, we lean over to speak for liberalism. Nevertheless, the niggle about whether I should be sitting there has persisted.

The difficulty lies in the characteristic British Syllogism or Shuffle, which goes like this: I am shocked; so this is obscene; so it must be banned. But some people can be shocked by many things, and it is a misuse of language to call more than a small number of such things obscene. That some language and some incidents in some television plays disturb some people does not necessarily mean they are obscene; upsetting, perhaps, disconcerting, distasteful.

I give that example to make the point sharper; which is the proclivity of people in this country to confuse matters of taste with matters which can properly be called obscene. We know that taste changes from generation to generation, sometimes broadening, sometimes narrowing, and has been for the last twenty or so years broadening; as in the fact that women's bare breasts came on to cinema screens only that short time ago, and that by now their pubic triangles are, late at night, fairly often seen on television. That has either been not noticed or not accepted by some people; they continue to believe taste immutable and to equate the many things of which they disapprove with that which deserves to be banned. My Aunt Ethel was a prime holder of this outlook: she could dismiss anything of which she in the slightest disapproved, and the range was enormous. With 'I think that's *disgusting*; they shouldn't allow it.' Out went everything from brassière ads to music-hall comics pretending to fart — or sparrow-fart jokes, I expect.

One video on which the appeals committee was asked to pronounce illustrates the point. The owner of the video, of women wrestling in mud, appealed against the restrictive classification the board had awarded; it would have cut out almost all sales and loans. The setting, real not a studio, was a West Country pub on a Sunday morning; the women were in bikinis which very quickly dripped thick mud; the brassière tops came off first, then the pants. By now the women were covered in mud from head to foot. The audience seemed to be from a wide range of ages, including some who looked like OAPs; perhaps they were allowed in at half-price. It was an extremely distasteful film, the oddest prelude to anyone's Sunday dinner. I do not think it could be called 'obscene', unless that word were being used as an intensifying image not an accurate label. To base the case against it on the charge that it 'exploited women' would have been an intellectually unacceptable over-simplification.

I wish people had better ideas on how to spend their time. But I did not feel my brother's keeper in this, and thought the restrictive classification should be lifted. So did the committee and the appeal was upheld. I am not, incidentally, suggesting the board are prudes; they have to work within an Act which itself encapsulates prudery. So it is easier to serve on the appeals committee than on the board itself.

A short byway. We tend to associate censorship chiefly with attitudes on the political Right, but for about thirty years now a special brand of censorship has been practised by some on the Left. Partly because that is my own political wing, I find this less attractive even than Right-wing censorship. It is not an example of 'repressive tolerance' to believe, to insist, that people have a right to be heard (as in universities) even if their views are anathema to us. After the Arts Council cuts a couple of students, prompted by Michael Croft, set out to bar me from giving one of my lectures at Goldsmiths'. I was persuaded, I now think mistakenly, not to push the point. I was angry to a degree that almost frightened me and would have made me useless as a mediator. Travels round the world for UNESCO, seeing that a majority of nations habitually and often brutally deny their citizens free speech, has made my fuse very short indeed for these silly and safe games in England. It is too easy to excuse undergraduates in Britain who behave like that – 'they're young, they're idealistic, they'll learn'. That sort of patronage reduces them; they are old enough to know and to think better.

In the course of fulfilling an invitation from the Publishers' Association, in the late Eighties, I examined activities of this kind *apropos* books. Attempts at censorship, especially by left-wing municipal authorities, were wider, more aggressive and more stupid than I had expected. The rules proposed showed that those who framed them were imaginatively inconscient, would accept a meritless book if it avowed the correct attitudes, and could not recognise writing of merit. Again, the cruelty of the unco' guid. Coleridge was more measured: 'I have seen gross intolerance shown in support of tolerance'; these had no tolerance. The Publishers' Association, sometimes rather nervously but on the whole very intelligently, produced a number of countervailing booklets for the benefit of authors, publishers, booksellers and librarians.

There are more subtle, because almost entirely hidden from the practitioners themselves, forms of censorship; or, perhaps better, distortion. Walking up Regent Street, in early 1976, to a small meeting in the BBC, just outside All Soul's I ran into a friendly acquaintance from the Corporation. His greeting was unusually muted, as if to one previously believed to be on our side but now revealed as a member of a terrorist cell. More amused than abashed, I went to the meeting, where the chairman, also a staff member, had the same betrayed air. A few days later yet another corporation executive repeated the reaction, and elaborated on it so far as to say I had allowed myself to be duped by a bunch on the far Left. All three men were devoted servants of the corporation, intelligent and honest.

The Glasgow University Media Group had just published *Bad News*, a study of the claims that television news is largely objective and neutral. They had asked me to write a preface. I agreed, on the understanding that I would not associate myself with their particular research findings – it would have taken too long to assess those – but would use the opportunity to write on the assumptions which lay behind their research: that, to a degree very few journalists whether in broadcasting or the press realised, what constituted their 'news' was a culturally conditioned construction (though some get nearer objectivity than others). Therefore more journalists should recognise two related processes in which they are involved – for each of which there is a handy sociological tag: 'agenda-setting' and 'the structuring of reality' – in determining what they called 'the news'.

I had not realised how deeply resistant the profession would be to these fairly simple ideas. Hence in part the BBC executives' sadness at what they saw as a blow to their professional integrity. It is fair to say also that they had thought the Glasgow Media Group's handling of evidence unconvincing, and so wished I had not associated myself with it, with no matter what qualifications.

A senior man in ITN said: 'But the news is out there and we simply report it as accurately as we can.' That the very process of selection – 'this is news, this is not' – were products of his time and place, not of illegitimate outside pressures but of all the unspoken assumptions of his class, of professional case-law and of society as a whole was, surprisingly, news to him and unacceptable. Not all the profession were so taken aback. A review of *Bad News* by a former Deputy Director-General of the BBC said, *apropos* the preface: 'Every sentence of it is absolutely relevant and right.' But he was a very rare bird in those circles and had always been regarded as exceptionally disinterested.

Of course, what we call 'the news' has to be artificially constructed, by a process of selection so speedy and instinctive as to seem almost natural, in the blood. There is simply too much material; filter determining subject, order, length and stress have to be employed. Several main types of filter: those determined by constraints of the medium itself, what it can and can't do, and constraints of time and place; the impressionistic judgment that this is 'good television material' but that is not, not visually interesting; and the filters which accept materials which are at home with the cultural air we breathe and reject others. There need be no political or authoritarian pressure to reflect society's assumptions; most of the press, of radio and of television, moves naturally towards confirming 'the ordinary man and woman' in their attitudes and in setting odd balls aside. In a street interview with a popular television anchorman, I once refused to accept that, because vast numbers of paperbacks of all kinds were now being sold, this showed we were a much more literate society; most of the paperbacks were trash. On that, the consummate television journalist turned to camera and, before introducing the next item, said: 'That puts us in our place, then.' A perfect Shakespearean *ducdame* – 'a cry to call fools into a circle'.

If, in the definition of news, the besetting error of most practitioners is to regard it as objectively 'out there', waiting to be plucked, with the aid of their well trained eyes for relevance, from the overloaded trees of daily events, the equivalent error in some students of society, usually among the less talented, is to look for 'low conspiracy theory' in any interpretation of events. One uses a restrictive set of filters, the other waters the rich brew so that it runs easily through their one determinist filter. The more intelligent use 'high conspiracy theory', which does not rely on secret telephone calls from Whitehall to newspaper editors and broadcasting chiefs, but marries the journalists' own assumptions about what news appears to be to 'hegemony' theory. The processes of defining and interpreting news are then unconscious expressions of the assumptions of the forces which really control society, not simply of the general and generalised climate of assumptions.

Most important, though, one has to remember that in this kind of society something very often escapes, something which cannot be explained by agenda-setting, the structuring of reality, low conspiracy theory or high conspiracy theory; but which is the expression of a personal will, of conviction, or of wit and imagination, or of bloody-mindedness. Which is why in the end these powerful elements of hidden censorship are no more than elements within a more complex and far more interesting whole.

'High conspiracy theory', though – by which the definition of news is believed to be influenced chiefly and usually implicitly by the major forces and drives of a society – leads directly to the most difficult of all types of censorship: self-censorship. That kind inspired from outside, by the high conspiratorial forces, is in turn the simplest kind of self-censorship. You would not perhaps yield to explicit directives or bullying, and they are rarely needed. You do begin instinctively to evade issues, opinions, positions not acceptable to those above or the body of those out there. All this is hugely practised in totalitarian states; but like persistent bad drains it also haunts open societies.

This does not mean you always appear to go along with the main impulses of your society. You are free to tear it apart but in a way which doesn't in the end get beneath the skin, and so gives the sense of being bold and honest, but without risk. Moral indignation and self-interest then come together. Open capitalist societies – especially the United States, as both the wealthiest of societies and the least secure in its collective psychology – produce, regularly, commercially successful books which reveal how rotten their societies are. The readers can enjoy them and say with the deflective wryness which acts as a lightning conductor against any real hurt: 'Well, that puts me/us in our place.'

At a conference of writers in Berlin, in the early Sixties, there was constant criticism of the USA, of its mass culture as massively exported and of its foreign military interventions. On the third day an American scholar responded: at least America was the most self-critical of nations, her writers far sharper in criticism of their own country than outsiders. There was a bark from Mary McCarthy, sitting next to me; I had begun to recognise that bark as the prelude to an intervention. 'Sure we're self-critical about our own sins. Means nothing. It's the mirror on the whorehouse ceiling. We do it and watch ourselves doing it. Get it both ways.' Switching through the simultaneous interpretation channels then was a compact lesson in cultural and linguistic differences. The French had no problems, the Germans needed longer so as to convert idioms and images into the abstract and polysyllabic, the Russians were at sea – 'Whereas in the capitalist West there are institutions which . . .'

Finally, the most disregarded form of self-censorship, of all kinds of censorship, is that designed to protect our own sense of ourselves. A related kind of personal censorship leads us to omit things which might hurt the living, or the dead, but we are usually fully conscious of that and of the moral ambiguity it can involve. Self-protecting censorship too is sometimes conscious, but more often unconscious. We are betrayed by what is false within, by the urge to protect that image of ourselves we wish not only to project towards others but also to sell to ourselves, even though we half-know it to be biased, partial, deceptive. Face-saving, phoney personae – to some degree these are inevitable for all of us or we would, to adapt George Eliot, 'die of the roar which lies on the other side of silence'. But, especially if we presume to present ourselves as a lens through which something in our common experience may be more honestly seen, we have to do all we can to correct the lens's distortions.

CHAPTER 9

LANTERN ON THE STERN: CONVICTIONS, LANGUAGE, GROWING OLD

The light which experience gives is a lantern on the stern, which shines only on the waves behind us.

Coleridge, 'Allsop's Recollections'

This is the use of memory:
For liberation – not less of love but expanding
Of love beyond desire, and so liberation
From the future as well as the past.

T. S. Eliot, *Little Gidding*

1

Coleridge also speaks, neatly as ever, about 'excursions in my own mind'. This tale has moved across three decades. The start of the Nineties is both an inevitable and a peculiarly convenient place to end: a turning-point in British political and perhaps social life, and the beginning of true old age for me; but, oddly, no less pressure to push on with some things.

The Sixties, and the lead-in to them from the late Fifties, seemed at the time one of the more cheerful decades. The first widely spread prosperity relaxed a lot of people, made British society feel more open. We even began to half-believe that some of the old restrictions, of the sense of division, would be substantially eroded. But it was a phantom relaxation or, better, remission; as so often. For the very respectable working class, the lower middle class and a little higher, Robbins and the huge expansion in higher education, rather than the emergence of a British style in pop music, would be one of the chief markers of that change. The sense of the power of 'Them', out there, weakened. A permissiveness which wasn't often promiscuity grew.

In the first volume of this sequence I quoted a working-class woman in her fifties, long married to a typically selfish, woman-misusing man, talking of a girl we knew who was 'living in sin' with her boy-friend, at least for the time being (the woman didn't use the redolently old-style expression I have put in inverted commas, but it is a useful way to mark the change she was illustrating). She said she thought that way of going on was all right: 'If I had my time again, I'd have tried that . . . and wouldn't have married him in the end.' Only ten years before she would not have been likely to say that or have thought it. That kind of relief was not conceivable, not to a respectable working-class girl. My Aunt Annie, about seventy, was sitting nearby. She could never have got her tongue round those words nor her mind comfortably round the idea. So she said, 'Ooh, fancy!' when her step-daughter-in-law made the assertion; she wasn't judging, just registering surprise at a very large change. The fifty-odd-year-old woman's position was more solid, more typical of the Sixties' enormous changes than, for example, the often-quoted fact that about that time girls from expensive boarding schools were adopting broad Liverpool or Cockney accents and other working-class odds and ends. Even if they too lived with their boy-friends without necessarily thinking of marriage they rarely broke the class divisions then or, even more rarely, in their eventual marriages.

About the Seventies there are fewer striking things to say, at least for the two of us. Looking back on living abroad in the first half of that decade, I recall we thought surprisingly rarely about Britain, except through our sense of our children and friends being over there on the island. The work was hard and engrossing; the perspectives world-wide. More and more, Britain seemed small, marginal and often confidently small-minded too, at least in its responses to the growing demand across Western Europe for wider than insular thinking. By the time we came back, just in the middle of the decade, the country was grey.

For me, the late Seventies and early Eighties were the time at Goldsmiths', with the national Advisory Council for Adult and Continuing Education and the beginning of the Broadcasting Research Unit. Small matters in a national perspective; but they also indicate that some more modestly fair kinds of hope were nurtured even in that drab period, pointers to a future which might assume again that, whatever the economic difficulties, we should feel responsible towards each other; little markers.

At the turn into the Eighties the air had changed more abruptly, more chillingly, than it had for a very long time. Initiatives such as those above now seem, over that trench, as old-fashioned as those socially earnest initiatives of the second half of the nineteenth century I have often invoked. Echoes of a less cost-conscious, a shabbier but a more humane era.

The Eighties were above all harsh and hard-nosed. Undoubtedly, they touched sympathetic nerves in the British collective personality; at the admirable end attitudes which believed in driven hard work and self-reliance, at the worst those which urged getting on at any price and at whatever cost to your neighbours (that word itself became out-of-date and out-of-place). Mrs Thatcher embodied both elements in her beliefs, projected them in her manner and, above all, in her voice. I belong to the few, especially among people on the Left, who thought, but on grounds not usually assumed to be hers by her enemies, that both the Falklands and Gulf campaigns and the attack on certain bad trade union practices were justified; and that the poll tax had some elements of sense to it.

There is little more to credit and much to deplore. Her reign was lacking at the heart. There is no need to say more here about that: it is well documented – the relentless economic determinism, the unshakeable assumption that letting the market rip will produce its own justifications; that these can be substitutes for difficult social and moral choices, for seeing society as more than a collection of individuals and atomised families. Among my own special interests, her treatment of broadcasting exemplifies the worst in her implacably self-confident, limited vision. The Broadcasting Act, we saw earlier, will irreparably damage one of the better social initiatives of the century.

Clearly, I do not feel an affinity with Mrs Thatcher; rather, the antipathy one feels towards a self-righteous, interfering neighbour. She is in many ways my Aunt Ethel come back to life. I was brought up with, precisely, hauntingly, that shrill, nagging, over-insistent way of speaking, that bossy-pants way of walking, that remorseless insistence on always being right. It seems surprising that so many upper-class Tory MPs were insensitive to the whole style, mistook it for a set of determinedly statesmanlike attitudes.

So: a decade to regret, a decade which damaged some of the best British attitudes. Three utterances, seen on television, sum up its more unattractive aspects: Lord Denning saying it was preferable that innocent men spend time in gaol rather than that the judiciary be brought into question; Arthur Scargill seeming reluctant to condemn directly and publicly the miners who threw a concrete block off a bridge on to a taxi, killing the driver (Scargill countered by talking of police brutality); and Mrs Thatcher quoting St Francis on civic harmony – in that voice. Worst of all was the gloating among some right-wingers, at the end of the decade – on the grounds that the collapse of authoritarian, repressive, Marxist regimes in Eastern Europe had discredited the ideas of socialism – in favour of let-it-rip individualistic capitalism.

Now we have to try to revive the damaged tissue. It will not be easy; we will be going against the thrust of social and cultural changes made in the last dozen years, whose style and structures are meant to last. But, more and more now, people – not only on the Left – seem to be turning against this bleak and uncharitable spirit, so perhaps change is on the way again. One can't prove this, only point to what look like straws in the wind.

In relation to deeper changes in society, the attitudes of the governments of the Eighties are only symptoms and consequences, a first exploitative phase in the new or at least the emerging social landscape. Many decades after it was first announced, and thirty years after the false near-dawn of the Sixties, the hold of the traditional kind of class division really does appear to be weakening in Britain and across Western Europe. Thirty years after Michael Young coined the word, a sort of 'meritocracy' can be seen moving into position. To which, yes, I belong; and probably you, since you are reading this book. But the sense of class or, more accurately, of division, does not fade so easily; it is transferred, its emotional charge included, to the new categories and groupings.

The new stratification is a pyramid with three parts. At the top, perhaps 15 per cent of us, well trained – especially for society's more complex new needs – at least comfortably paid and likely to have arrived at this point by virtue of some quite high competence – very often in one type or another of communicating, technological or verbal. Below us, the majority, perhaps 70 to 75 per cent, less trained but adequate to society's needs so far, and again quite comfortably off. Below them the underclass, the outsiders, the out-of-work, for whom modern society cannot find a place; and the old and the very poor – none of them worth much wooing, politically or commercially.

As always, what look like minor cultural phenomena can be revealing. They show unmistakably the persistence of the sense of division, the thrust towards transferring old class attitudes to new status divisions. Hence the layering of television advertising by channels – for cars, for kinds of holiday, for foods and feeding, for the different supermarket chains, for clothing, for sports and leisure, for every aspect of taste which can be marketed. All these are now divided by status and allotted to their apt broadcasting channels. The process can easily be seen in the other mass media too, in newspapers and, even more strikingly, journals; and so out from goods to the stratification of assumed opinions and tones of voice, to almost all other kinds of communication right across to popular fiction and popular religion.

There is a further refinement. Modern technology makes possible, especially for those who have more than the average of disposable income, for that top 15 per cent, a more and more finely tuned range of provisions. Any large railway station bookstall shows the hugely increased and hugely subdivided body of journals for those with sophisticated leisure pursuits, and freedom to spend a good few pounds a week pursuing them. In one London station bookstall I counted 6 different journals each on guns, hi-fi and video; 7 on photography; 8 on music; 9 on horses; 12 on cars; 14 on computers, and 20 on sports of various kinds. Among the many journals on golf there was a clear front-runner: *Executive Golf*. At first there came the intriguing thought that executives must play golf differently from others; but it's only the ads being segregated. There was also, and unsurprisingly, among 37 journals on aspects of health care, one on Health Care for Executives.

More and more varied, finer and finer layers of provision for the top group goes along with more and more coagulated provision for the next and much the biggest group. For the more literate executive: not only the existing 'quality' papers but also the *Independent*; not only BBC 2 and – for a minority within a minority – Radio 3, but also Channel 4; and all those semi-specialist journals. The most important casualty in all this is the assumption of a general audience, of the general reader with a range of responsible interests outside job or particular leisure pursuits. With the decline of that assumption have gone also, or are failing, the journals of opinion (such as the *New Statesman*), those which assumed a band of respectably educated and widely interested people at all levels of society. We might do well to revive the word 'hobbies' to describe those more circumscribed interests, dominant today, which are outside work but also internal, detached from any interest in social meanings.

At the same time, the popular press grows shoddier, the more popular broadcasting channels on both networks drive each other lower in pursuit of the same mass audiences; so do videos for home viewing, so far as the Act allows. The top 15 per cent in society can produce a tidy profit on relatively small but expensive sales; the great body of people have to be kept consuming and changing what they consume. Vast sales, small profits on each, quick returns, so very large profits overall. To stress the point yet again: these audiences live in a world which endlessly tries to persuade them to buy according to fashion, and to change those fashions according to regular instructions from their phoney mates in the mass media. Reading, listening, watching, we see inescapably that almost a hundred years of literacy have brought this, for most people. This only near-literate mess is what we have made, are making, out of all those good efforts and intentions.

Three images sum up the new divisions: mushy peas, theme parks and Channel 4. I described earlier the way in which mushy peas latch on to and develop a traditional taste. Theme parks hit the dead centre of the middle range of people: packeted again, but with a nod to history . . . film- and television-style history, processed nostalgia. Channel 4 is, it hardly needs saying again, for the selective 15 per cent.

The movement is towards solidifying, congealing, the tastes of the great majority of people, so that they do not object to anything fed to them, no matter how bland, tasteless, prefabricated. They aren't as foolish as that may suggest but they put up with such things and reserve their critical faculties for more private interests, from football to pop music. We have plenty of studies which show how well developed those critical abilities can be in those, finally unimportant, areas. Too many of the authors of those studies then invoke or imply that 'stay as sweet as you are' assumption. People can be, are, highly discriminating in their personal interests, it is said, so stop criticising them as though they accepted all the public mash fed to them, and as though your kind of critical literacy is the only acceptable kind. But they do in a certain sense accept that stuff; it may not at bottom seem real to them but they don't blow it away contemptuously; they are almost always ill-equipped to confront the admen, the PR men, the politicians selling them duff programmes, and all the other hucksters. They are not discriminating in public and political matters; and those who try to be soon become cynical, as though walking through and against a flood of mud. Either way, the sense of the community weakens yet again. If Herbert Read were able to come back, he would be reminded of his own prophecy of several decades ago:

It will be a gay world. There will be lights everywhere except in the minds of men and the fall of the last civilisation will not be heard above the incessant din.

That rapid run through the last three decades makes me feel as though I have wakened, suddenly and startlingly, to the way my own life has run; I had not seen the road so clearly until making this backward scamper. Thirteen years of university extra-mural teaching, eleven years of internal teaching, five and a half years of the international civil service abroad and eight and a half years running a university college. Teaching outweighed administration; but I never intended administration to take up so much time. I slipped into it all, was pulled out of teaching without expecting to be, or expecting it to be for so long. Would I have done better to refuse, in particular, the invitation to UNESCO in Paris? The question is misguided, and regrets beside the point. You take this branch rather than that; and then the third branch along from the new one – and gradually you are further and further away from your original main stem. Questioned at this point, we all tend to say, 'Well, I wouldn't have wished it otherwise' and 'It all turned out for the best in the end.' Things acquire their own inevitability and rightness simply by being lived in and through. A fully faced regret, if that is what threatens to emerge in the end, is hardly to be borne. I might have stayed at Birmingham, resisted what later invitations might have come and, above all, continued to help build the Centre for Contemporary Cultural Studies. That is the one thing I might feel a twinge of regret about, rather than regretting leaving the straight academic life in itself. But on the whole regrets are few. All things had their interest and, as one always says at these times, their 'challenges'. That word deserves better than its too-frequent routine appearances in public farewell speeches. It can mean that each job seemed worthwhile enough to call for all your energies and whatever intelligence you could muster. To use another over-used but still exact word, a favourite of Lord Reith, it 'stretched' you; or an Oxonian friend's very Oxonian summing-up of parts of his life: 'Well, after all, it was *fun.*'

The academic who allows those kinds of exterior roads to call him is always an ambiguous figure, and especially if he is thought actively to have sought to tread them. One meets such people now and again, in committees, some hoping they are climbing a ladder which could lead to a vice-chancellorship, others just pleased to be in an activity which, though they would hardly be likely to admit it, seems more real than academic life. They are the ones who over quickly propose a tough, slick solution to a problem and glance at the businessmen, the high executives, on the committee for recognition of their lack of what might be thought the indecisive niceness of the ivory tower, rather than the firm smack of the market-place. A small corruption.

Much more interesting are those who are not pushers but were pulled. To me, that always recalls Charles Frankel, of the OECD report and much else. His friendship with Lionel Trilling captured the idea of two different but worthwhile kinds of university inhabitant: Trilling a superb academic, quiet, soft-spoken, rather withdrawn until he knew and trusted you, an admirable writer but one to whom lecturing to an audience seemed likely to be less agreeable than teasing at meanings in print. Frankel, large, ebullient, hearty, outgoing, thoroughly at home in political corridors, in public negotiations and utterances; yet also one who loved teaching so much that, even at the height of his reputation when he could have left almost all teaching to others, he tried always to do some lecturing to first-year students. I first met them together in the Trillings' flat on Morningside Heights and sensed their rapport, their mutual respect and affection; nothing guarded either way.

No doubt Frankel, for all his public eminences, failed to do some things he might have done. He seemed, though in a larger way, to have felt much as I have: that it was a duty to answer calls which seem worthwhile, but that it was even better to teach and write in your subject; that was both a duty and a love. For an English academic the public-service tradition is more habitual and well-trodden than for an American. We have long had not only a Literary Happy Family but a Public Service Happy Family; we are small and know one another; we have assumed there should be a constant interplay between those who are paid to think and those paid to do. Partly, perhaps chiefly, this is because recruitment to senior academic life and to the higher offices of state has been from so relatively small a circle, from Oxbridge and the main schools which fed it. An old boys' network, but one which had some worthwhile results. The height of this worthwhileness, the point where the narrowness can be partially excused, lies in the assumption that the academic in those corridors does best when he acts most thoroughly as an academic not as a putative statesman or politician, acts as one who has claims to have learned something about trying to think objectively – odd though that may make him seem from time to time.

That is why I have been led to defend the quango tradition. I started by wanting to say only that there were more good quangos than most people realised, and that a good quango was a useful tool of an open society. I was led to defend them further precisely because in the Eighties this instrument of the idea of democratic consensus was badly damaged, in the interests of that confrontational model of government. There is a more important significance: quangos emerged from more than the consensus idea; they emerged from and could only work where there was an assumed pattern of values about the nature of the good society and the good life. As, for example, at that moment when the Pilkington Committee had examined all the ways it could think of to improve the squalid state of commercial television in the early Sixties, and had come to the conclusion that the most radical solution was the only proper one. Sir Harry was able to look round his mixed group and say that though this solution would certainly be unacceptable to the government the members all seemed agreed that it, not a more digestible one, should be proposed. He was able to do that because he knew – perhaps without knowing – that he was talking a language of values, of the attempt at true judgment, which was shared (he would not have put it like that, nor wished to). The real reason for the weakening of quangos over the last one or two decades is that the assumed consensus itself has been progressively lost in the fog of relativism; that has fed, in reaction, the crude aggressiveness of contestatory politics. Democracies can only work well, be true to their declared nature, when they are underpinned by a sense of some common values. Without those, they look like democracy but become, as I have said again and again and again, a pattern of shifting populisms – which can be exploited by the hardest-mouthed.

2

I have argued for many years about the strength and continuity of the sense of class division in Britain; and have now, only a few pages back, argued that in some ways that sense is being eroded or at least taken over by a new sense – of stratification, based on profession, position, executive status. It is just as well that the process will be slow, because the new looks likely to be no better than the old; perhaps worse, because its indicators are more lightweight than those they are succeeding. One can meet upper-class people who are simply snobs; or others with an admirable, lived-out sense that *noblesse oblige*. Eliot's *Notes Towards the Definition of Culture* may still be unpalatable, but especially bears re-reading now.

Nor has the sense itself of class, of division, anything like disappeared; it flourishes, especially in comfortable middle-class enclaves, and will flourish for a long time alongside the new stratifications. As I wrote the first draft of this chapter I came upon two instances, both concerning Mrs Thatcher who had just left government. The first was from one of her own junior ministers. After the usual tribute to Mrs Thatcher's abilities and achievements, this woman added: 'Not quite the sort of person one would invite to dinner, though.' The other was from a staunch Tory, also a woman, admitting that on balance she was glad Mrs Thatcher had gone or she might have had to think of voting for one of the centre parties. For Mrs Thatcher, she added, 'is, after all, common.' There the striving, respectable working class meets, linguistically, the hide-bound secure middle class – my Aunt Ethel's routine dismissal of those working-class people whom she saw as below even her, and of whose manners she disapproved, was 'common'.

My own constant concern with the nature of class has obviously been nurtured by my background; not only that of the poor working class but of an orphan within that environment. There is an obvious danger here, the danger of putting too much weight on social factors in examining your own attitudes. Anger about class divisions, and this is only one example, can be fed by early experiences, but not wholly explained by them. It can be only part of a more deep-seated set of attitudes, of thin-skinnednesses; and those may owe more to nature than to nurture, be less social than personal.

It is easier to identify shortcomings than any strengths we may have, partly because to recognise a single small strength easily seems like arrogance and, more important, because many of us live with the sense of our own weaknesses more at the front of our minds than with a disposition to pat our own backs. My own greatest intellectual regret is for a limitation it took many years to recognise; my mind does have a narrow range of interests, tends to go round and round the same old tracks. It is a clear lack, can to some extent be worked against but not completely overcome.

There is occasionally a certain expression on some academics' and no doubt others' faces, especially when they are still under thirty-five – a surprised, lifted smile which seems to be directed more at their inward sense of themselves than at anyone outside. It says: 'Gosh, I'm so pleased that I've got where I am, especially from a standing start.'

The reverse of the first smile can be seen in the kind of person who looks hesitant but grave, and withdrawn, as though wondering when and whether the next insight will come. I tend to live between the two. It is not disputable that a certain cleverness got me out of Hunslet. That has not, I think, given me the first sort of smile but it can make me sharp, over-sensitive to slights, more willing to give than to receive. But the limits are now plainer than they used to be. I enjoy meeting people whose perceptions, and powers of expressing them, plainly outrank mine. The best can even lie fallow without always pushing for quick certainties; their minds are sinuous and flexible not snip-snap; they do not jump at conclusions, can afford to – are undemonstratively confident enough to – ruminate; they can deal in half-tones.

Above all, they do not feel threatened by intellectual challenges, by disagreements with whatever position they may have taken. That kind of assurance I still find hard to reach much of the time, though I have learned ways to live with it. Yet I still have to gird myself to face a discussion which may challenge views I hold hard by. They may be threatening a platform I have built to hold a set of opinions on a subject which greatly interests me, which seems important beyond all personal considerations. But, to an extent others may not themselves experience, do not recognise and do not have to recognise, that platform, that position, is closely tied into the sense of the personality built up over the years. The sense of self-protection is then stronger than the urge towards truth, especially in an environment which seems, if not alien, then still not a home.

I will be neither surprised nor put out by those who take the opportunity to dismiss this kind of self-examination. Only a few, a very few, have the right to do that, though; some others do it because they have begun to feel uneasy. If I look over my own career yet again, this time to produce a summarising judgment, it would run something like this: 'Probably like many others, I have seemed always to be holding under tension the ends of several different and often countervailing threads – the public and the private, family and profession, the living and the dead, the local and national and international, the Left and what seems the best in the Right, the quietly unknown and the evidently powerful, the present and the past, flux and – a little – stillness'. Given my nurture, my background, I have achieved a fair amount; given my nature, my natural limits, I have worked too narrowly but have ploughed that ground fairly thoroughly. The oddest job of all I've had – that at UNESCO – is a good instance of the pros and cons. I did some things well there, but my limits also showed, in the things I did not manage to do as well as I would have wished. 'Not bad, but might have done better,' might be the Great Head Teacher's comment.

That may, of course, be too charitable; we can all allow ourselves indulgences, absolutions, benefits of the doubt, repetitive self-justifications. We almost all feel we have fallen short in some ways, not done all the worthwhile things we might have done; but again we get ourselves over it.

Fallings short: my own most practical wish, if I could be born again, would be to be six inches taller. If, as very occasionally happens, I find myself the tallest in a group, the effect is heady. The Cleopatra's nose effect. No doubt it would soon wear off.

There are some who seem to have no need of face-saving habits, few moments of self-doubt. They tend to have no private lines on the face or expressions of the eyes; they never look vulnerable. Some give off a brusque masculine energy, as though they have muscles or an erect penis in the brain. They are great brushers aside of hesitancies, or indecisiveness based on a touch of what they regard as excessive, small, moral scruples. They seem not to have read many of the great novelists, and never poetry – or, if they have, not to have absorbed a sense of imaginative malleability from them. If they are public people then a combination of determination and optimism seems called for. I remember one saying, as he removed a difficulty with a bromide brush: 'Ah, but you forget – I believe in people.' How could he seriously get his tongue round that banality? The steadiness of the half-shut eye.

There is also a decisiveness characteristic of parts of the professional middle class which can sit with very great sensitivity in other areas of the personality. Auden saying briskly that you should kill new-born kittens with one twist or blow on the neck, and without hesitation, is my own most remembered encounter with that style. I would even make a cross-national comparison: French intellectuals have that edge of decisive hardness much more than British.

The people we admire without being at first aware of it tell us most about what we lack (just as we attack hardest those who have our own kinds of weakness); these tend to be, through their writings, our austere elder brothers and sisters; for me, Tawney and Titmuss, for instance. They seem to have a security which prevents them from bolstering their own egos by gossip about others, gossip malicious or self-consciously charitable. But at the same time they do not give the impression of having to consign most others to the flat backcloths of their lives; they do not write off others they dislike; they do not feel moved to tell funny anecdotes for effect in company. They are short on righteous indignation and not prone to harangue, to lecture people rather than talk to them, ever to use a formulation such as 'so I told him straight'. But they can rebuke us silently by a look which has more of understanding and regret than of dismissive judgment. That is quite different from the setting-aside glance which categorises you, sums you up, and declares you do not belong to their kind of group, are not to be admitted.

But what makes less secure people tick, especially if they have no sense of a God or Church to look to? They are the opposites of the once-born, the simply assumptive believers, who appear to go through their lives without ever being shaken to their roots with the temptation to agnosticism, let alone atheism; they have a special smile, too. Some others with no trace of religious feeling also have their own smile, one which dryly accepts the pointlessness of the world as they see it; but they rub along easily and creaturely, like the central character in Camus's *The Outsider*. Such an attitude seems at home in North Africa but no doubt can be found in Castleford, Yorks.

Yet others inhabit that odd region where we are likely to say: 'I appear to have no religious sense. But if I were moved to join any church in the West it would be the Roman Catholic; that is at least fully and uncompromisingly eschatological.' I like to think my apparently unshakeable puritanism, with that small 'p', is because I try to be responsible for my own conscience, but have a suspicion that that may be a fancy way of describing a self-involved intractability. Among other effects, it makes me suspicious of over-tolerance, too easy moral generosity; 'the world is not our oyster' is a basic cracker motto.

So does one feel, as to religious belief, like a Bisto kid, looking in at the warm scene, pressing the nose against the glass? Not really, though occasionally that mood came, a long time ago. It has not been encouraged to stay by acquaintance with European or American religious groups. So there we are, no joining. One can still just imagine, though, that it would be good some time to be surprised by joy; that does not seem at all likely, nowadays.

A sort of solitariness, then; at least as the bedrock. A touch of modified unexpectancy, certainly no progressivism, nothing which would make you utter, 'I believe in people,' though in a certain sense you do, and in another just as important sense you do not. Neither Newman's 'terrible aboriginal calamity' of a godless world, nor Thoreau's vision of the mass of men leading lives of quiet desperation; nothing very melodramatic. Yet sometimes the world can seem loveless, going on going on without meaning or justification. Then Mrs Moore in Forster's *A Passage to India* is our psychological great-aunt: 'Boom, boom', no more. But equally we like, respect, almost admire, precisely those who go on going on, creaturely, shabby in dress but not entirely shabby in spirit, in some important ways resilient, not soon willing to give in, companionable, tolerant, undemanding, capable of gentleness and pity, of fellow-feeling; Joyce's Leopold Bloom rather than the painfully trapped Little Chandler in his 'A Little Cloud'. And weak people like my Uncle Walter who are 'their own worst enemies', drinkers, over-generous with money they cannot afford to squander, but not pompous or self-righteous or stiff with rectitude; minor Dostoevskyan figures, rather, on his comic-sad side.

Their great-uncle, their very great-great-uncle, is Lear at the end, after he had lived out in all its horror and accepted that 'Men must endure / Their going hence, even as their coming hither: / Ripeness is all', and so finally came through to a state of grace. Years ago I heard a fine lecture by the then professor of English at Bristol, D. G. James, on *King Lear*. I now understand what he meant by his final sentence: '*King Lear* marks the limit of secular art.'

We all, those of us without the comforts of religion and no doubt many who sincerely believe themselves to be religious, live our lives according to our own selected fictions. The centre of mine is about the importance of going on going on. 'Stoically' would be too large a word: 'stubbornly' will be better, sometimes perkily and cheerfully, sometimes grumpily.

Behind all this is the conviction, the blind assumption, that life should be morally coherent – that we should try to make it so for ourselves and should try to make it possible for others to go on the same road, if they wish; against all the odds. I do not look for a common culture if that means uniformities; better to be socially ecumenical. But the divisions, the traditional chasms, in British society are not often a form of rich diversity; they are far more often inhibiting, belittling; they block whatever way there may be to an uncomplicated pluralism and a kind of unity within it. In this perspective, the most surprising historical fact of British life and those of most European countries is that for centuries most men have gone to war for a set of prejudicial principles, asserted by others, which were patronising to them and false to the true strengths in their lives and of their countries.

From this group of convictions a whole range of subsidiary beliefs come: that most people are capable of rising to better ways of life if the expectation and the possibility are there; that all have a right, a birthright, to the best; that we should all be as free as possible to make our own choices and shape our own lives. It follows that all of us must be given the chance to become more self-aware; and, finally and yet again, that each bell tolls for us all. That last may not be so hard to translate into modern circumstances as some of the other convictions, because it has its own tap-root: in the traditional neighbourliness of British life. That still lives strongly, in both working-class and middle-class areas, but almost entirely enclosed within those areas. The wider sense of its meanings and implications has been damaged in the last half century by the false mateyness of the persuaders and, more, by that greatest of all weaknesses in an open commercial democracy, by populism – egalitarianism gone mad and gone soft, the Parkinson's disease of the body politic, which now lies over all we think and say, like molasses. The definition of fraternity in Wordsworth's 'Republic' should be more often recalled: 'Where all stood thus far / Upon equal ground; . . . we were brothers all / In honour, as in one community / . . . Distinction open lay to all that came. / And wealth and titles were in less esteem/Than talents, worth . . .'

Any discussion of personality and especially of elements in one's own personality, runs one overwhelming risk: of setting the picture in amber, of rigidity. The moment we stand back from such a portrait we realise, though we have really known all along, that we are all of us several kinds of person, chameleons, different characters at different times; and they are all true. It is for most of us embarrassing to look over our own personae, to run along the line of masks. We can seem as knowing as an Oxford Street huckster and as fumblingly unsure as a seventeen-year-old boy, can hate dogs in the manger but often feel like one, particularly when faced with aggressive confidence in younger people. In managerial mood, we can feel like a bright tycoon; or then assume the figure of a steady old traditionalist. We can be cautiously prudential or wantonly bohemian, greatly hopeful one day and entirely unhopeful the next. Above all, for me, both Martha and Mary, a slightly harassed Martha much of the time but one moved to defend the Marys rather than rebuke them; they are what most Marthas would prefer to be, at bottom. All this will surprise no one who has even only slightly thought about his own styles, moods, changing impulses.

In the end, with no larger sense of meaning, one does, most of the time, just go on and on. There is a strangely comforting rightness and acceptance, not depression, in the thought of that going on, that flux of time. As so often, Chekhov caught not only the substance but the mood (in *The Three Sisters*):

'Yes, we will be forgotten, such is our fate and we can't help it, and the things that strike us as so very serious and important, they will be forgotten one day or won't seem to matter. The curious thing is we can't possibly know just what will be thought significant and important or what will seem pathetic or absurd.'

But we can easily see why that limpid resolving prose will do nothing to satisfy those who hunger after a firmer truth.

3

For last year's words belong to last year's language
And next year's words await another voice.
                                    T. S. Eliot, *Little Gidding*

By our words will we be known. Language, the language of others
and my own, has proved much more powerful in my thoughts
than I had suspected before beginning to write this sort-of-life.
Two ideas appear now to have run throughout: how much language shows the way society is changing, and how in the course
of writing you learn more about yourself through your own use
of words.

If anything would make me at last give up taking part in the
arts/culture debate it would be the thought of having to push
around yet again those tired counters which do duty for clearer
or new thoughts, the to'ing and fro'ing as in an endless verbal
tennis game, with worn-out balls on a badly marked-out court.
Many of those words have run throughout this story but are
worth finally gathering together: community, caring, grass-roots,
supportive (one of many insidious and very popular "ives"), amen-
ity, alternative, gender (often mistakenly preferred to 'sex'), ethnic
(usually wrongly used, to mean 'different from the English, Welsh
and Scots'; we're all ethnics of one kind or another), participant
and participatory, authentic, campaigning, militant, committed
and commitment, dialogue, outreach, liaise, praxis (often misused
for 'practice'), bonding, unwaged (to avoid 'out of work' and
'OAP'), senior citizen (of course; it would be good to see 'retired'
or 'elderly' back, or just 'old').

Antagonistic words in the same debate include: élitist, state
patronage bureaucracy, bourgeois (especially in phrases such as
'bourgeois crap'), conspiracy ('conspiracy theory' is the most
common use), orthodoxy, confrontation (as in 'seeking confrontation' for 'not accepting my point of view'), provocation (the
translation here is 'refusing to agree to my proposals and suggesting modifications'), controversial (much like 'provocation' but
slightly softer), paternalistic, patronising, Bourbons, divisive
(because right is on our side and most people know it; or at least

those people we habitually talk to), highbrow arrogance, dull, solemn, heavy, earnest and 'emotional' (which means making a judgment of value. I most recently came upon that in a management paper from an Institute of Higher Education, in response to a staff complaint that academic levels were being allowed to fall. That was, 'the management' said, merely 'an emotional assertion').

At the extreme are one or two words which must never be used because they sound superior or are labelled racist or sexist. At a drafting group I heard a man rebuked for writing that many people in Britain are artistic philistines. It was a cliché and he should have avoided it. But the rebuke was because the word is racist, since in pre-Christian Palestine the Philistines were an ethnic group whom the Hebrews despised; and here he was, doing it again. The same person rebuked another man for male chauvinism (it was during a working group on the report prepared for the British Council) for referring to the enormous unpaid contribution to the work of the council by what have for long been known, almost always with sympathetic admiration, as 'council wives' in overseas posts. That patronised the wives and insulted the women professionals in such posts, it was argued (there were at the time only a handful of women professionals abroad but several hundred wives). We wanted to retain the tribute so, I think, settled for 'partners'.

In such a climate substitutes have to be found, since there is no value-vocabulary for words which validate our seriousness and honesty. Statements have to be almost always individual, personal, once you are forced outside the circle of totemic words of the sort listed above. 'I actually think . . .' means 'Because I am stressing it as my personally-arrived-at conviction I do ask you to believe it, even though I have brought forward no argument about shared judgments on value.' Its brother phrase is 'I definitely think..'. Others, more idiomatic, are 'This *has* to be . . .' and 'This has got to be . . .'. Insecurity shows itself in 'I happen to think', the nervous version of 'actually think', and in the more formal but still tentative 'My perception is . . .'. Only the very swish will say, 'I have a perceived notion that . . .'. Any locution will serve to avoid saying 'believe' or 'am convinced'.

Those last are two of the verbs which can hardly be spoken,

the words which are 'moral' or, in the favoured dismissal-jargon of the day, 'judgmental'. They can also be crept up to by substitutes, not synonyms but vague words which do a foggy duty. As in 'that is a very meaningful/real/moving incident'; or, a rather ineffectual gesture at the void, 'That is a very/interesting/intensely/ *human* story'.

Out of the same embracing mood come the evasive and disguising phrases. They exist at any time, naturally; they are particularly drawn on at insecure periods. So today the old-fashioned 'spilt milk' and 'water under the bridge' are put into service not just as tolerant acceptings that some things simply are not worth making an issue of; they foreclose any item of conversation whose pursuit might involve making a stand rather than a deal.

There are more self-deceptive evasions: 'Let's face it' can mean the opposite – 'Let's not face the complexities. Let's settle for a simple explanation'; 'It's as simple as that', which again means the opposite, 'Let's stop going over the ins and outs, which I find embarrassing to my taste for easy answers.' The best-known public self-deceptions include 'nuclear-free zone' for 'anti-nuclear local council'; 'positive discrimination' for introducing, into making a decision, factors hitherto thought irrelevant (that may be justified; the verbal cover-up isn't); and 'direct action' for 'violence'.

There are many cheating evasions. One of the more common today, to come back to arguments about broadcasting where this kind of cheating is rampant, is the use of 'ensuring more freedom for the air-waves in a democratic society' for 'clearing away regulatory obstacles to my making a lot of money quickly'; and 'enlarging choice for the viewer and listener' which means 'allotting channels to me so I may exploit them for gain'. One of the worst examples is the White Paper *Broadcasting in the Nineties*; like a well oiled semantic one-armed bandit, it moves on a succession of 'weasel' words and phrases, as befits a document produced for a government which has no languages except those of the market and of a narrow moral illiberality.

We all know about the procession of catchwords from television and radio; they are rarely interesting in themselves, slightly more interesting as indicators of late-twentieth-century leisure-culture, especially as they affect children. Or as they grip the broadcasters themselves.

Between finishing the last chapter and starting this, I heard the particularly smooth presenter of a radio programme, meant to reach the minority of listeners at present interested in the arts, use these phrases within three minutes: 'punters'; a 'magicked' something; something '-wise', as in 'stylewise'; 'on a face-to-face basis' for 'face to face'. The presenter went on to refer to 'the whole picture-postcard bit', to 'pulling out all the stops' and to 'frame-by-frame' thinking. There can be a jerky vitality as some of these come and go month after month. Used as they were here, they were more like a string of verbal jellied-eels, a confetti of anxiously up-to-the-minute clichés whose tattiness shows up the moment you listen even half carefully as the litter falls around you.

The judgments presented in the programme were as facilely fashionable as the language; Ezra Pound again: 'When the language goes rotten . . .' so does the thought. Most broadcast arts programmes are uncritical celebrations, passing puffs. If Radio 4 addresses its more thoughtful listeners in this way, how do Radio 1 presenters talk? Perhaps they have arrived at a Labovian subtlety all their own.

Among adults in the more modern professions, the main cluster of new words and phrases picked up for general rather than exact professional use have to be value-free also, not weighty and three-dimensional but two-dimensionally pushing things along, lightweight, un-humanised, committed to the medium but to no message. Along comes, on cue, the language of cybernetics, of communications technology, of computers and word-processors. Speech acquires the air of what can be called the 'scientocratic', a form of imitation-scientific linguistic sterilisation induced by relativism and the urge towards germ-free words. Where PR dominates, the scientocratic and the matey cohabit: 'Let's establish enhanced demand mechanisms and roll back this lousy trend.'

That kind of utterance is much less common and illustrates less in the mental climate than the cybernetically neutral, as in the continuous loops of everyday speech to be found from just above the manual worker level: 'spin-off, fine tuning, time-warps, the new generation of (meaning "this year's very slightly modified model"), feedback, foregrounding and backgrounding, menus, interfaces, scenario, module, on stream, in synch., up-front, down-side, time-frame, state of the art (meaning, again, no more than something which has just been given a new "image", so that selling can be "hyped up"), window of opportunity, mind-set, blip, "hands on" experience and "experiential learning" (for "practical training"; much used by teachers and educational administrators who wish to convince the politicians and business-men they are "right in there")', and 'rolling' or 'scrolling back'. In two days' fairly casual listening I heard virtually all those several times.

The more PR-affected phrases include: 'giving a higher profile, giving a steer to, sexy, seminal, tranche ("slice" is out, and if you can say you are about to "vire a tranche", you score many "brownie points"), ongoing ops, hanging in there, promising to give someone a bell (to 'phone them), kicking the ball about, brainstorming, strengthening the infrastructure, the flavour of the month, bouncing off, taking on board, being up-front, going down-market or up-market, recognising the bottom line, the name of the game, increasing visibility, on the back-burner, saying "our thinking was . . .", targeting maximising contacts, saying "micro and macro" even if not always accurately, defining some new objects for sale as "designer this . . .' and "designer that . . .", "cotton rich" (that fooled me, buying underpants in Marks and Spencer. I had bought them before I realised it meant ' "This is a mixture of cotton – for the large part – and artificial fabric"); 'clever' or 'serious' as in 'serious – or clever – money' – that is, a lot".' Again, only a selection. Some are lively; almost any word or phrase, technical or demotic, can be useful in the right context. Used so much, their spray gets in your eyes. It is their repeated use as crutches which wears them out. There is a fascination with words and images in all this, but not for 'the images that hurt and connect'; these have had a smooth plastic coating put over them. Consumer images will last longer, especially in the arts. Promoters will go on claiming for some time that they are present-ing 'a well balanced diet of the traditional and the new in our products for arts consumers'. In the face of all this, those MPs – and they are many – who still utter, 'I take the view that . . .', 'I am seized with . . .', 'at the end of the day' and 'in this day and age', sound as though they have walked out of a Disraeli novel.

All that is about the cultural uses of words. They intertwine with personal uses which can be identified in us all; personally favoured words and phrases which tell something about the way the culture, this time, this place, interact with our particular personalities. My own favourites are much over-used; perhaps many people hear their own repetitions frequently. Fairly active and instrumental words, to begin with: 'focus, filter, interact, intertwine, interconnect, wrap-around and mesh'. 'Secular': I had been missing a word to express a long movement through time, saw this in a piece by a professor of philosophy, looked it up and appropriated it for good; and 'demotic' (to avoid 'democratic', which has other uses).

Then, epithets which mark qualities I admire more than I knew before I made the list; and also use too much: decent, respectable (both heavily over-used), unaffected, companionable, liveable, comely, flexible, unexpectant (the working-class version of 'stoical', putting up with things so as not to have hopes fall even lower), elegant (a mathematicians' favourite but useful for others because it avoids more obviously aesthetic words, and quirkily picks up a word which in its lay contexts is suspect, being fancy). Come to think of it, 'quirky' is another favourite. Then there are 'telling, revealing and striking', all over-used because in my kind of writing you are always trying to find some significance beyond themselves in individual incidents. And there is 'feeling things on the pulses' which I picked up from Bonamy Dobrée and have not let drop.

Words and phrases to indicate dislike are just as 'revealing': brittle, self-indulgent, evasive, illiberal, snide, populist (those top the lists of, respectively, epithets of individual and social misconduct), wide, knowing, smart Alec, disconnected, at ease in Zion, damp, dispirited, and 'insurance policy behaviour' (face-saving qualifications).

'But still the heart doth need a language, still / Doth the old instinct bring back the old names.' Coleridge again; the pleasure of remembering the words which recall a lost world. I made an hour's trawl: 'whippet, flat cap, snot, chapped (as in "chapped knees"), chilblains, Meccano, fretwork, impetigo, verruca, conkers, outgrowing his strength, Woodbines, humbugs, licorice allsorts, kippers, herrings, black pudding, thick-seam tripe, cowheel, corns, Andrews Liver Salts, Beecham's Pills, tinned salmon and pineapple, condensed milk and Carnation milk, California Syrup of Figs, vanilla slices, fancies (iced buns), rabbit hutch, coal 'ole and coal scuttle, false teeth, "Me feet are killing me", stays (corsets), ginnel and snicket, tits, knickers, Phulnana, Parma violets, scarlet fever, clip rug, gas mantle, rag-and-bone man, Parrish's Chemical Food, to mash (tea), Oxo, Bisto, Woollies (Woolworth's) and "woollies", as in "I've got me woollies on, it's that cold", to fend for yourself, larking about, penny duck (savoury rissole, made mainly of cereal and animal fat), scraps (of fried batter from the fish and chip shop), beer-off (off-licence), senna pods, commode, eau de Cologne, tick ("Can I have it on tick, please?"), darning and, inevitably, 'shabby'.

Other words and, especially, phrases and passages, one remembers from reading, chiefly because they are startling or funny or both. Or they capture an idea more sharply than you had known before, without necessarily giving you the feeling they are tied closely to your own time and character, though some are. Ibsen's 'One should never put on one's best trousers to go out to battle for freedom and truth'; Sterne's 'There is a North-west passage to the intellectual world'; La Fontaine's 'A hungry stomach has no ears' whose English equivalent is more vulgar: 'a stiff prick has no conscience'; 'Il faut tenter de vivre' ('Men must endure . . .').

And two which move over into another kind of importance: 'He hath a daily beauty in his life / That makes me ugly'; most of all, the line of Coleridge I have quoted before, about weighing not counting men. The largest single group of passages which persist are sad, regretful. This may indicate no more than that elegiac verbal music is more memorable than happy. Strange how potent sad music is. 'Call no man happy'; 'Oh call back yesterday, bid time return'; 'The sigh of the oppressed creature, the heart of a heartless world'; Thoreau on 'quiet desperation', also quoted earlier and much quoted by others. He had many other good lines.

Emily Brontë's Mrs Dean's flatly dour: 'We must all be for

ourselves in the long run'; 'I have seen him that is beaten, him that is beaten . . . Set thine heart after letters'; 'How quick bright things come to confusion'; 'Time that is intolerant / Of the brave and innocent . . .'; 'All, all of a piece throughout / Thy chase had a beast in view / Thy wars brought nothing about / Thy lovers were all untrue'; 'That it should come to this'; 'Othello's occupation gone'; 'The death of friends or death / of every brilliant eye / That made a catch in the breath'; 'Action is transitory . . . a step, a blow . . . / Suffering is permanent, obscure and dark / And shares the nature of infinity'; and finally, one that insists on being hopeful against the odds: 'The truth is great, and shall prevail, / When none cares whether it prevail or not'.

Counterpointing, but fewer, are the joyous passages, most of them large, generous invocations: 'Ah love, let us be true to one another . . .' Arnold goes on to lament the lack of certitude and hope in the world, but it is the first line one remembers at least as much as the others. 'Dear friend, Elizabeth, dear friend / These days have brought me . . .'; 'Oh, everyday in peace and labour / Our life and death are with our neighbour / And love illuminates again / The city and the lion's den / The world's great rage, the travel of young men'. 'Dear dead women, with such hair too . . .'; again, it becomes elegiac . . . 'What became of all the gold. I feel chilly and grow old.' And, as I can hardly ever forbear quoting, from my near penniless Aunt Annie on the great operatic arias: 'That sort of music makes you want to give all your money away.'

4

About Time, growing old and the oddities of it all, we may best start with yet more quotations, stuck in the mind because, first heard, they captured a truth nearer to us than we had realised. The old chapel injunction 'Live this day as if thy last' sits oddly with a fine more current phrase, 'He played around as if there were no tomorrow', and with another from my childhood: 'He always went about things as though he had all the time in the world.' More often, life is seen as bracketed between the coming out and the going back: 'a traveller between life and death'; 'History is the lengthened shadow of a man.' And all the regrets which flow from that sense of the shortness of time and the impossibility of going back on our tracks, calling back yesterday. One of the most poignant common phrases desperately offers what cannot now be given: 'I'll make it up to you, I promise.' 'O man, that from thy fair and shining youth / Age might but take the things Youth needed not!'; 'The almond tree shall flourish, and the grasshopper shall be a burden, and desire shall fail; because man goeth to his long home'; 'Ronsard me célébrait, du temps que j'étais belle'. The pathos of dying young: Keats to Fanny Brawne: 'if I had had time I would have made myself remembered'; Hamlet's injunction to Horatio before the fell sergeant takes over; and 'These walk the earth and know themselves defeated'. No doubt the long syllables help.

There are more bracing attitudes. 'We owe God a death.' 'It is time that I wrote my will; / I choose upstanding men . . .'; 'I have prepared my peace / with learned Italian things / And the proud stones of Greece'; Yeats put on the mantle of age quite early, but 'Lapis Lazuli' makes up for the more obvious histrionic gestures: 'Hamlet and Lear are gay; / gaiety transfiguring all that dread.' I do not fully understand Kundera's 'The old are innocent children of their old age', but it sounds beautiful, and I can just grasp at a possible meaning.

The commonest clichés about growing old seem even more boring than most; but they are mostly true and, like most clichés, come up new-minted once they are directly relevant. Life gets shorter and shorter and goes faster and faster. We find ourselves surprised to be so old at thirty, forty, fifty, sixty and seventy. We redraw the playing field, 'move the goal posts', at each decade but without really kidding ourselves – even though the commonest cliché of all, that the policemen look young, is a faded memory; now the Foreign Secretary does. At the same time, life can seem long, especially if we are tired, as we are more often than before. Sometimes we think we should try to be 'nice' all the time; there's so little time left that to be nasty is a pitiable waste. Then we recognise yet again that is a coward's attitude, as if we said not to someone else but to ourselves: 'Don't hit me, I haven't long to go.'

What we now know as we did not earlier is that we have only temporary use of the earth, briefly share a patch of land, are living on borrowed time, all short-term tenants, casuals in rented property with the landlord not around much – until we walk off the edge of the world. Aunts Ethel and Annie and all the others possessed the place in their day and have gone; as must we.

It is true too that some of the time we feel as young as we ever were. It's not that there's a young man trying to get out of the carcass of the old – that's an over-dramatic cliché – but we rarely feel grave and reverend, no matter how grey our hair, nor want to feel like that; better to feel somewhat raw and unfinished. Though, from the way they have their hair cut, the suits they choose, and the voices they develop, I suppose some people do want to feel grave and reverend; and manage it, often from quite early.

We still haven't got to the point. It isn't that a young man insists on popping up occasionally in the old body; rather, there is a feeling that you are old and middle-aged and young all at the same time, seeing with trifocal eyes, multifocal eyes. All time eternally present. Against the flux of time and the eating away at our physical well-being which, the increasing aches and pains of daily life do not allow us to forget, is going on all the time – against that I find Eliot's line on the eternal presence of all our days not only sober and chastening but comforting, something of a stay within the flux. Eliot goes on to talk of the unredeemable, but that is a word and a concept I cannot use. I pick up, though, that line on the eternal presence of all our ages and find it more consoling than the sense of an endless progression, even if that were to a better material condition.

Which is partly why, I suppose, Arnold Bennett can be so attractive. I quoted from *The Old Wives' Tale* when this story began, as I saw Aunt Annie dying in St James's Hospital, Leeds. Bennett concentrates on the sad, poignant 'riddle' of life. It always does come to this or that and one way or another but, whether Bennett fully knew it or not, that sense of the remorseless flow of time and the way it wears us out – Tithonus' 'the woods decay, the woods decay and fall . . .' – transforms the often pedestrian prose and perceptions into poetry, the poetry of pity. Not the pity Graham Greene so mistrusts because, if directed at individuals and individual circumstances, it can reduce them; the phrase 'an object of pity' was not coined accidentally. But, for Bennett, a sense of pity for the individual is born out of the sense that, small and wilful, we are carried along by forces we can have no hope of influencing, let alone controlling; like a non-swimmer in a slow, not very deep but powerful stream. But the non-swimmer does what he can, treads water and moves along with the flow. Tithonus was right to regret his immortality; he was missing something, the chance to stretch himself up to a certain end. We need time, finite time, for that stretching. It is a dimension of our spirits as space is of our bodies.

You don't need to be possessed by death. Yet I find in myself a need to keep in touch with the dead; they are, in a sense, always there, not necessarily consciously thought about, but a sort of presence, an awareness, all the time. New deaths bring this feeling more and more frequently to your attention, like unsolicited mail dropping quite regularly through the slit in your mental letterbox. I think it was E. M. Forster who said, perhaps on the night we ate at the Reform Club over thirty years ago, how conscious he was of people dying to left and right. Falling out of the column. Soon, many of the names in the obituary columns are of people younger than you. You wonder whether you should ask editors to let you bring up to date the two or three obituaries you have written, now it's becoming so late; you wonder whether someone is doing that for you. Feeling surplus to requirements. Push off; you disturb the order here; someone else has booked this place. A look some young people give you, as though you are another kind of being, as though they wonder why you still require house-room. Lear asking his daughters to forgive him for being old.

I was a late recogniser of the procession of the dead. Then it happened suddenly, when I had just turned sixty; back in Paris for a day's talk about adult education in the two countries, and alone. The hotel was only half a mile from UNESCO so, feeling pushed by an instinct I did not understand, I dropped my bag in the bedroom and started to walk. I knew I was tired; within twenty yards I knew I was nostalgic; I did not know how suffused with memories I would become. I found myself facing the apart-ment in the Rue Casimir-Périer where we had last seen Francis Hope; he was correspondent for the *Observer* and also writing his poetry all the time. The main recollection is of him playing with his baby girl whilst the two Marys looked and smiled in the way mothers do when the father is spoiling the child. That was a few days before he was killed in the crash of the Turkish Airlines DC 10. That Sunday afternoon, twenty miles out of Paris, we had caught the announcement over the car radio and soon could hear the ambulances howling like mad cats up the motorway; to several hundred dead. We both felt someone we knew would be involved.

For a while, in that unusually lambent couple of February days, Paris became a city of deaths. Maheu of UNESCO had not long gone. Bonamy Dobrée, my first professor, and patron, seemed there too because it was there I had belatedly heard of his death, at eighty-three, wanting to go. Billy Mayfield, who had given me my first job, in Hull, and been a marvellous teacher of teachers, seemed to be there because he had loved sitting and talking in the Paris apartment; he too was not long dead.

Then, Lionel and Diana Trilling having lunch with us on a pavement near UNESCO not long before he died. He was neither well nor happy, and still sad about the breach with Leavis over the Two Cultures debate of more than a decade before. That had not been healed, though he felt he had tried hard. Always watchful for him, Diana had said, 'Tell him some of your funny stories about UNESCO. He enjoys those.' He smiled, and I was moved as always by the dignity of his face and bearing.

And Charles Frankel, shot dead with his wife in their apartment – in the New York they could not bear to leave for a home elsewhere – by two drug-crazed robbers. Characteristically, Charles had sat up in bed and tried to reason with them.

The next day, heading for Charles de Gaulle and the 'plane, the car went up the Rue Francois Ier. That was where Christopher and Jane Ewart-Biggs had lived when he was at the Embassy. We had not known them well but he had sought me out to talk about his great non-professional love, writing. And now he also was dead, killed by the IRA not long after he had become ambassador to Dublin.

The dead who have moved through this story are often those who showed something about intellectual honesty and toughness, or about the dues owed to the sympathetic imagination, or about grace in extreme situations. These things are true of relatives as much as of friends. So, apart from those above: Boyle, Humphreys, Fraser, Shonfield, my brother Tom. As I was drafting this section I came, unexpectedly, upon a note by Andrew Shonfield from the early Seventies. It caught the amused, courteous and generous among his styles, as he broke some surprising news: 'Imagine the most unlikely thought we could have had when we first met as gunners in that field in Italy almost thirty years ago – that we would each give the Reith Lectures in successive years! It pleases me enormously. . . .'

As to grace: Joyce Grenfell making light of her ailments to the end – demonstrating her movable glass eye, for example – and then slipping out quietly; and the artist Peter MacKarell of Goldsmiths' who suffered years of increasingly disabling decline with multiple sclerosis but saved himself from despair partly by painting the whole process step by step and partly by refusing to stop being visually intrigued by life and people. At my last visit, just before he died, he said, 'I reached the bottom at the beginning of this week. But I'm up again and drawing.' Again, that dread transfigured.

Of the family, most have gone now; Aunt Annie in her mid-eighties and Aunt Ethel in her nineties. They live long, those Northern working-class women, longer than the men. Then a cold snap in February makes them slip on the icy front step, they break a hip and do not recover; or the great reaper pneumonia takes them after a few weeks in bed. Tom died in April 1990, much sooner than we had expected, but he had proved to be riddled with cancer. I knew I admired and loved him but did not realise how much I would feel, when he went, that a sheet-anchor had gone; how much I would, quite simply, *miss* him. We did not meet often but he was my big brother and that feeling never went. It took many years to realise he was tougher, less family-sentimental, than I am. He was best man at our wedding and I assumed I would be his. But he had a very close friend from his otherwise lonely and unsympathetic schooldays in Sheffield, and that mattered more even than family habit or his undoubted affection for me. As the older son of the older son, his son had by tradition the middle name 'Longfellow', after the poet we believed was related to us. Tom said he would not burden a child with that oddity; I would have. When I told him the story of the foolish temporary lecturer at Goldsmiths' and the, to me, immoral role his union had played, Tom said, 'That's all right. That's their job.' But I never heard him speak slightingly of anyone and he gave almost all his free time in eight years of retirement to the Samaritans, to those who had had strokes, and to wounded people of many kinds. He was not a churchgoer, though his wife was, and they had the funeral service in the great Parish Church of Grantham. It was crowded with people who loved him and many of whom he had helped. I spoke 'Fear no more . . .' and could hardly get through it. He had remained more cheerful than that. A couple of days before he died, when he was on a powerful morphine drip but intermittently in possession of himself, he came to the surface and asked his wife and children to come in, with two bottles of champagne. He spoke to each separately, saying how much and why he loved them and mildly admonished the children for what he thought were weaknesses which should be watched. His son became embarrassed, thinking it all sounded too much like *This is Your Life*, and was ticked off: 'This is my last speech and I mean to make it properly.' On the day before he died, he managed to look at the ten of us gathered round the bed and whisper, 'I love you all.' That was the older brother who, more than half a century ago, held Molly's hand and mine and shepherded us as, just orphaned, we left our tiny stone cottage for a new, separated, life.

Molly is still up in Leeds and I see her as often as I can.

The physical business of ageing shows, most of all, in what is done to our faces and, even more, in what we do to them. Some can carry the inner essence of their beauty through to old age. Helen Corke, D. H. Lawrence's early love, looks ethereally beautiful in the photo of her in Lawrence biographies. She appeared one night on television, now a very old lady walking with an old man, Malcolm Muggeridge. He had carved out a pixie, foxy, cheeky, smiling face for his old age; she still looked shy, contained, surprised by life, beautifully hesitant. There are old men, rather like Muggeridge, who look like withered pippins until they cock their chins and grin; then they are twenty years old, not yet settled into their own characters.

The opposite can be seen in those people I mentioned earlier, who seem only to have been waiting until they could put on, physically and psychologically, an air of great middle-aged consequence, could be large and portly and broadclothed, boss figures, managers of men. They probably look of consequence even when paddling about the bathroom naked; they've grown into the persona. The Germans slip into this manner most easily of all Western Europeans; and the Mercedes Benz is their exact automobile visual equivalent. Broad-faced, large, muscular, middle-aged farmers in any European country – were they ever slim? – look right, as though never shaken in themselves, not quarrelling with themselves. The English archetypal male professional look is the ageless Head Prefect, energetic, smiling, lean.

We sculpture our faces by the pattern of our loves and dislikes, by cutting out certain habits and extending others, by believing some things about ourselves, whether they are true or not, and resisting others. We all have a best age, that time in our lives when we are most at ease. We are all used to the truism that for some all life after thirty seems an anticlimax. We recognise less that for others the best time of their lives is in their fifties, forties, seventies, or sixties.

We all have three or four faces ready at any one time; but only one or at the most two define the particular phase of our lives we are passing through. The ten-year passport photograph is no more than a rough indicator. Two successive passports may show little difference, because face-change phases are each of about fifteen years in most people. The next passport shows that the shutter has clicked over. This is more than saying simply, 'You look older'; of course you do. It is the recognition that life, the manner of confronting life, has taken a major turn; the eyes and the mouth, not the wrinkles or the extra folds of flesh, are the critical signs.

For men, the most typical shock is to see a woman whom you have known to be beautiful, after a fifteen- or twenty-year gap, after her face has entered a new phase; to see that she is now and will be for some years to come, until the next switch, middle-aged. But if she smiles, and you see that she still feels secure in love, then it is as though an illusionist has passed his hand over the face; the younger face shines out, or a new kind of beautiful face.

It takes longer to accept our own new faces – until a new photograph or a certain angle of light on a mirror make the change no longer escapable. Our editing – a cheating photographer air-brushing out the lines, blotches, double chin, the thickening at the neck – no longer works. We realise one day that the crows'-feet under the eyes, which used to disappear after a night's sleep, are now there for good. At that point we begin to accept that we must start calling ourselves middle-aged, at the least. The head itches intermittently, as though we have beetles in the rafters; odd hairs appear on the comb and the open pages of the book, looking coarser than they did before and drier. Then hair and dandruff fall around like snow; at low periods we feel like a moulting duck. We don't necessarily have Yeats's rage at being fastened to a dying animal, but know what he meant. A friend says suddenly that we all become less fresh as we grow older, especially round the crutch, and need to bathe more often. A smelly dying animal. Then one day we overhear someone say, 'You know, he suddenly looked an old man' or 'He does look his age now, doesn't he' or 'He's aged, seemed to shrink, this last year or two' or 'Ooh, hasn't he changed? I'd never have recognised him.'

Perhaps it's all worthwhile if we can tot up cheerfully what we have learned from the journey. But that's easier said than done, and always intermittent. Sometimes we feel we have learned nothing at all along the way, sometimes are surprised at what we do seem to have picked up. Sometimes the power to respond, especially to calls upon imagination and fellow-feeling, seems to have dried up, as though an inner palate has become dulled. Sometimes doors seem to be successively closing behind as we inch forward, and will not reopen. We feel less inclined to accept new challenges, unable or unwilling to make new friends, disinclined to consider other than the mildest change in the manner of our lives. It is tempting to call all this the recognition of limits, at least a small part of the wisdom that can come with age, but that is an unjustified making the best of a bad job. Unless we fight very hard we lose entirely the sense that we are going somewhere, anywhere, that there is always another place over the hill or round the corner. Without being fully aware of it, our spirit steadily narrows its focus, tells us we are short of time. We know that moment has come when we find ourselves thinking: 'Well, this suit will probably see me out.' Or this car; or the decoration of this room; and perhaps this bunch of lazily unrevised opinions. 'There are so few who can grow old with a good grace,' Richard Steele said, and by and large was right. There are some, though.

Some remain busy, busy not simply to keep the black dog off their backs; that would be self-deception and soon exposed even to most who pursue it, but busy with something about which they have not the slightest doubt that, even if they died the next day, it would have been worthwhile. That can mean not only doing things, good works and all the rest, but being things, things they had not been before, widening and if they can deepening their sense of themselves, their family and friends and world. E. M. Forster once said, of Lampedusa's *The Leopard*, 'This book has changed my life.' He was in his late seventies when the book appeared. Impressive as are some of Dylan Thomas's poems challenging death, Forster's sentence is more startling, more tonic, than 'Do not go gentle into that good night . . .' or the refusal to mourn the death of a child.

5

Someone suggested that people of my persuasion should be depressed at the way in which many of the causes we have tried to advance over all these years are now in decline: not only public service broadcasting, public support for the arts, the approach to censorship, weakening the sense of class and especially its effect on education, and much else; the fading away of the spirit which informed those nineteenth-century initiatives, usually freely provided, which I have listed several times; initiatives which, in spite of the inequalities and brutalities of the time, did indicate a commitment to the idea of the Commonweal, to Wordsworth's Republic.

It can be saddening, yes; but not depressing, because not permanent. No one with a sense of the movements of the Condition of England debate over two centuries will be surprised, or put into depression, by the last decade. One could see it coming, and it will go as it came. The more liberal sides of the English character will reassert themselves. Until the next setback. But sometimes the sliding back is to a point a little bit ahead of where we were before. Not a sunny uplands progressivism, but enough to be going on with.

As for myself, I can't and don't grumble. The love of words got me out. I was accepted as a classless something-or-other, but did not join an Establishment. Doors opened; the world opened. I have odd scars, external and internal, but they were all worth getting; the fights were more enjoyable than perhaps they should have been. I had more 'fun', to use my Oxford friend's word, than would have seemed possible at the start.

Over all, for me, is the example of Tom. He would not have claimed to have been going anywhere in particular throughout his life; he had struggled through to a job for which he felt suited and believed unquestionably worthwhile; he became the first headmaster of a rural secondary modern school, not because he was particularly ambitious but because he liked the idea of that job, and presumably the appointing committee recognised his disinterested devotion. His first wife died in the most tragic of circumstances. He married again after half a dozen lonely years, and they had a very happy going on until his death fourteen years later. He carried out all he did honestly and patiently. Though he wasn't 'going anywhere', he was being something; that ensured he remained cheerful and open and apparently untouched by regret to the very end of his life, to the champagne party, to the last expression of love and the few hours that then remained.

'He that puts on a public gown must put off a private person.' I hope Thomas Fuller was wrong. It will have been obvious that home and family have been the most stable elements in my life. After having totted up the various businesses I became involved in over thirty years, I realise with surprise and pleasure that the way we lived was overwhelmingly unfashionable, 'ordinary' if that means our everyday life was much as it would have been if I had never written a line, or served on a committee or been hoisted into a large job. A stable family was new to me and, though Mary had had a loving home, a 'proper-sized' family as distinct from a one-child family was new to her. Another not so usual element was that there was in me a strong personal drive not only to look after the family in a way I had always felt a

father and husband should, but also to do something beyond even
the large demands of the family and the job; to write. There were
bound to be tensions; each family has its own sorts of those. But
tensions can, by the adjustments of time and if you are lucky,
became more and more manageable. These are intensely difficult
things to write about. Even the images which first come to mind
sound, most of them, arch. But the experience, the longest and
most intense of a life such as this, is not to be ignored and should
not be undervalued.

In an earlier book I had one longish chapter entirely on the
nature of family life as we had come to know it. It was like trying
to take hold of something which slipped away all the time, and
would probably leave you with a spoonful of goo in your hands.
Perhaps I should have turned to poetry for that part. It is easier
to say such things in poetry than in the novel, and very much
easier than to put them down autobiographically. Too close;
warm breath. Poetry distances by its form; and is allowed greater
emotional freedom in its language.

A few years ago I had a series of conversations on television
with half a dozen writers with whom I felt an affinity. One was
another product of the Leeds working class, Tony Harrison. He
talked easily, not only about his poetry but also about the sense
of being both out of and still within his background. At the end,
after I had asked about the powerful place of women in his life,
and added that his second wife was appearing more and more in
his poetry, he produced a memorable sentence. He was speaking
of the struggle to come to terms with conflicting elements in your
own personality: 'You learn to do that by loving. I've found a lot
of love in recent years and I'm trying to write about it.' An apt
note for the programme to end on, and said with sureness. Prose,
but from a poet.

So I shall be economical about home and family, in this final
chapter. Their meanings should have come out incidentally all
along. No need to do much more or the cake will be over-egged.
I still have a powerful and always-present sense of that old, odd,
unhappy home in which the years from seven to going to university passed. It sits with the new sense of what a family can be,
and the two do not quarrel. Of course some relationships are
better won-through-to than others. There should be no setting of

them against each other. There were several kinds of baffled love struggling to get out in that Hunslet home; and a flow of direct love; my grandmother and Aunt Annie – and, in her own way, Aunt Ethel – lived that out.

Now we are a family of sixteen, eight of them grandchildren, from seventeen to two years old. From now on we are likely to decrease not increase, in our life-times. The voice of the first grandchild broke two or three years ago; we two now get around less sprightly than we like. Physically, the two groups have passed each other, going in opposite directions, the distance between widening each year.

We have learned, as we all have to, a way of detaching from the children and they from us; and that can be long drawn out and painful, especially for the parents. But you would not wish it otherwise. And some main threads hold; we all move up and down them, with pauses but not breaks.

Emotionally, we all seem as close as ever, and all seem to find pleasure in each other's company, up and down and across the range of ages. For me, home and family have provided a firm centre I had not expected, though I have not entirely lost the sense of loneliness which first struck when our mother died on the clip-rug up in Chapeltown, Leeds. Even now, if left alone for long, I can feel as if slowly coming apart. Not an admirable condition, a form of self-absorption, but so it is; grappled with, it has allowed to grow a small network of relationships outside the self which are far better than the isolation, less self-centred. But it is probably the sense of a self apart which has pushed me to write, to write chiefly about a narrow range of things intricately involved with that loneliness, its social and personal origins and ways out from it. That impulse sometimes quarrelled with family duties; it could not do other. But the sense of the family would not have been the same, would have been weaker, if there had not been that tension. So the complex meshing over years goes on, the effort to avoid also the inturned, nervy, uxoriousness which can be a substitute for the continuing attempt to do right by and embrace both the home and the outside world. I am not saying we have succeeded entirely, or all the time; but we have gone on trying to find that balance.

We learn, too, from the children. At about twelve years old one of them turned to me and said, 'I wish you wouldn't find a moral point in everything we do or don't do. Can't we take it easier?' I suppose I'd been asking heavily why he hadn't dried the pots as promised but had lain on his back hearing a record out. It was a notch up, another of those small revelations (we had been very puritanical moralists indeed in the respectable working-class bit of Hunslet). Cheerfulness kept breaking in on our family life, though; it's been a more cheerful business than not. After reading my pages on family life, one of the children said, 'You forgot to say we laughed a lot.'

We had decided to get married in the summer of 1942. I knew, but did not say, that we were due to go on an invasion somewhere in a few weeks. There was no engagement ring but, one day when I was let out from a very economical kind-of-commando type training, I went into Stirling, armed with a piece of cotton, sent by Mary to indicate the size, and bought a wedding ring. The jeweller shook his head, but it did fit, though loosely; it cost a pound.

We bought the engagement ring in 1988, a better one than we could have envisaged all those years ago. In 1990 we asked what an equivalent wedding ring, one of the cheapest because we did not want to break that long hold, would cost. Between fifty and sixty pounds. And how much to have the present ring enlarged, using the same, not very good quality, gold? About sixty pounds. We chose that.

Not long ago I went back to Hunslet for a week, to make a small study of changes. That house, 32 Newport Street, had long gone, bulldozed with hundreds of others so they could build Hunslet Grange, one of the worst large housing developments of Sixties Britain. That too has gone, its demolition helped on by building deficiencies and the refusal of people after the mid-Seventies to accept rabbit-hutch housing foisted on them by planners who had not looked at them or the way they ran their lives. The new housing, on the same twice-blasted heath, marries the best of the old scale, family and neighbourhood-sized, with the conviction that those who live there are not second- or third-class citizens and deserve the best that can be afforded.

It was in the nature of the work that I spent much of the time with the older people. They gave two contrasting impressions. Though they rarely went to church and chapel now, they pronounced as firmly as ever the old moral rules, most taken over from their parents; and then added: 'Of course, it's only my opinion.' A very late-twentieth-century, not a Thirties, axiom. They still roared at every possible opportunity to laugh, usually led by the recognised anecdotalist from a few doors away, whose timing was always precise. They often mentioned Aunt Annie, and their voices dropped in respect for a couple of seconds. Then the gatekeeper would say, 'Eh, but she did like a good laugh, didn't she? Do you remember the day when . . . ?' and the voices would lift again.

I remembered then, as so often (but the writing of all this may, usefully, have put some of these memories more into the background), our mother's last words to Tom and me: 'Look after your sister.' We have tried, and I go on trying now Tom has gone; naturally. I remembered the tortured Aunt Ethel, the weak but engaging Uncle Walter, the still point of love which my grandmother stood for and the nervy but similarly loving Aunt Annie – whose final illness set me off at last on writing this sequence. It has proved to be an eight-year journey of discovery, of remembering and forgetting, and of celebrating; but, above all else, a record of the continuity of love. So the first line of the first book, emerging without premonition as I sat on the top of a London bus and setting me off on this long internal exploration, had best be the last of this: 'My Aunt Annie is dying in St James's Hospital. . . .'

INDEX

OXFORD

MORE OXFORD PAPERBACKS

This book is just one of nearly 1000 Oxford Paperbacks currently in print. If you would like details of other Oxford Paperbacks, including titles in the World's Classics, Oxford Reference, Oxford Books, OPUS, Past Masters, Oxford Authors, and Oxford Shakespeare series, please write to:

UK and Europe: Oxford Paperbacks Publicity Manager, Arts and Reference Publicity Department, Oxford University Press, Walton Street, Oxford OX2 6DP.

Customers in UK and Europe will find Oxford Paperbacks available in all good bookshops. But in case of difficulty please send orders to the Cash-with-Order Department, Oxford University Press Distribution Services, Saxon Way West, Corby, Northants NN18 9ES. Tel: 0536 741519; Fax: 0536 746337. Please send a cheque for the total cost of the books, plus £1.75 postage and packing for orders under £20; £2.75 for orders over £20. Customers outside the UK should add 10% of the cost of the books for postage and packing.

USA: Oxford Paperbacks Marketing Manager, Oxford University Press, Inc., 200 Madison Avenue, New York, N.Y. 10016.

Canada: Trade Department, Oxford University Press, 70 Wynford Drive, Don Mills, Ontario M3C 1J9.

Australia: Trade Marketing Manager, Oxford University Press, G.P.O. Box 2784Y, Melbourne 3001, Victoria.

South Africa: Oxford University Press, P.O. Box 1141, Cape Town 8000.

OXFORD LETTERS AND MEMOIRS

Letters, memoirs, and journals offer a special insight into the private lives of public figures and vividly recreate the times in which they lived. This popular series makes available the best and most entertaining of these documents, bringing the past to life in a fresh and personal way.

RICHARD HOGGART

A Local Habitation
Life and Times: 1918–1940

With characteristic candour and compassion, Richard Hoggart evokes the Leeds of his boyhood, where as an orphan, he grew up with his grandmother, two aunts, an uncle, and a cousin in a small terraced back-to-back.

'brilliant . . . a joy as well as an education' Roy Hattersley

'a model of scrupulous autobiography' Edward Blishen, *Listener*

A Sort of Clowning
Life and Times: 1940–1950

Opening with his wartime exploits in North Africa and Italy, this sequel to *A Local Habitation* recalls his teaching career in North-East England, and charts his rise in the literary world following the publication of *The Uses of Literacy*.

'one of the classic autobiographies of our time' Anthony Howard, *Independent on Sunday*

'Hoggart [is] the ideal autobiographer' Beryl Bainbridge, *New Statesman and Society*

Also in Oxford Letters and Memoirs:

My Sister and Myself: The Diaries of J. R. Ackerley
The Letters of T. E. Lawrence
A London Family 1870–1900   Molly Hughes